THE WOODS

JAMES **TYNION IV** • MICHAEL **DIALYNAS**

VOL. 9
THE WAY HOME

BOOM!
STUDIOS

BOOM! STUDIOS

THE WOODS Volume Nine, March 2018. Published by BOOM! Studios, a division of Boom Entertainment, Inc. The Woods is ™ & © 2018 James Tynion IV. Originally published in single magazine form as THE WOODS No. 33-36. ™ & © 2017 James Tynion IV. All rights reserved. BOOM! Studios™ and the BOOM! Studios logo are trademarks of Boom Entertainment, Inc., registered in various countries and categories. All characters, events, and institutions depicted herein are fictional. Any similarity between any of the names, characters, persons, events, and/or institutions in this publication to actual names, characters, and persons, whether living or dead, events, and/or institutions is unintended and purely coincidental. BOOM! Studios does not read or accept unsolicited submissions of ideas, stories, or artwork.

BOOM! Studios, 5670 Wilshire Boulevard, Suite 450, Los Angeles, CA 90036-5679. Printed in China. First Printing.

ISBN: 978-1-68415-127-1, eISBN: 978-1-61398-866-4

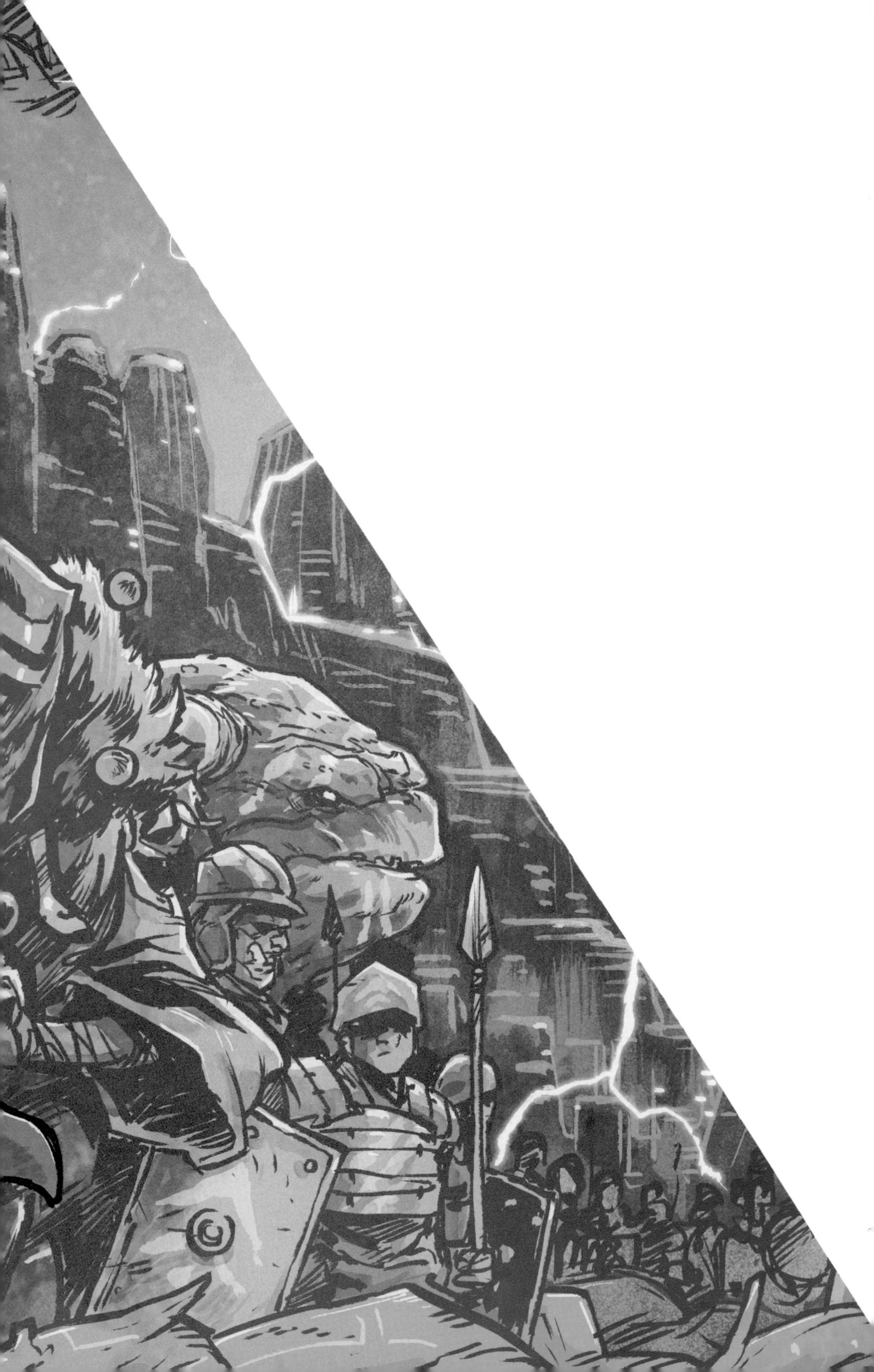

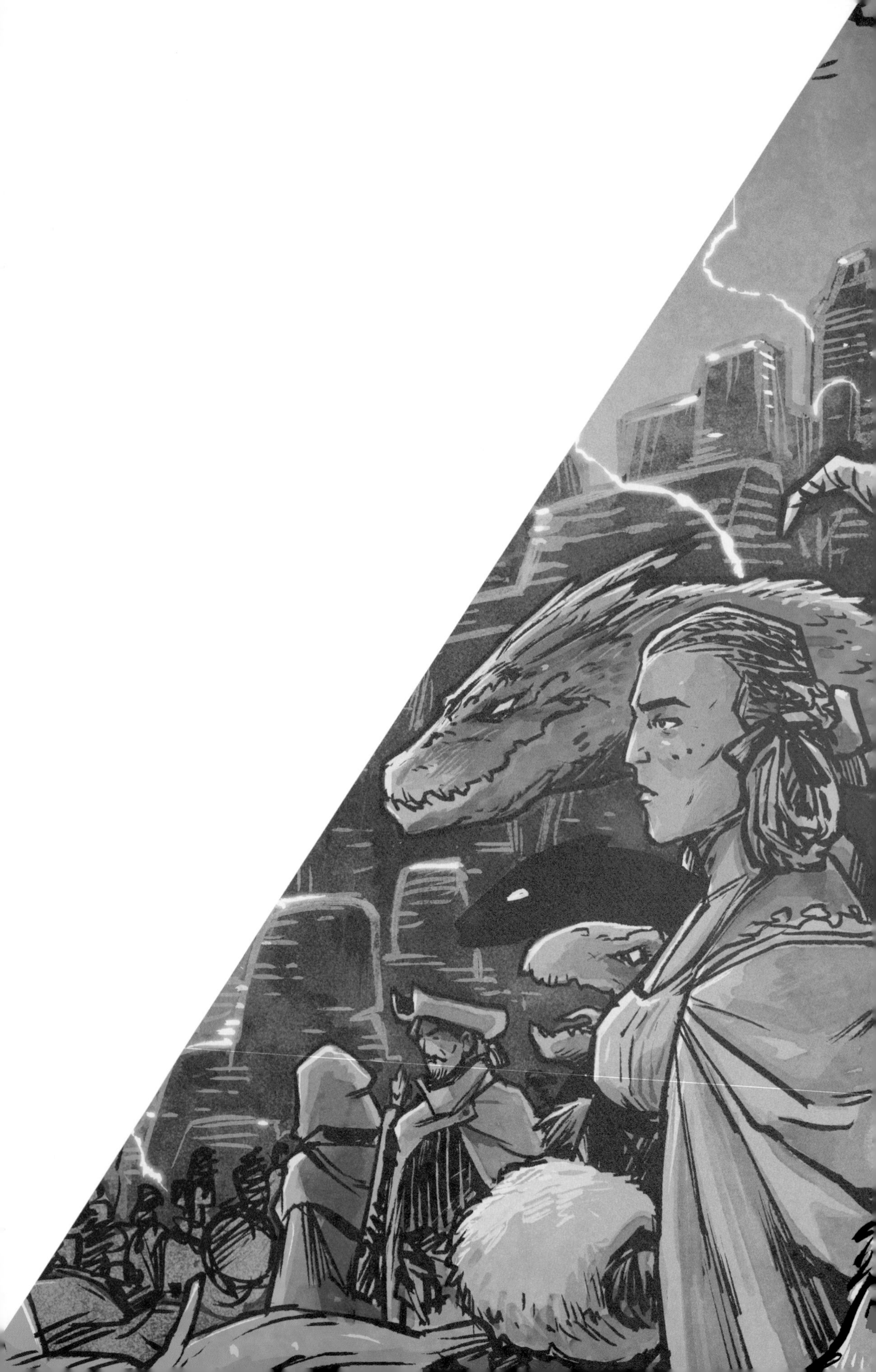

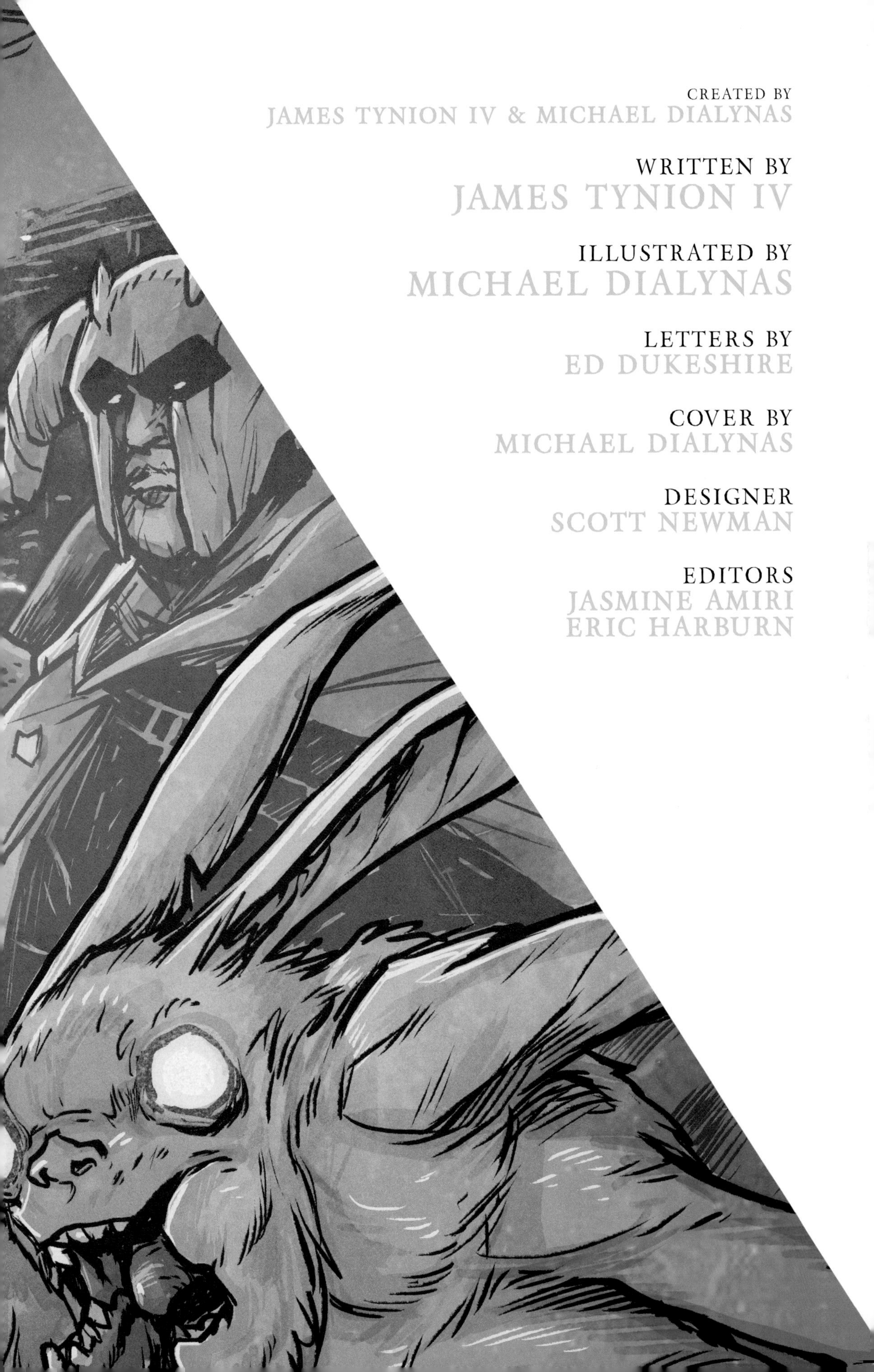

CREATED BY
JAMES TYNION IV & MICHAEL DIALYNAS

WRITTEN BY
JAMES TYNION IV

ILLUSTRATED BY
MICHAEL DIALYNAS

LETTERS BY
ED DUKESHIRE

COVER BY
MICHAEL DIALYNAS

DESIGNER
SCOTT NEWMAN

EDITORS
JASMINE AMIRI
ERIC HARBURN

CHAPTER
THIRTY-THREE

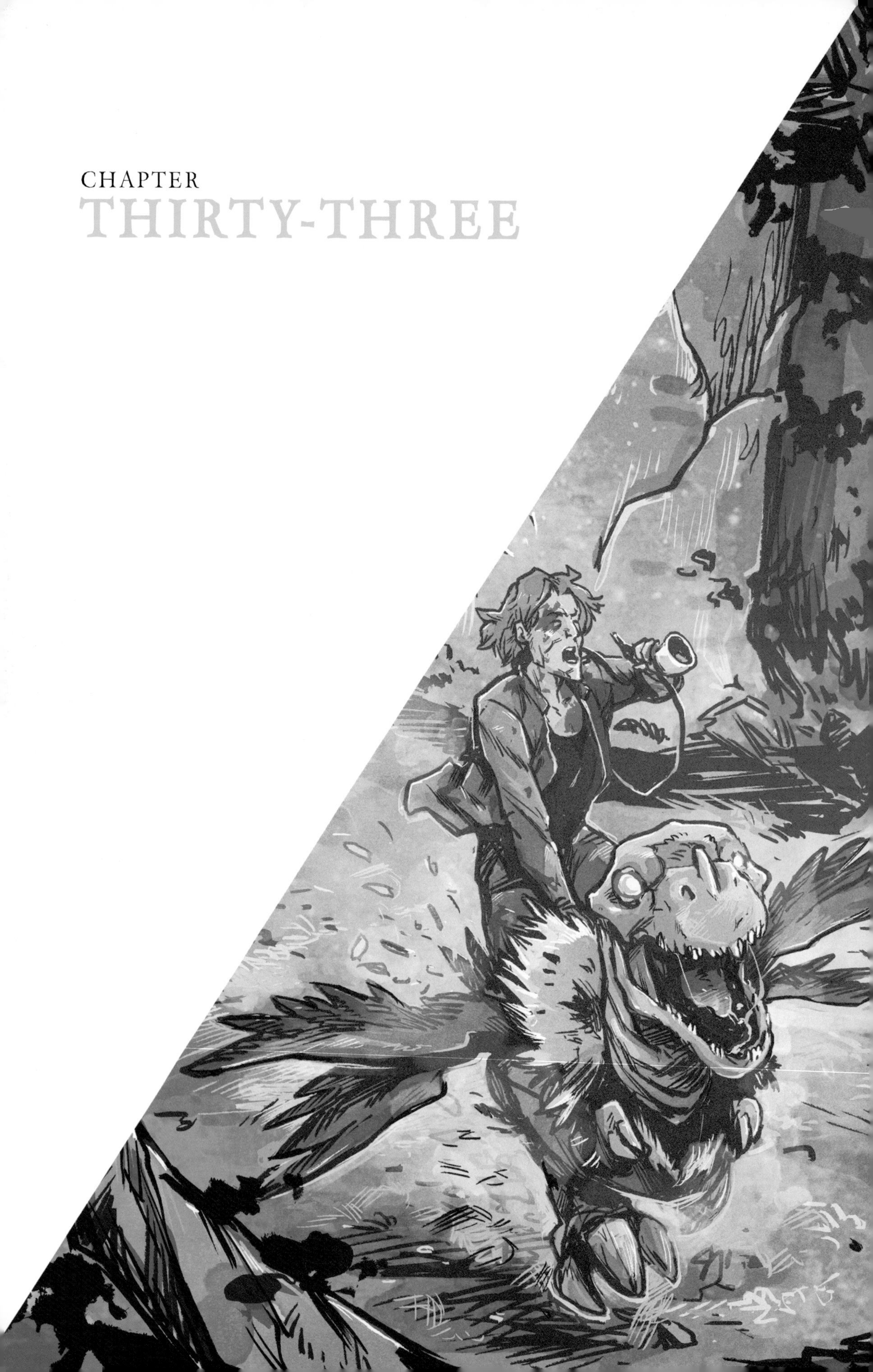

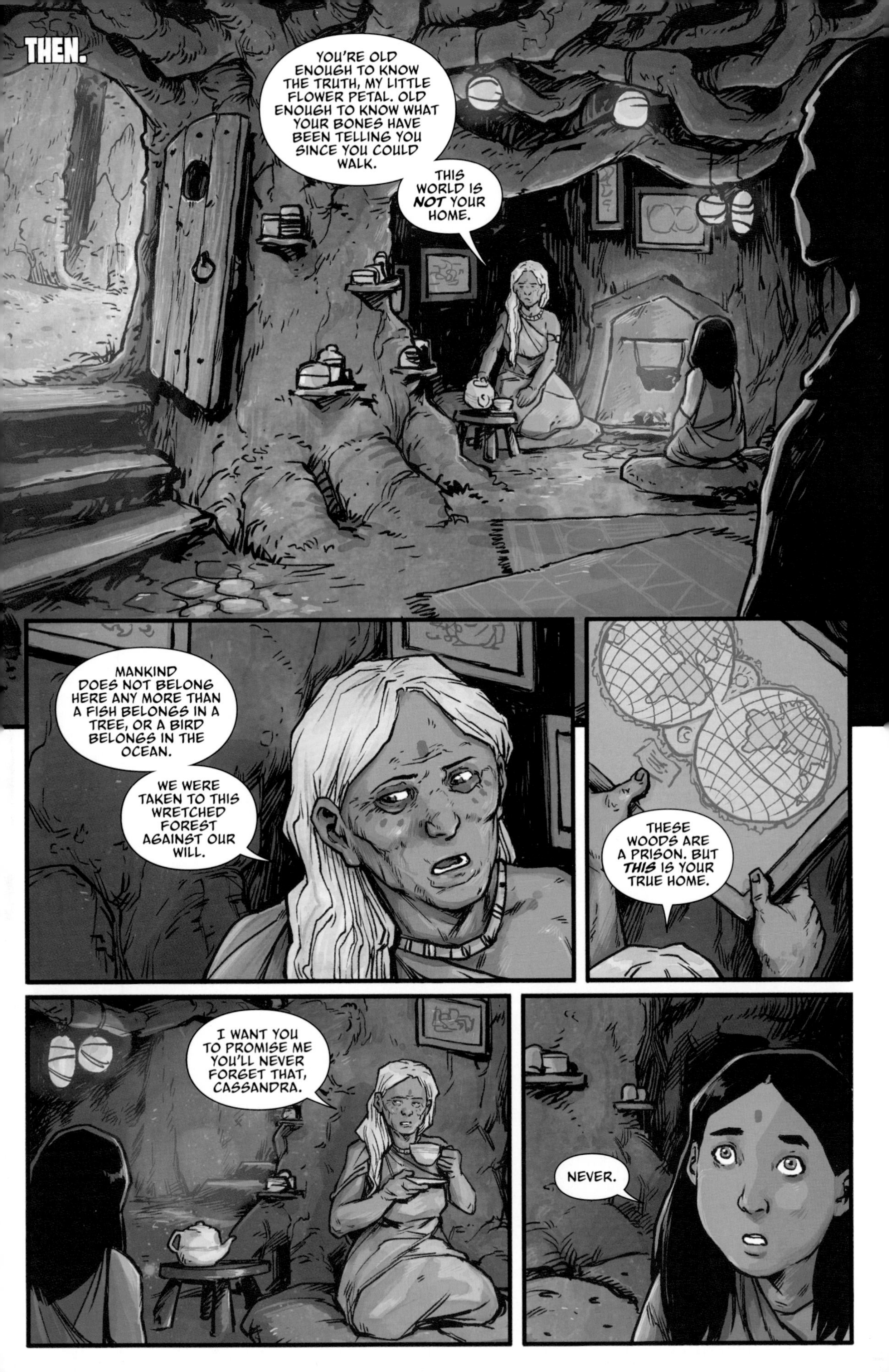
THEN.
YOU'RE OLD ENOUGH TO KNOW THE TRUTH, MY LITTLE FLOWER PETAL. OLD ENOUGH TO KNOW WHAT YOUR BONES HAVE BEEN TELLING YOU SINCE YOU COULD WALK.
THIS WORLD IS NOT YOUR HOME.
MANKIND DOES NOT BELONG HERE ANY MORE THAN A FISH BELONGS IN A TREE, OR A BIRD BELONGS IN THE OCEAN.
WE WERE TAKEN TO THIS WRETCHED FOREST AGAINST OUR WILL.
THESE WOODS ARE A PRISON. BUT THIS IS YOUR TRUE HOME.
I WANT YOU TO PROMISE ME YOU'LL NEVER FORGET THAT, CASSANDRA.
NEVER.

I TOLD HER, TIME AND TIME AGAIN, TO COME INSIDE THE WALLS OF THE CITY...

SHE WAS FAR TOO STUBBORN FOR THAT. SHE LIKED HER INDEPENDENCE.

SHE LIKED THE CONFLICT. SHE LIKED NEVER BEING ABLE TO REST IN THIS PLACE.

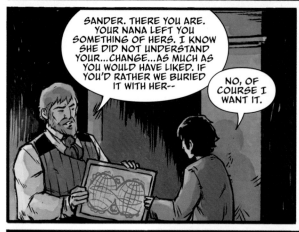

SANDER. THERE YOU ARE. YOUR NANA LEFT YOU SOMETHING OF HERS. I KNOW SHE DID NOT UNDERSTAND YOUR...CHANGE...AS MUCH AS YOU WOULD HAVE LIKED. IF YOU'D RATHER WE BURIED IT WITH HER--

NO, OF COURSE I WANT IT.

WAIT.

I NEED YOU TO PROMISE ME SOMETHING, SANDER. PROMISE WITH ALL YOUR HEART.

THIS IS YOUR HOME. THESE ARE THE PEOPLE WHO LOVE YOU, AND THESE ARE THE CIRCUMSTANCES WE MUST LIVE WITH.

LIVE IN THE MOMENT AND ENJOY THAT LIFE. DON'T WASTE YOUR LIFE DREAMING AFTER THE IMPOSSIBLE.

...

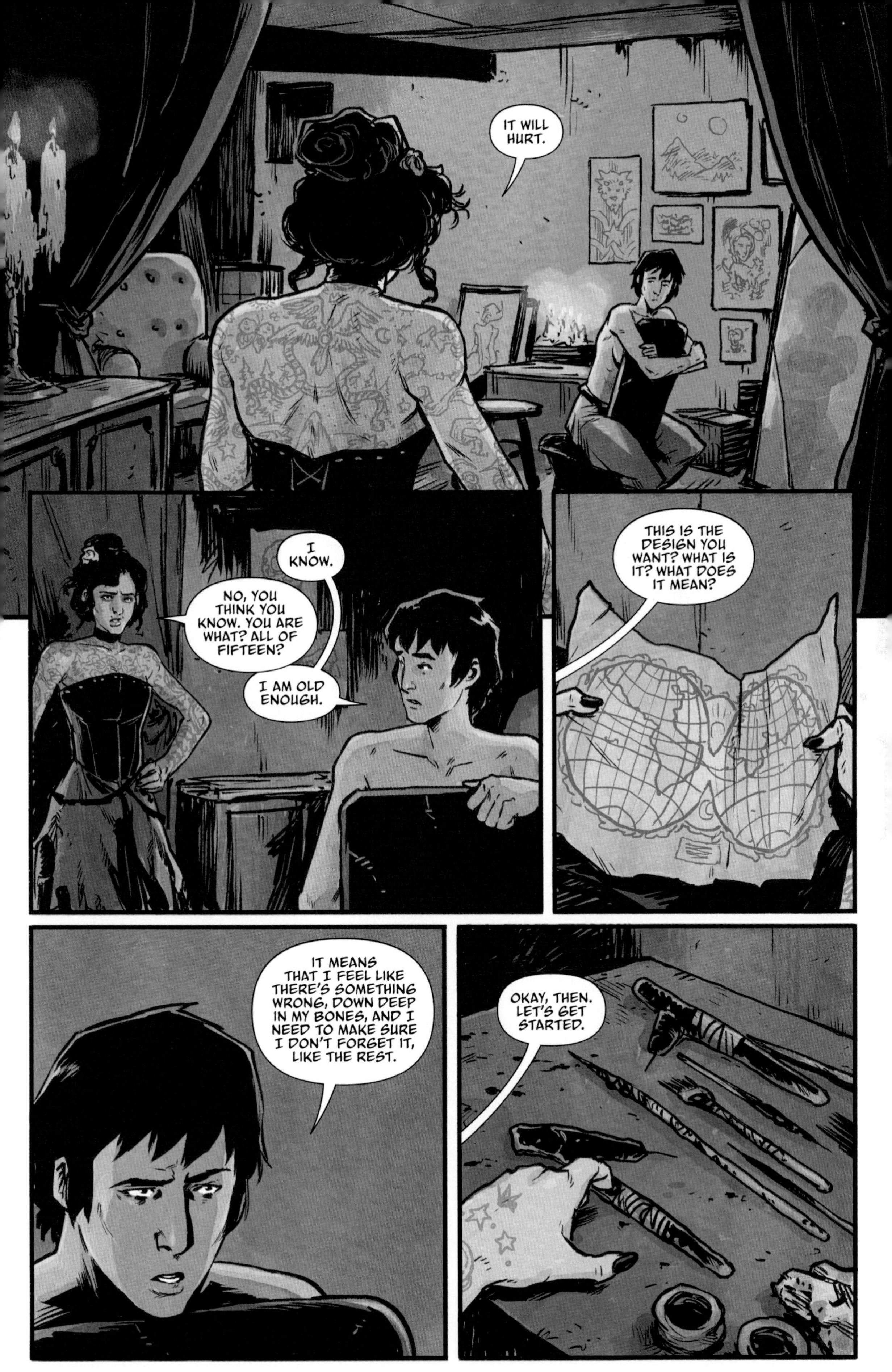
IT WILL HURT.
I KNOW.
NO, YOU THINK YOU KNOW. YOU ARE WHAT? ALL OF FIFTEEN?
I AM OLD ENOUGH.
THIS IS THE DESIGN YOU WANT? WHAT IS IT? WHAT DOES IT MEAN?
IT MEANS THAT I FEEL LIKE THERE'S SOMETHING WRONG, DOWN DEEP IN MY BONES, AND I NEED TO MAKE SURE I DON'T FORGET IT, LIKE THE REST.
OKAY, THEN. LET'S GET STARTED.

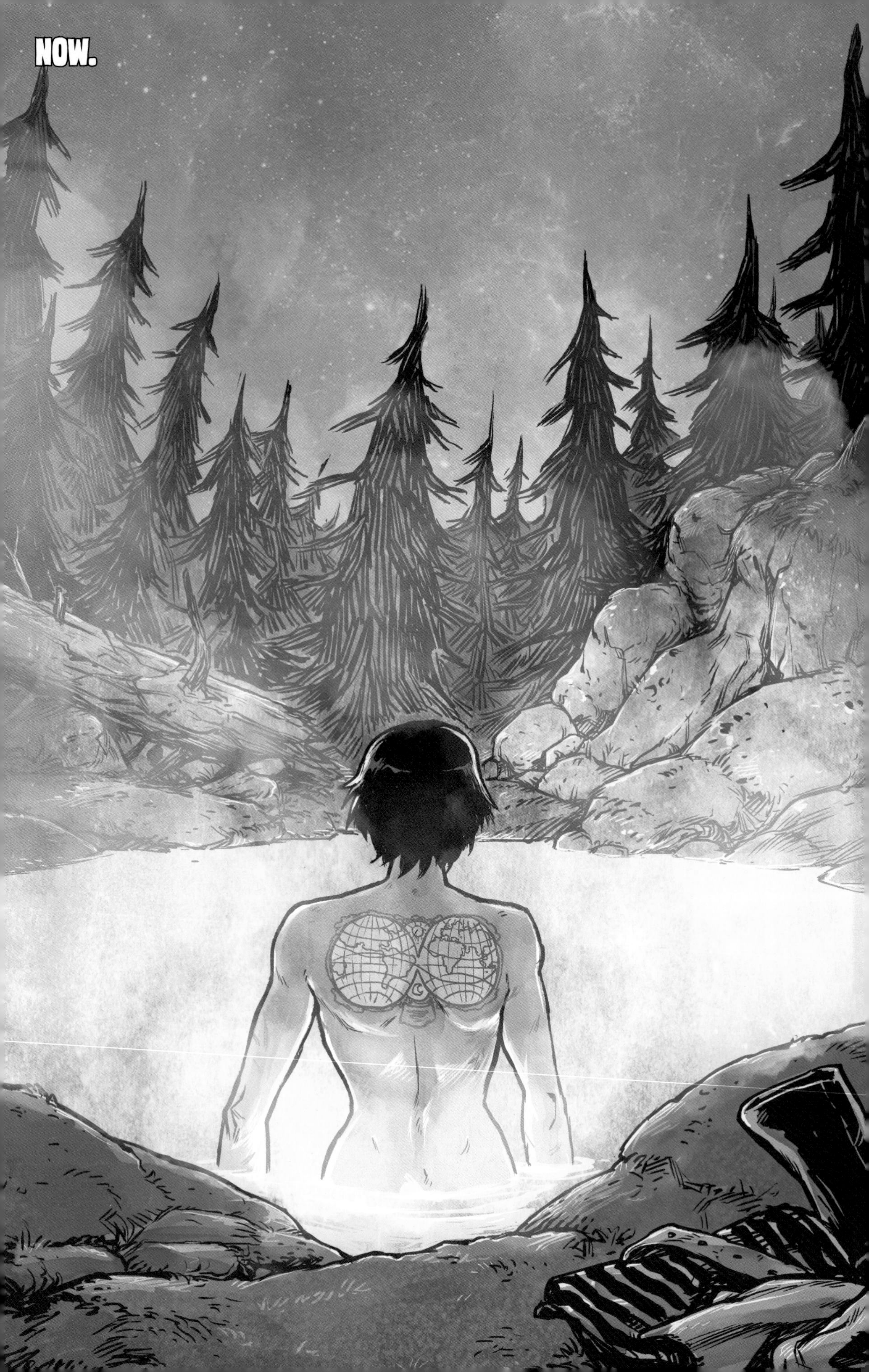
NOW.

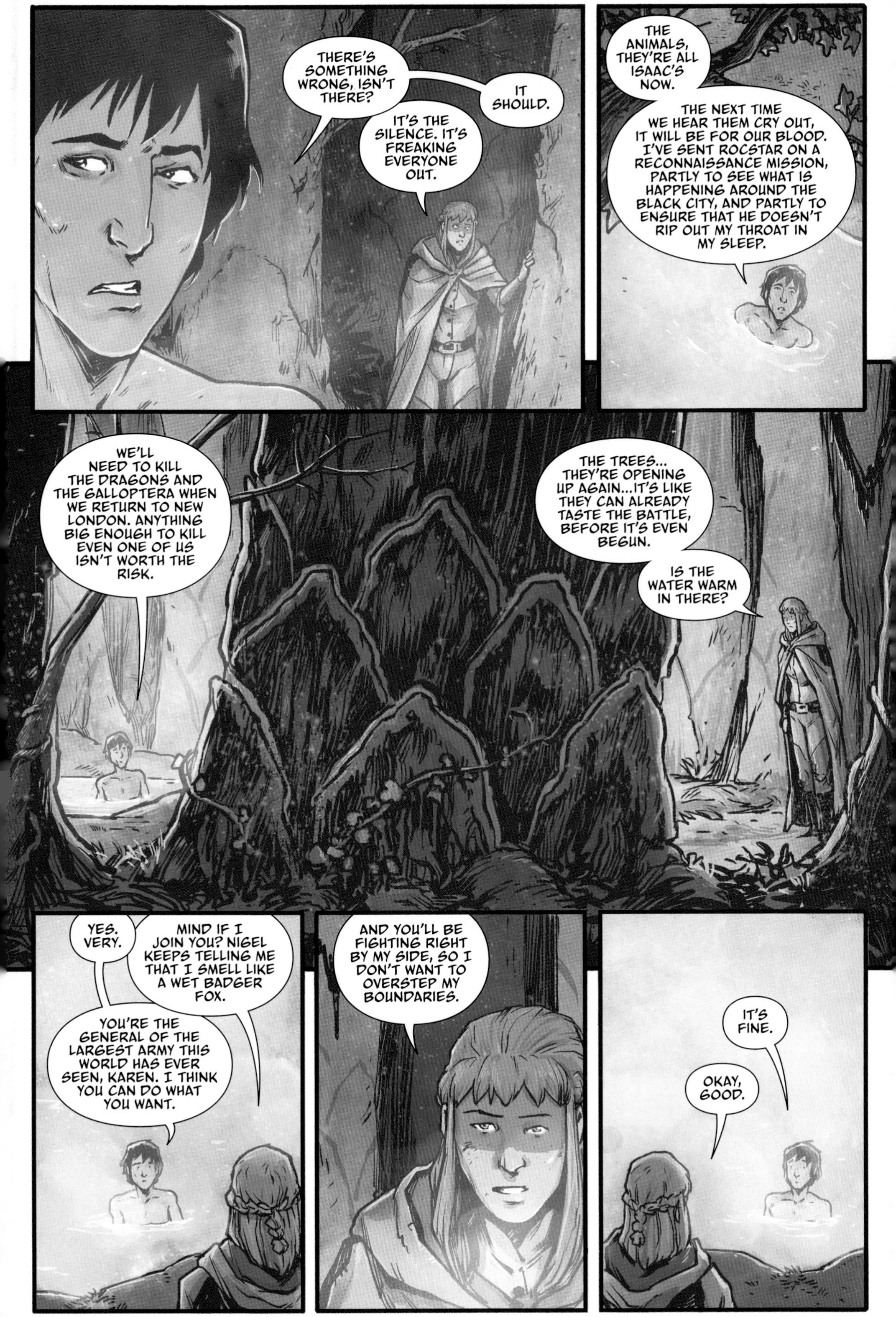
THERE'S SOMETHING WRONG, ISN'T THERE?
IT SHOULD.
IT'S THE SILENCE. IT'S FREAKING EVERYONE OUT.
THE ANIMALS, THEY'RE ALL ISAAC'S NOW.
THE NEXT TIME WE HEAR THEM CRY OUT, IT WILL BE FOR OUR BLOOD. I'VE SENT ROCSTAR ON A RECONNAISSANCE MISSION, PARTLY TO SEE WHAT IS HAPPENING AROUND THE BLACK CITY, AND PARTLY TO ENSURE THAT HE DOESN'T RIP OUT MY THROAT IN MY SLEEP.
WE'LL NEED TO KILL THE DRAGONS AND THE GALLOPTERA WHEN WE RETURN TO NEW LONDON. ANYTHING BIG ENOUGH TO KILL EVEN ONE OF US ISN'T WORTH THE RISK.
THE TREES... THEY'RE OPENING UP AGAIN...IT'S LIKE THEY CAN ALREADY TASTE THE BATTLE, BEFORE IT'S EVEN BEGUN.
IS THE WATER WARM IN THERE?
YES. VERY.
MIND IF I JOIN YOU? NIGEL KEEPS TELLING ME THAT I SMELL LIKE A WET BADGER FOX.
YOU'RE THE GENERAL OF THE LARGEST ARMY THIS WORLD HAS EVER SEEN, KAREN. I THINK YOU CAN DO WHAT YOU WANT.
AND YOU'LL BE FIGHTING RIGHT BY MY SIDE, SO I DON'T WANT TO OVERSTEP MY BOUNDARIES.
IT'S FINE.
OKAY, GOOD.

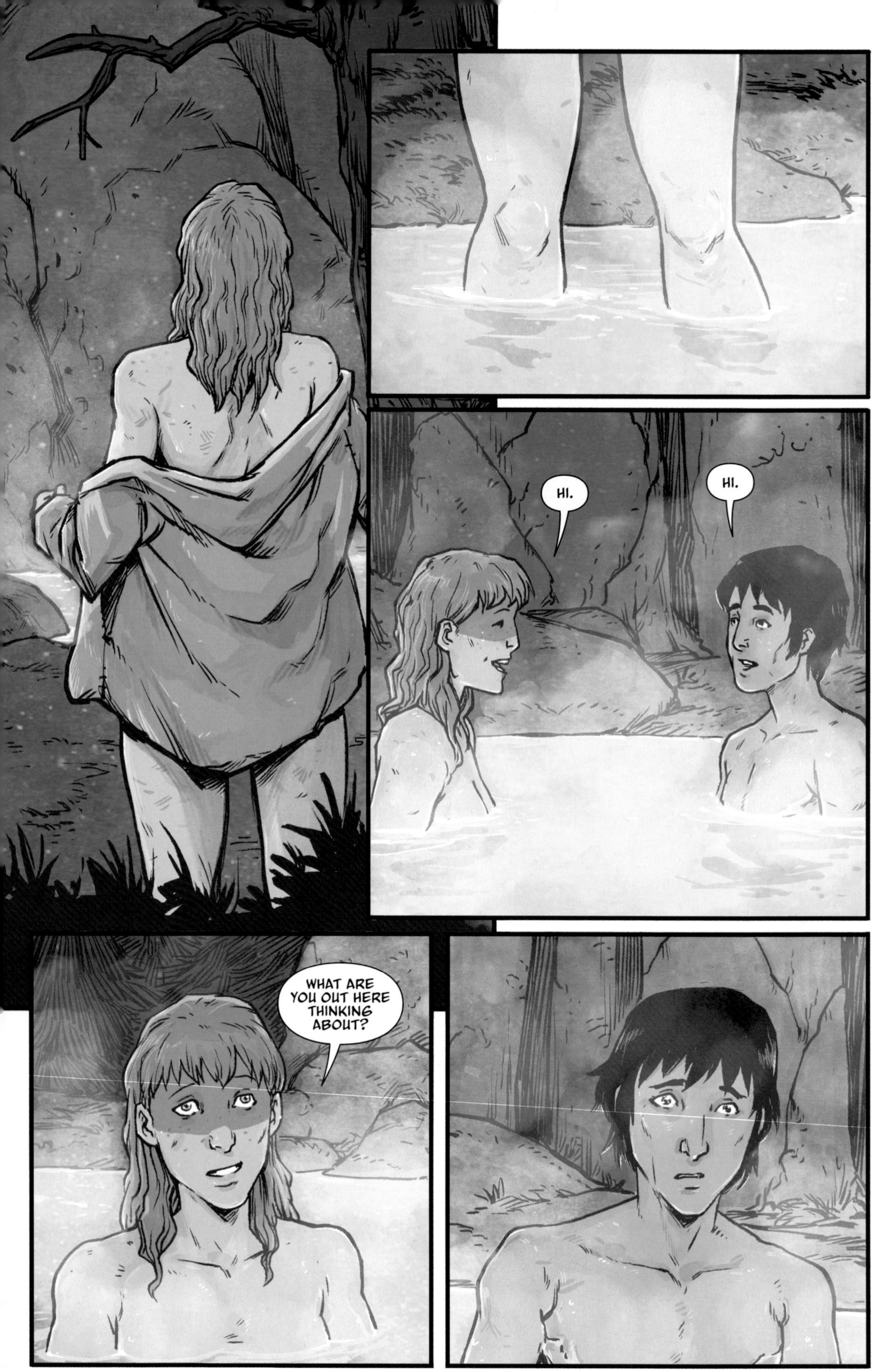
HI.
HI.
WHAT ARE YOU OUT HERE THINKING ABOUT?

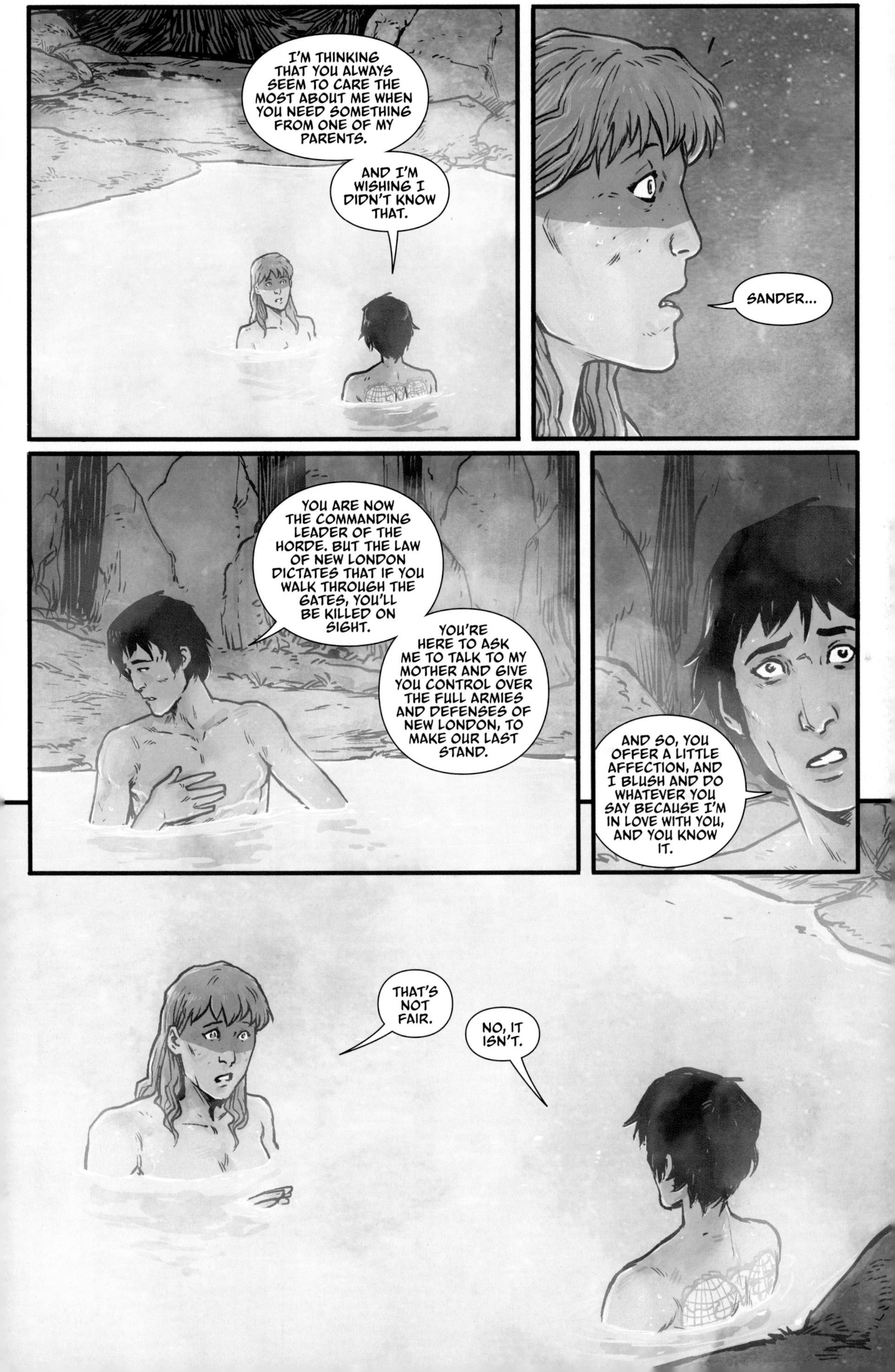
I'M THINKING THAT YOU ALWAYS SEEM TO CARE THE MOST ABOUT ME WHEN YOU NEED SOMETHING FROM ONE OF MY PARENTS.
AND I'M WISHING I DIDN'T KNOW THAT.
SANDER...
YOU ARE NOW THE COMMANDING LEADER OF THE HORDE. BUT THE LAW OF NEW LONDON DICTATES THAT IF YOU WALK THROUGH THE GATES, YOU'LL BE KILLED ON SIGHT.
YOU'RE HERE TO ASK ME TO TALK TO MY MOTHER AND GIVE YOU CONTROL OVER THE FULL ARMIES AND DEFENSES OF NEW LONDON, TO MAKE OUR LAST STAND.
AND SO, YOU OFFER A LITTLE AFFECTION, AND I BLUSH AND DO WHATEVER YOU SAY BECAUSE I'M IN LOVE WITH YOU, AND YOU KNOW IT.
THAT'S NOT FAIR.
NO, IT ISN'T.

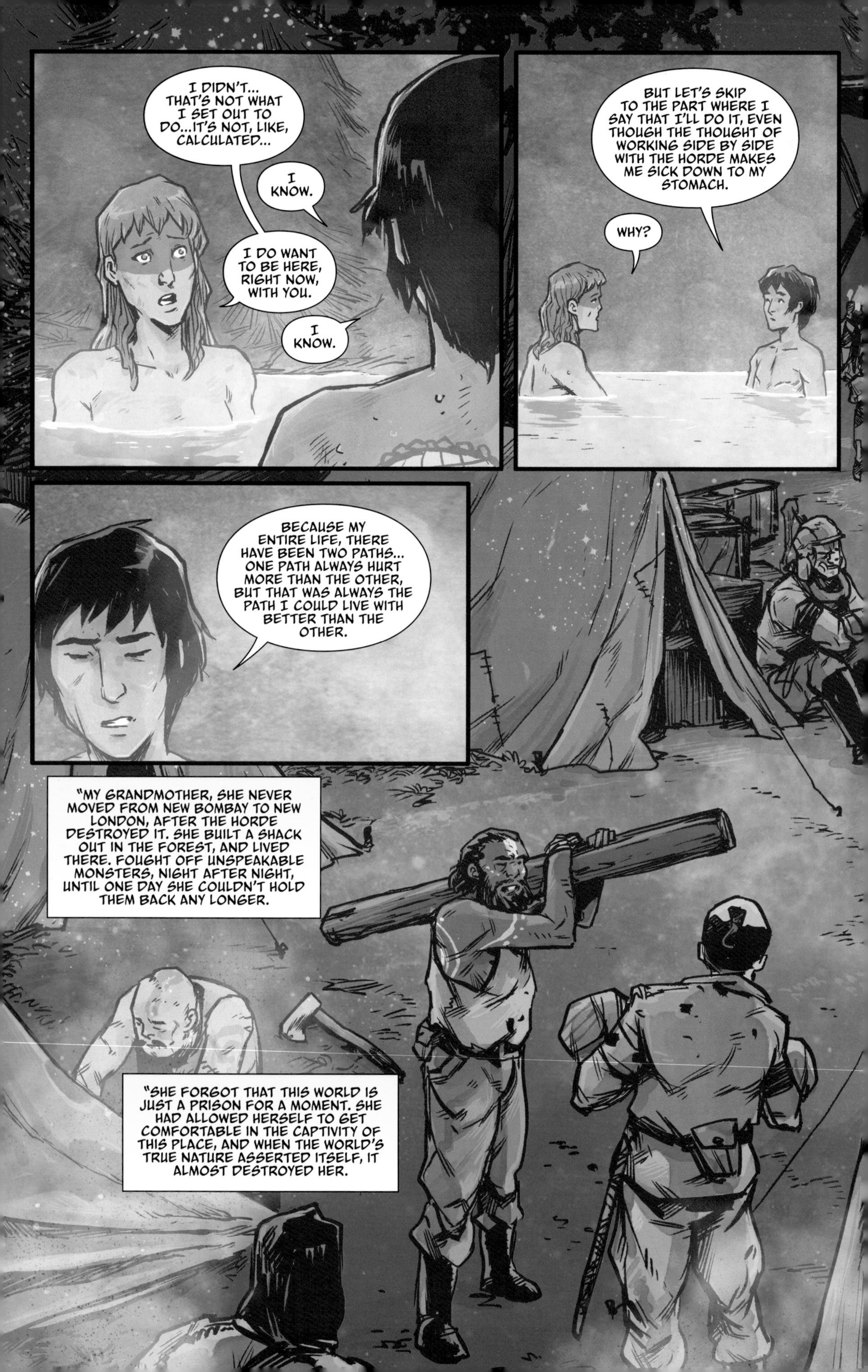
I DIDN'T... THAT'S NOT WHAT I SET OUT TO DO...IT'S NOT, LIKE, CALCULATED...
I KNOW.
I DO WANT TO BE HERE, RIGHT NOW, WITH YOU.
I KNOW.
BUT LET'S SKIP TO THE PART WHERE I SAY THAT I'LL DO IT, EVEN THOUGH THE THOUGHT OF WORKING SIDE BY SIDE WITH THE HORDE MAKES ME SICK DOWN TO MY STOMACH.
WHY?
BECAUSE MY ENTIRE LIFE, THERE HAVE BEEN TWO PATHS... ONE PATH ALWAYS HURT MORE THAN THE OTHER, BUT THAT WAS ALWAYS THE PATH I COULD LIVE WITH BETTER THAN THE OTHER.
"MY GRANDMOTHER, SHE NEVER MOVED FROM NEW BOMBAY TO NEW LONDON, AFTER THE HORDE DESTROYED IT. SHE BUILT A SHACK OUT IN THE FOREST, AND LIVED THERE. FOUGHT OFF UNSPEAKABLE MONSTERS, NIGHT AFTER NIGHT, UNTIL ONE DAY SHE COULDN'T HOLD THEM BACK ANY LONGER.
"SHE FORGOT THAT THIS WORLD IS JUST A PRISON FOR A MOMENT. SHE HAD ALLOWED HERSELF TO GET COMFORTABLE IN THE CAPTIVITY OF THIS PLACE, AND WHEN THE WORLD'S TRUE NATURE ASSERTED ITSELF, IT ALMOST DESTROYED HER.

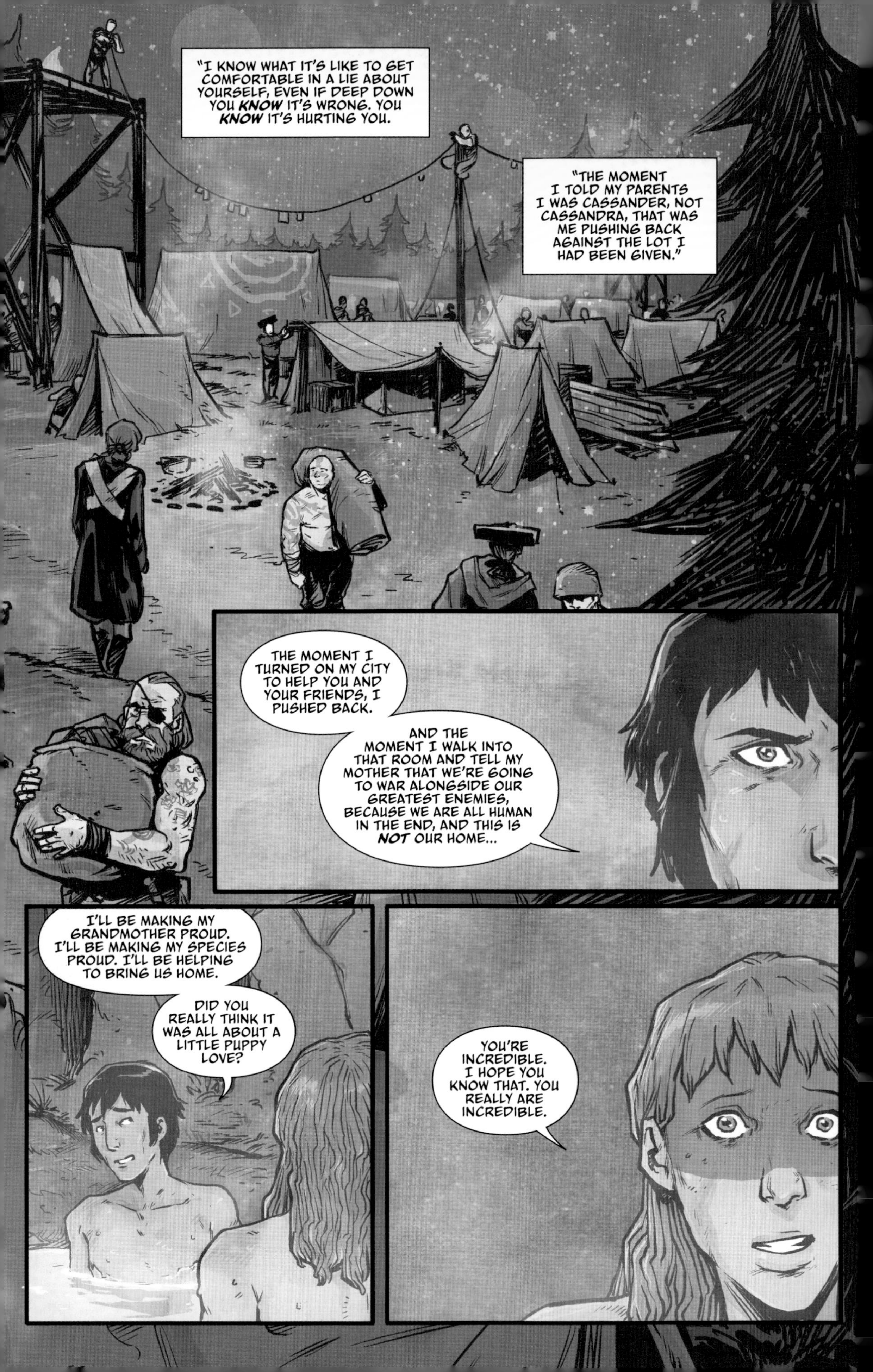
"I KNOW WHAT IT'S LIKE TO GET COMFORTABLE IN A LIE ABOUT YOURSELF, EVEN IF DEEP DOWN YOU **KNOW** IT'S WRONG. YOU **KNOW** IT'S HURTING YOU.
"THE MOMENT I TOLD MY PARENTS I WAS CASSANDER, NOT CASSANDRA, THAT WAS ME PUSHING BACK AGAINST THE LOT I HAD BEEN GIVEN."
THE MOMENT I TURNED ON MY CITY TO HELP YOU AND YOUR FRIENDS, I PUSHED BACK.
AND THE MOMENT I WALK INTO THAT ROOM AND TELL MY MOTHER THAT WE'RE GOING TO WAR ALONGSIDE OUR GREATEST ENEMIES, BECAUSE WE ARE ALL HUMAN IN THE END, AND THIS IS **NOT** OUR HOME...
I'LL BE MAKING MY GRANDMOTHER PROUD. I'LL BE MAKING MY SPECIES PROUD. I'LL BE HELPING TO BRING US HOME.
DID YOU REALLY THINK IT WAS ALL ABOUT A LITTLE PUPPY LOVE?
YOU'RE INCREDIBLE. I HOPE YOU KNOW THAT. YOU REALLY ARE INCREDIBLE.

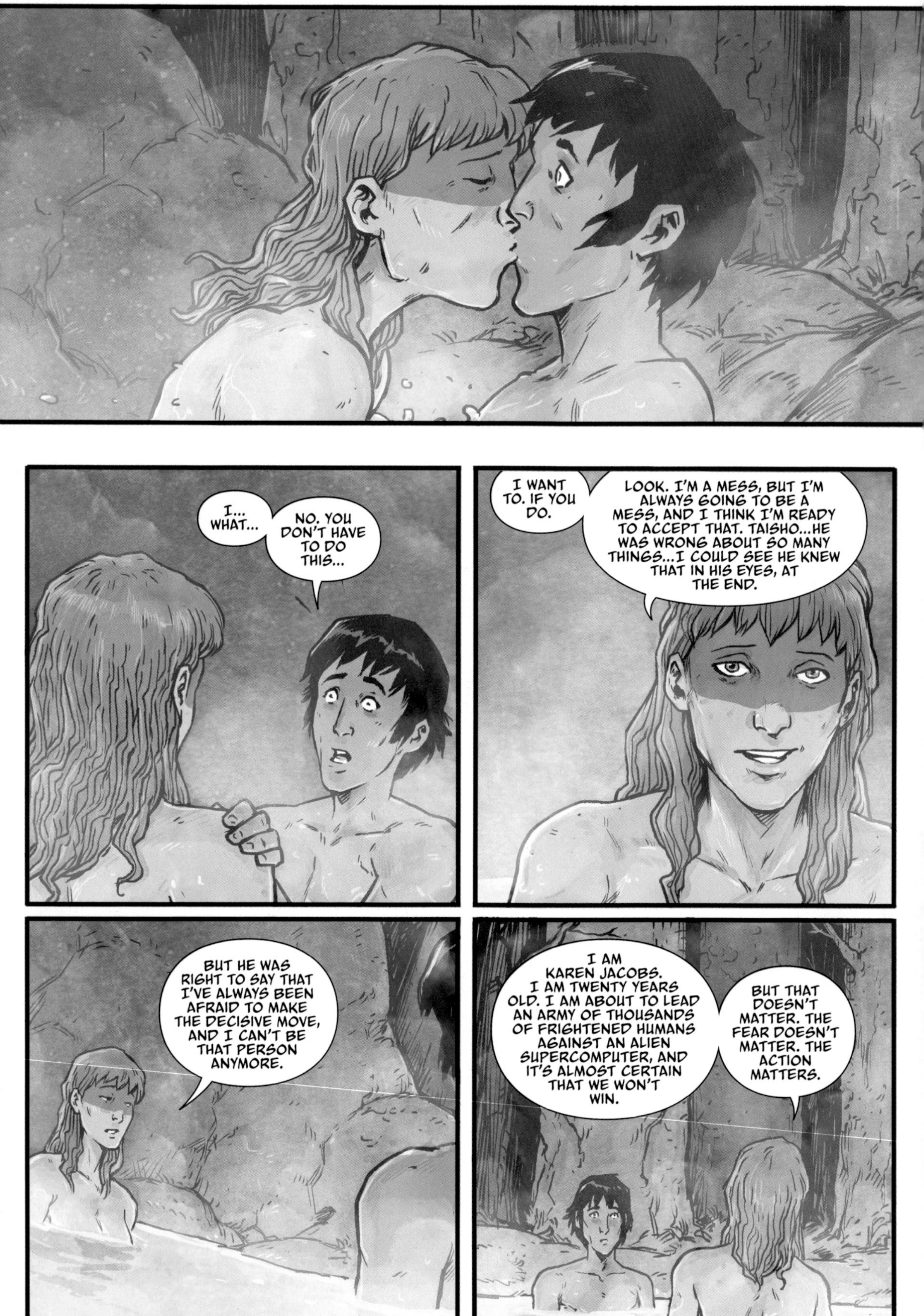
I... WHAT...
NO. YOU DON'T HAVE TO DO THIS...
I WANT TO. IF YOU DO.
LOOK. I'M A MESS, BUT I'M ALWAYS GOING TO BE A MESS, AND I THINK I'M READY TO ACCEPT THAT. TAISHO...HE WAS WRONG ABOUT SO MANY THINGS...I COULD SEE HE KNEW THAT IN HIS EYES, AT THE END.
BUT HE WAS RIGHT TO SAY THAT I'VE ALWAYS BEEN AFRAID TO MAKE THE DECISIVE MOVE, AND I CAN'T BE THAT PERSON ANYMORE.
I AM KAREN JACOBS. I AM TWENTY YEARS OLD. I AM ABOUT TO LEAD AN ARMY OF THOUSANDS OF FRIGHTENED HUMANS AGAINST AN ALIEN SUPERCOMPUTER, AND IT'S ALMOST CERTAIN THAT WE WON'T WIN.
BUT THAT DOESN'T MATTER. THE FEAR DOESN'T MATTER. THE ACTION MATTERS.

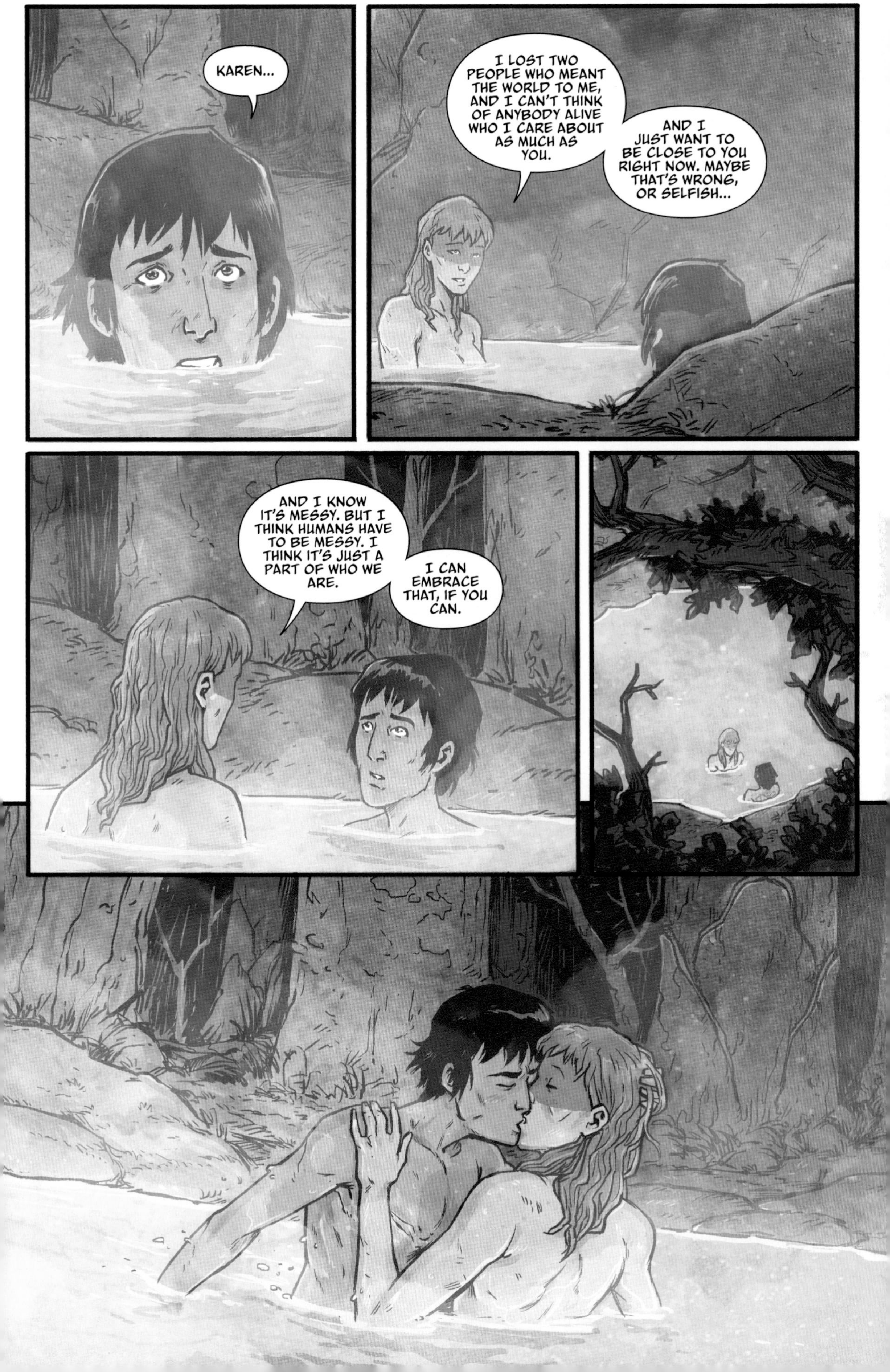
KAREN...
I LOST TWO PEOPLE WHO MEANT THE WORLD TO ME, AND I CAN'T THINK OF ANYBODY ALIVE WHO I CARE ABOUT AS MUCH AS YOU.
AND I JUST WANT TO BE CLOSE TO YOU RIGHT NOW. MAYBE THAT'S WRONG, OR SELFISH...
AND I KNOW IT'S MESSY. BUT I THINK HUMANS HAVE TO BE MESSY. I THINK IT'S JUST A PART OF WHO WE ARE.
I CAN EMBRACE THAT, IF YOU CAN.

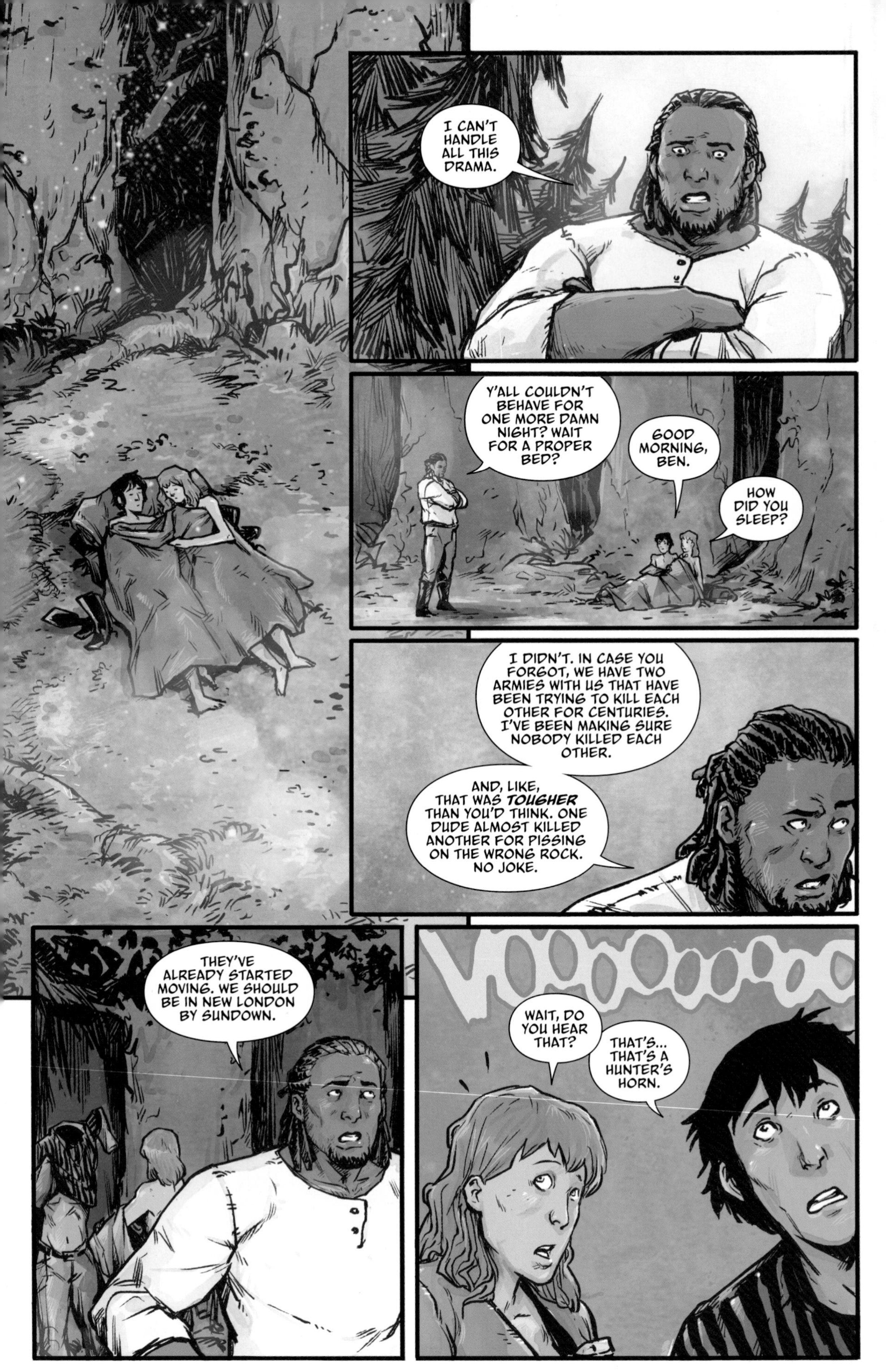
I CAN'T HANDLE ALL THIS DRAMA.
Y'ALL COULDN'T BEHAVE FOR ONE MORE DAMN NIGHT? WAIT FOR A PROPER BED?
GOOD MORNING, BEN.
HOW DID YOU SLEEP?
I DIDN'T. IN CASE YOU FORGOT, WE HAVE TWO ARMIES WITH US THAT HAVE BEEN TRYING TO KILL EACH OTHER FOR CENTURIES. I'VE BEEN MAKING SURE NOBODY KILLED EACH OTHER.
AND, LIKE, THAT WAS TOUGHER THAN YOU'D THINK. ONE DUDE ALMOST KILLED ANOTHER FOR PISSING ON THE WRONG ROCK. NO JOKE.
THEY'VE ALREADY STARTED MOVING. WE SHOULD BE IN NEW LONDON BY SUNDOWN.
VOOOOOOOO
WAIT, DO YOU HEAR THAT?
THAT'S... THAT'S A HUNTER'S HORN.

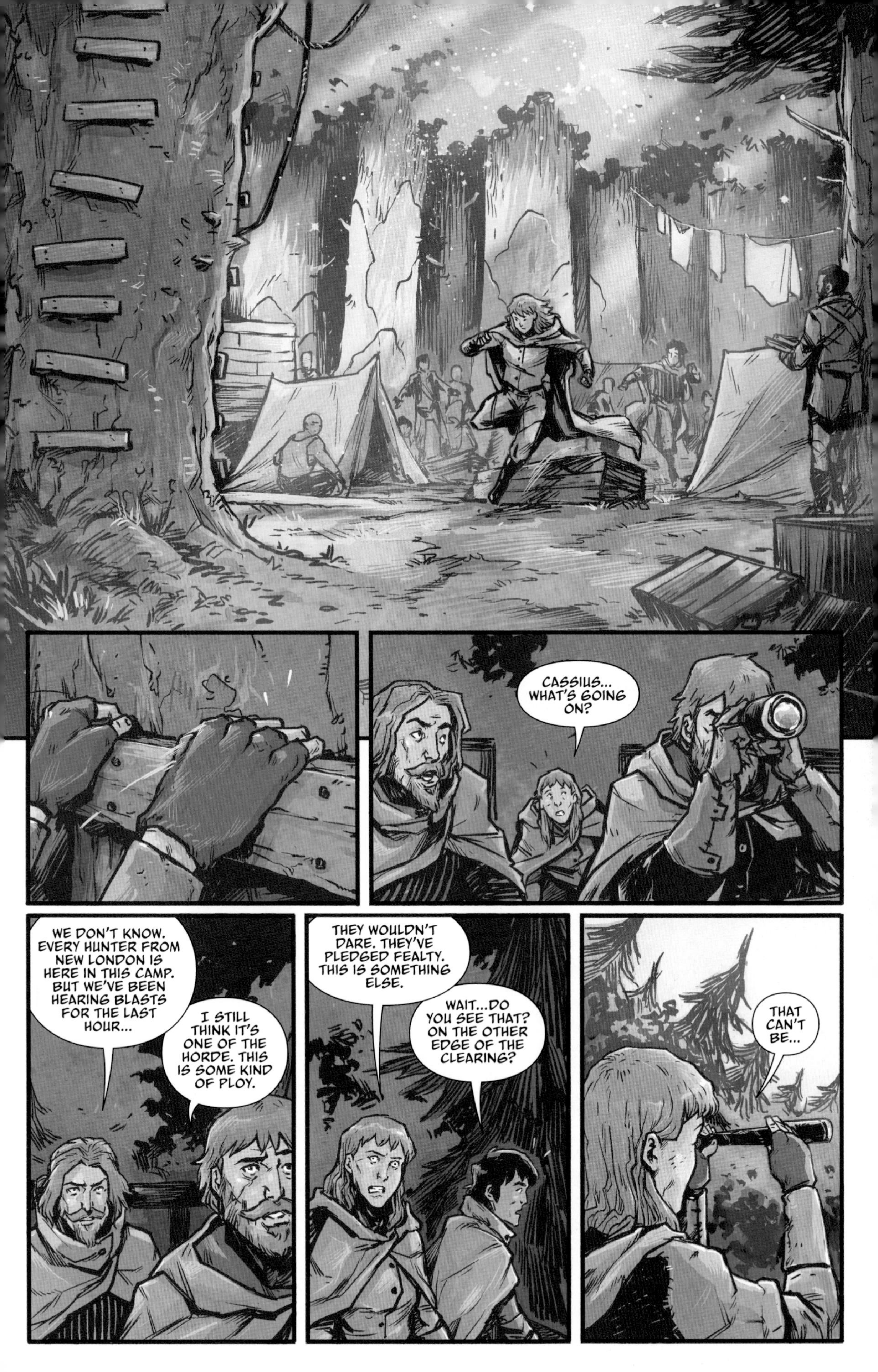
CASSIUS... WHAT'S GOING ON?
WE DON'T KNOW. EVERY HUNTER FROM NEW LONDON IS HERE IN THIS CAMP. BUT WE'VE BEEN HEARING BLASTS FOR THE LAST HOUR...
I STILL THINK IT'S ONE OF THE HORDE. THIS IS SOME KIND OF PLOY.
THEY WOULDN'T DARE. THEY'VE PLEDGED FEALTY. THIS IS SOMETHING ELSE.
WAIT...DO YOU SEE THAT? ON THE OTHER EDGE OF THE CLEARING?
THAT CAN'T BE...

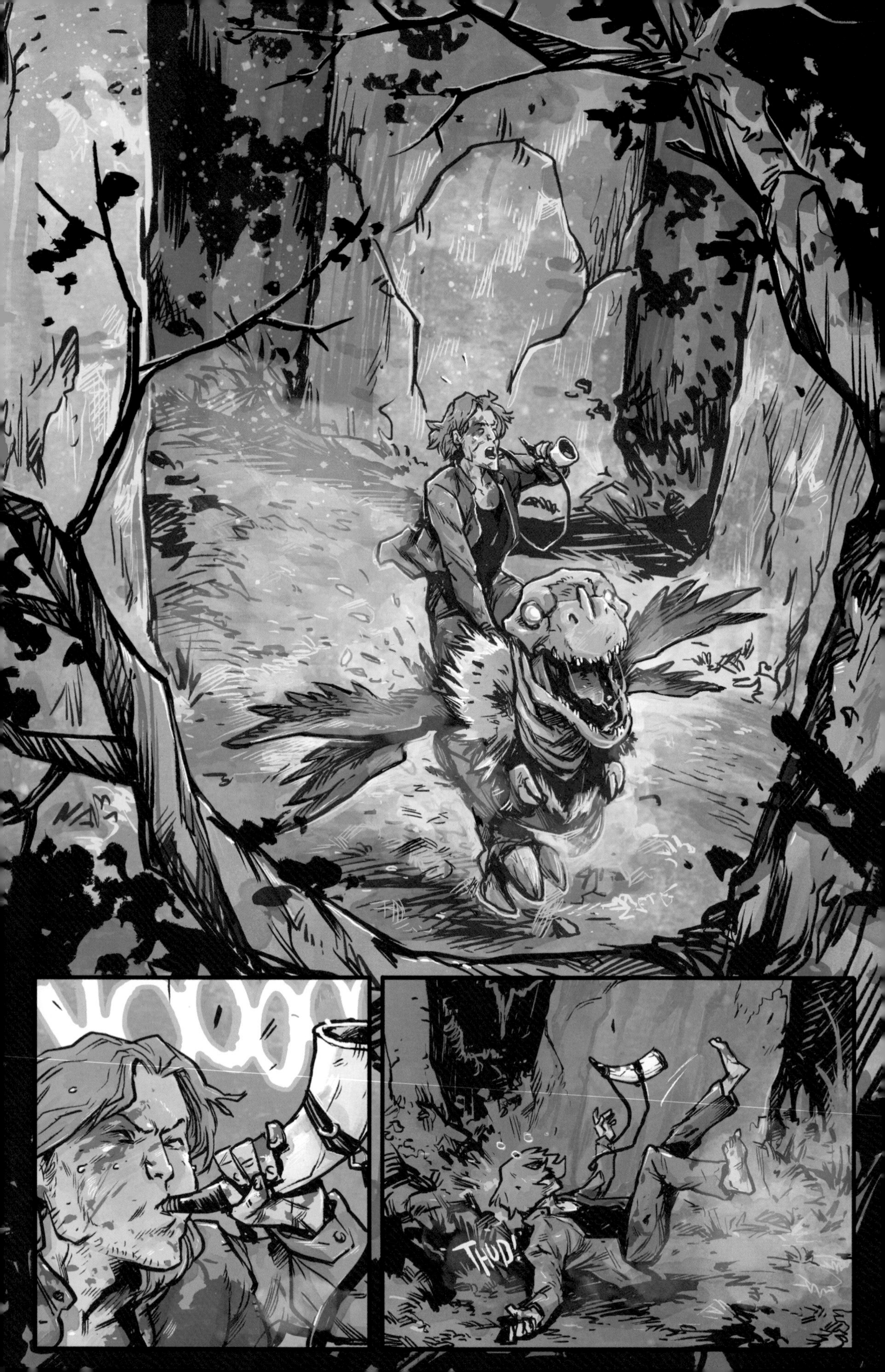
THUD!

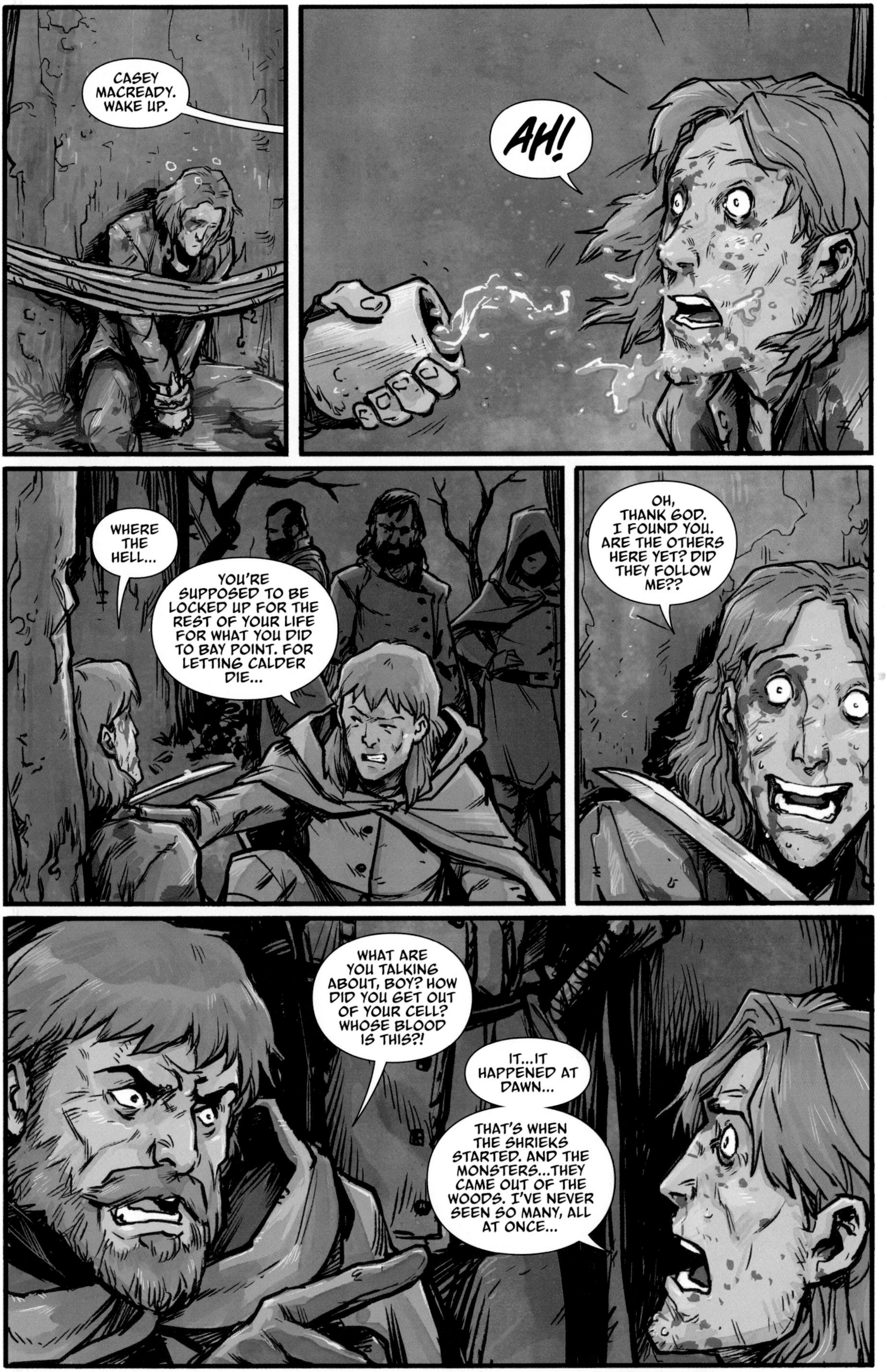
CASEY MACREADY. WAKE UP.
AH!
WHERE THE HELL...
YOU'RE SUPPOSED TO BE LOCKED UP FOR THE REST OF YOUR LIFE FOR WHAT YOU DID TO BAY POINT. FOR LETTING CALDER DIE...
OH, THANK GOD. I FOUND YOU. ARE THE OTHERS HERE YET? DID THEY FOLLOW ME??
WHAT ARE YOU TALKING ABOUT, BOY? HOW DID YOU GET OUT OF YOUR CELL? WHOSE BLOOD IS THIS?!
IT...IT HAPPENED AT DAWN...
THAT'S WHEN THE SHRIEKS STARTED. AND THE MONSTERS...THEY CAME OUT OF THE WOODS. I'VE NEVER SEEN SO MANY, ALL AT ONCE...

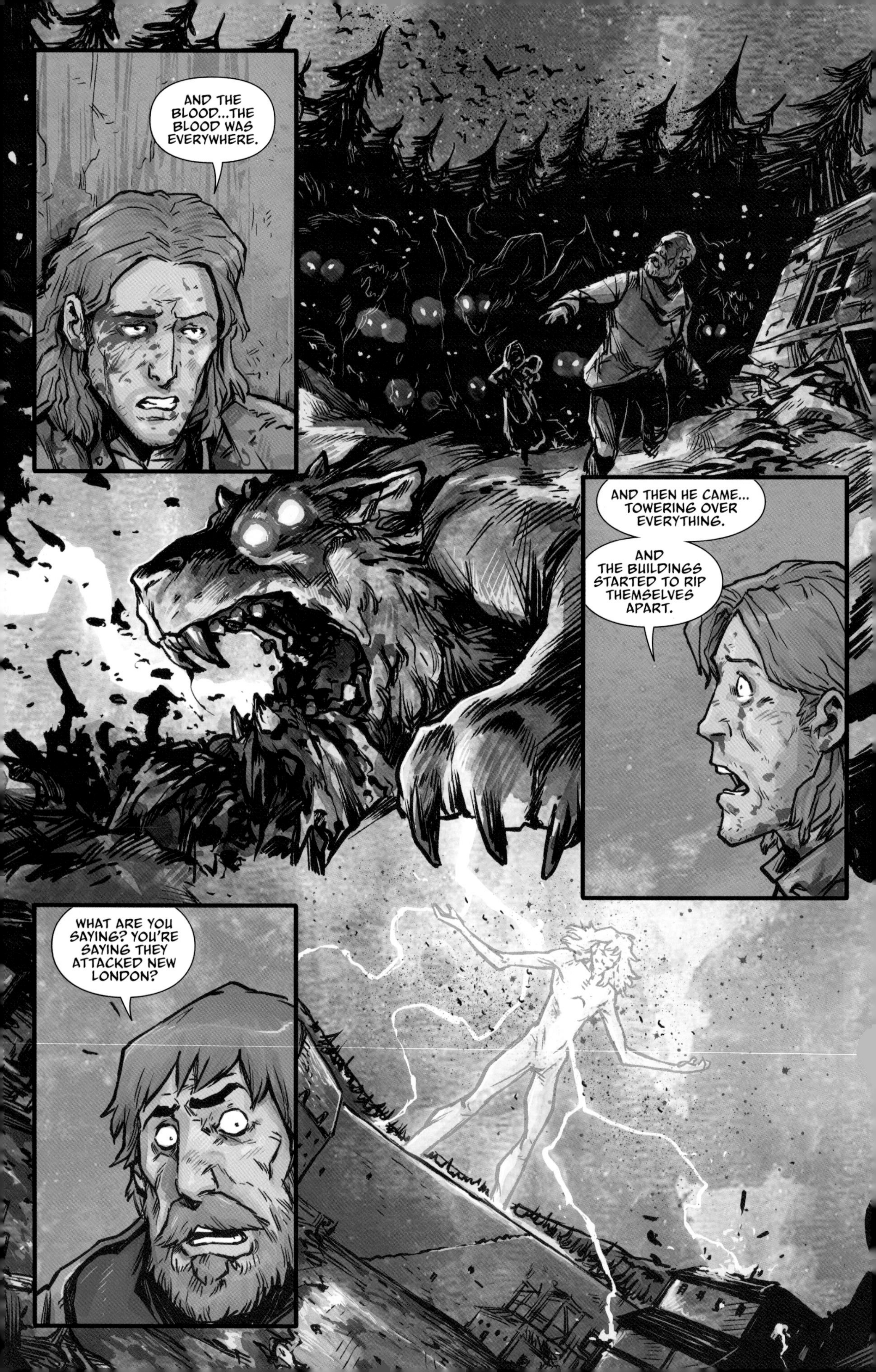
AND THE BLOOD...THE BLOOD WAS EVERYWHERE.
AND THEN HE CAME... TOWERING OVER EVERYTHING.
AND THE BUILDINGS STARTED TO RIP THEMSELVES APART.
WHAT ARE YOU SAYING? YOU'RE SAYING THEY ATTACKED NEW LONDON?

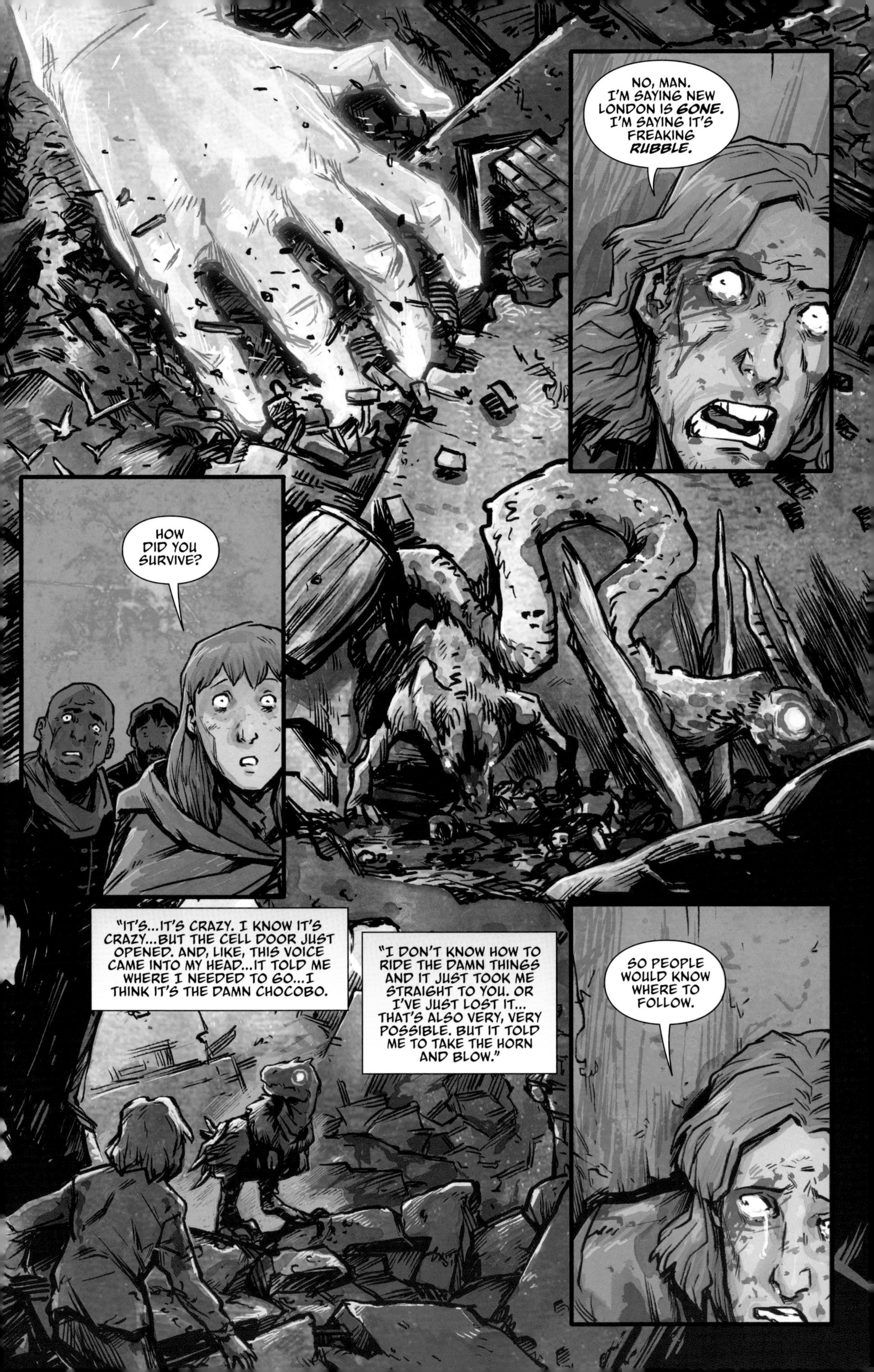

NO, MAN. I'M SAYING NEW LONDON IS GONE. I'M SAYING IT'S FREAKING RUBBLE.
HOW DID YOU SURVIVE?
"IT'S...IT'S CRAZY. I KNOW IT'S CRAZY...BUT THE CELL DOOR JUST OPENED. AND, LIKE, THIS VOICE CAME INTO MY HEAD...IT TOLD ME WHERE I NEEDED TO GO...I THINK IT'S THE DAMN CHOCOBO.
"I DON'T KNOW HOW TO RIDE THE DAMN THINGS AND IT JUST TOOK ME STRAIGHT TO YOU. OR I'VE JUST LOST IT... THAT'S ALSO VERY, VERY POSSIBLE. BUT IT TOLD ME TO TAKE THE HORN AND BLOW."
SO PEOPLE WOULD KNOW WHERE TO FOLLOW.

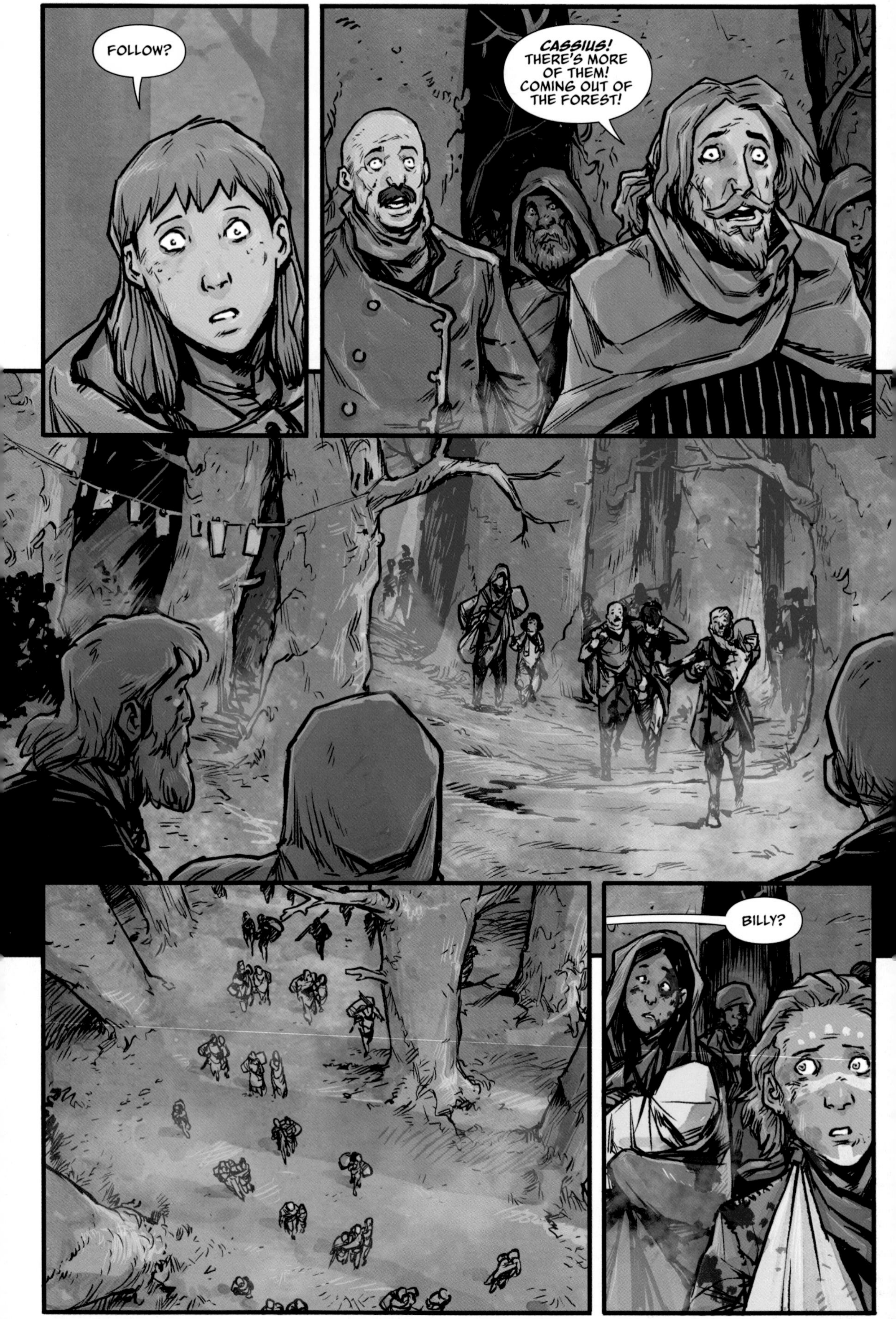
FOLLOW?
CASSIUS! THERE'S MORE OF THEM! COMING OUT OF THE FOREST!
BILLY?

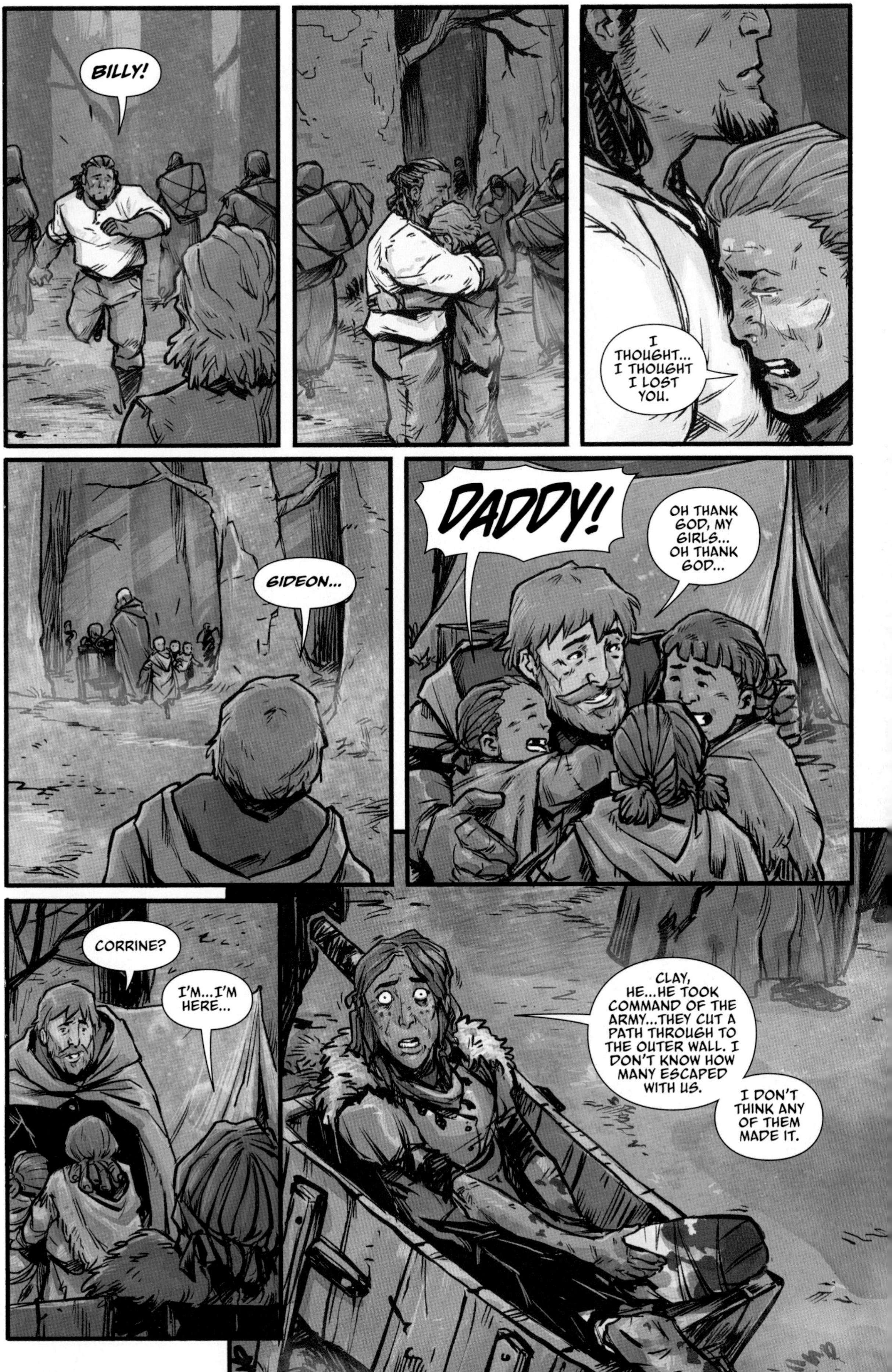

BILLY!
I THOUGHT... I THOUGHT I LOST YOU.
GIDEON...
DADDY!
OH THANK GOD, MY GIRLS... OH THANK GOD...
CORRINE?
I'M...I'M HERE...
CLAY, HE...HE TOOK COMMAND OF THE ARMY...THEY CUT A PATH THROUGH TO THE OUTER WALL. I DON'T KNOW HOW MANY ESCAPED WITH US.
I DON'T THINK ANY OF THEM MADE IT.

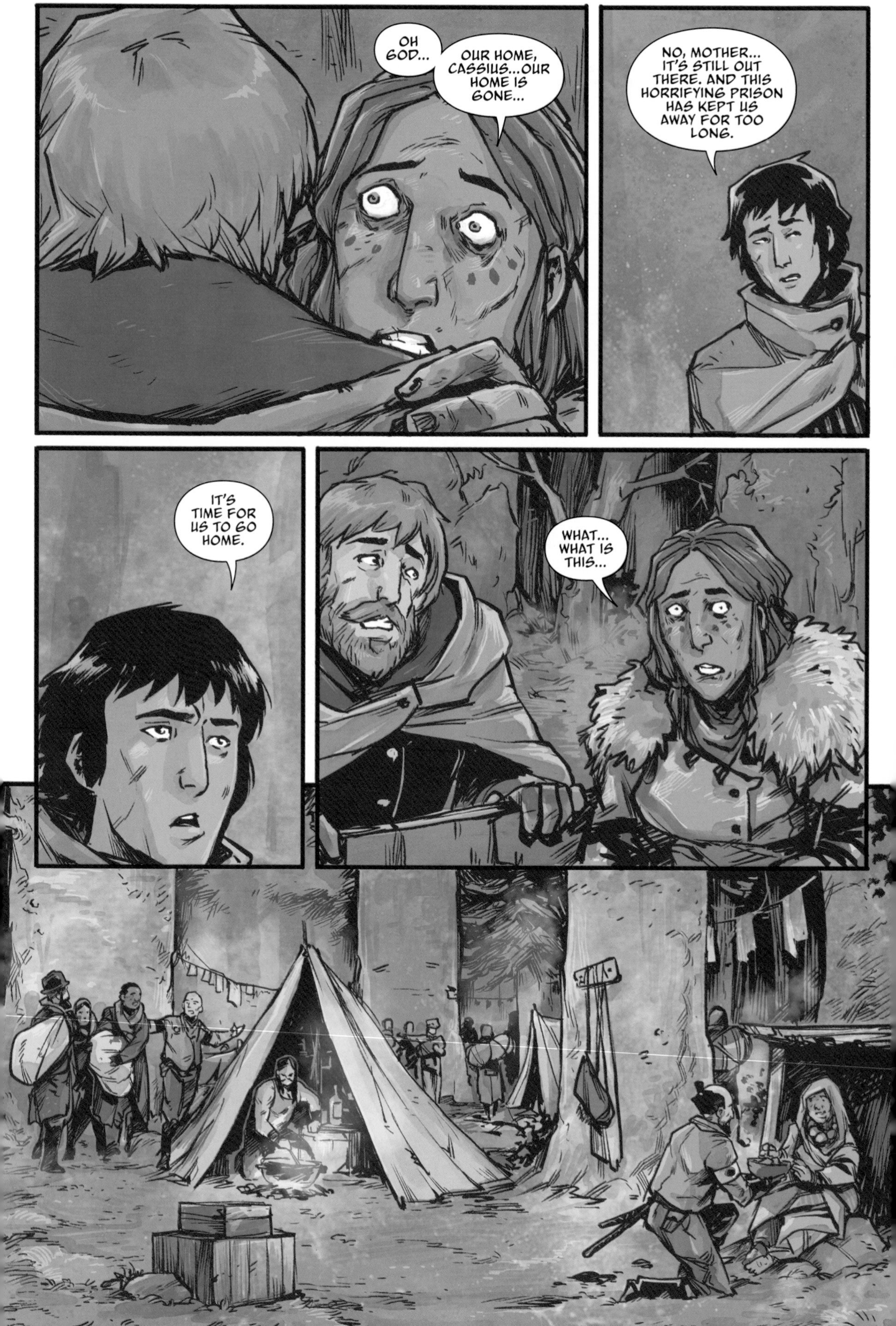
OH GOD...
OUR HOME, CASSIUS...OUR HOME IS GONE...
NO, MOTHER... IT'S STILL OUT THERE. AND THIS HORRIFYING PRISON HAS KEPT US AWAY FOR TOO LONG.
IT'S TIME FOR US TO GO HOME.
WHAT... WHAT IS THIS...

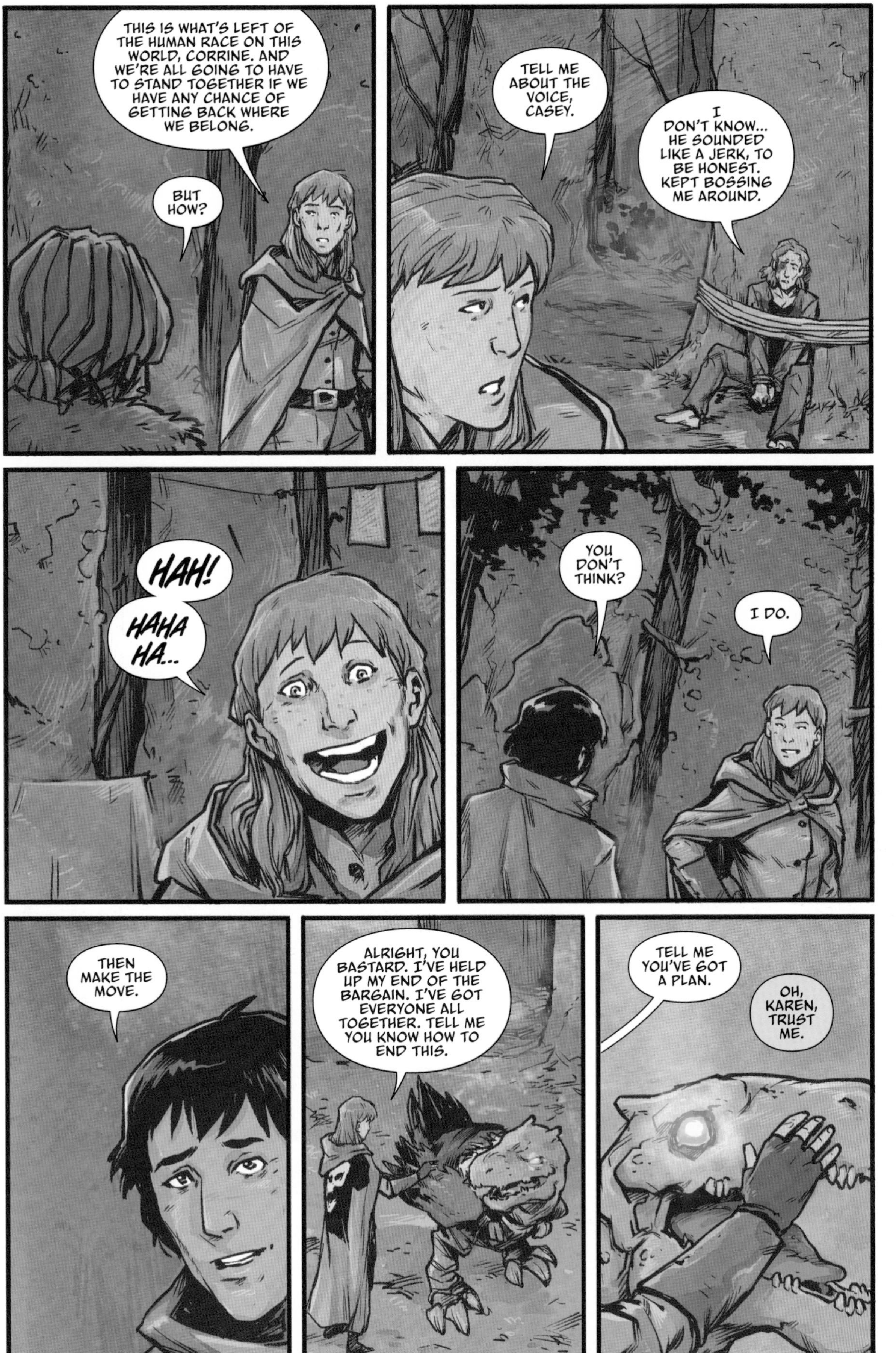
THIS IS WHAT'S LEFT OF THE HUMAN RACE ON THIS WORLD, CORRINE. AND WE'RE ALL GOING TO HAVE TO STAND TOGETHER IF WE HAVE ANY CHANCE OF GETTING BACK WHERE WE BELONG.
BUT HOW?
TELL ME ABOUT THE VOICE, CASEY.
I DON'T KNOW... HE SOUNDED LIKE A JERK, TO BE HONEST. KEPT BOSSING ME AROUND.
HAH!
HAHA HA...
YOU DON'T THINK?
I DO.
THEN MAKE THE MOVE.
ALRIGHT, YOU BASTARD. I'VE HELD UP MY END OF THE BARGAIN. I'VE GOT EVERYONE ALL TOGETHER. TELL ME YOU KNOW HOW TO END THIS.
TELL ME YOU'VE GOT A PLAN.
OH, KAREN, TRUST ME.

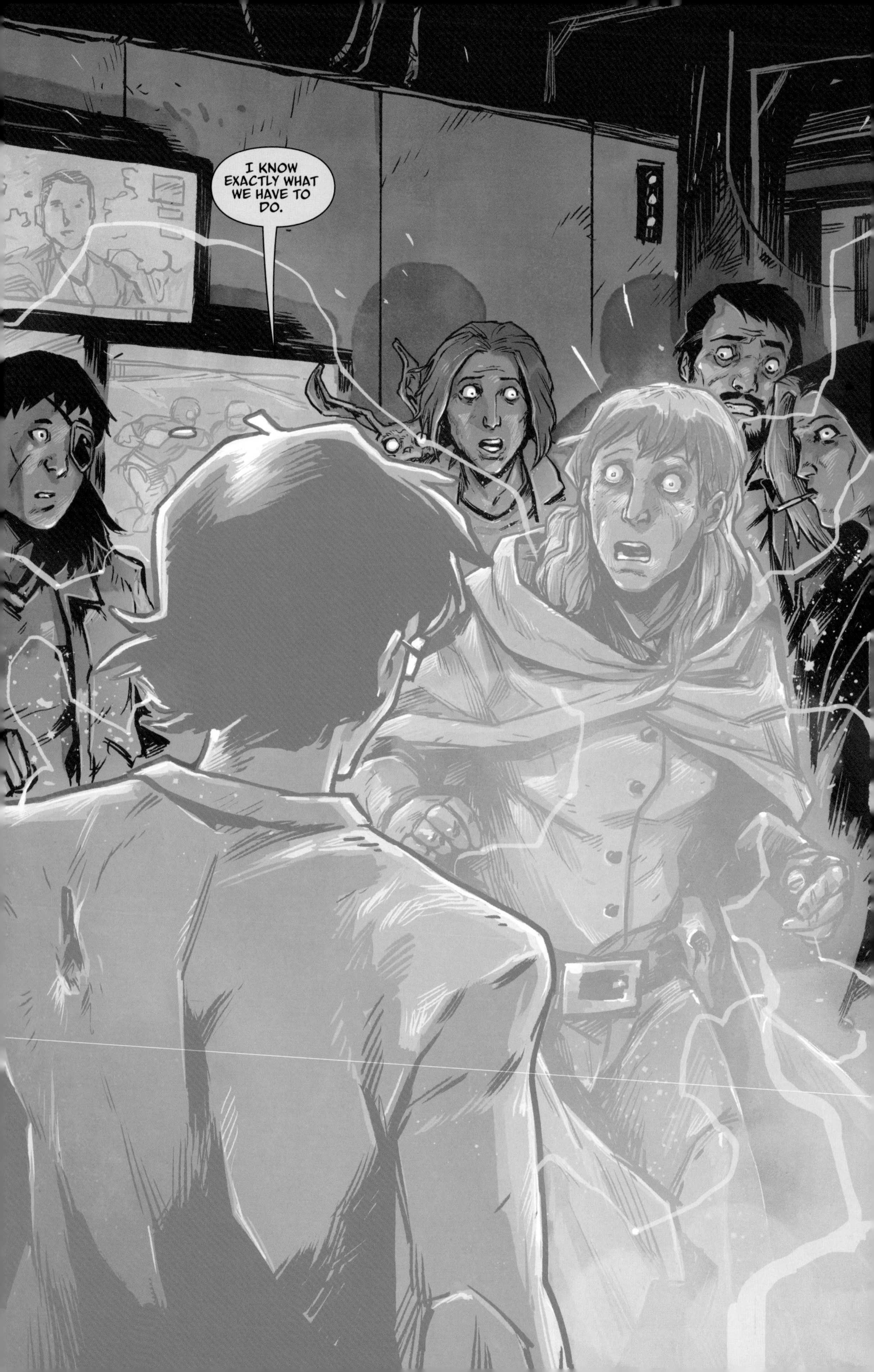
I KNOW EXACTLY WHAT WE HAVE TO DO.

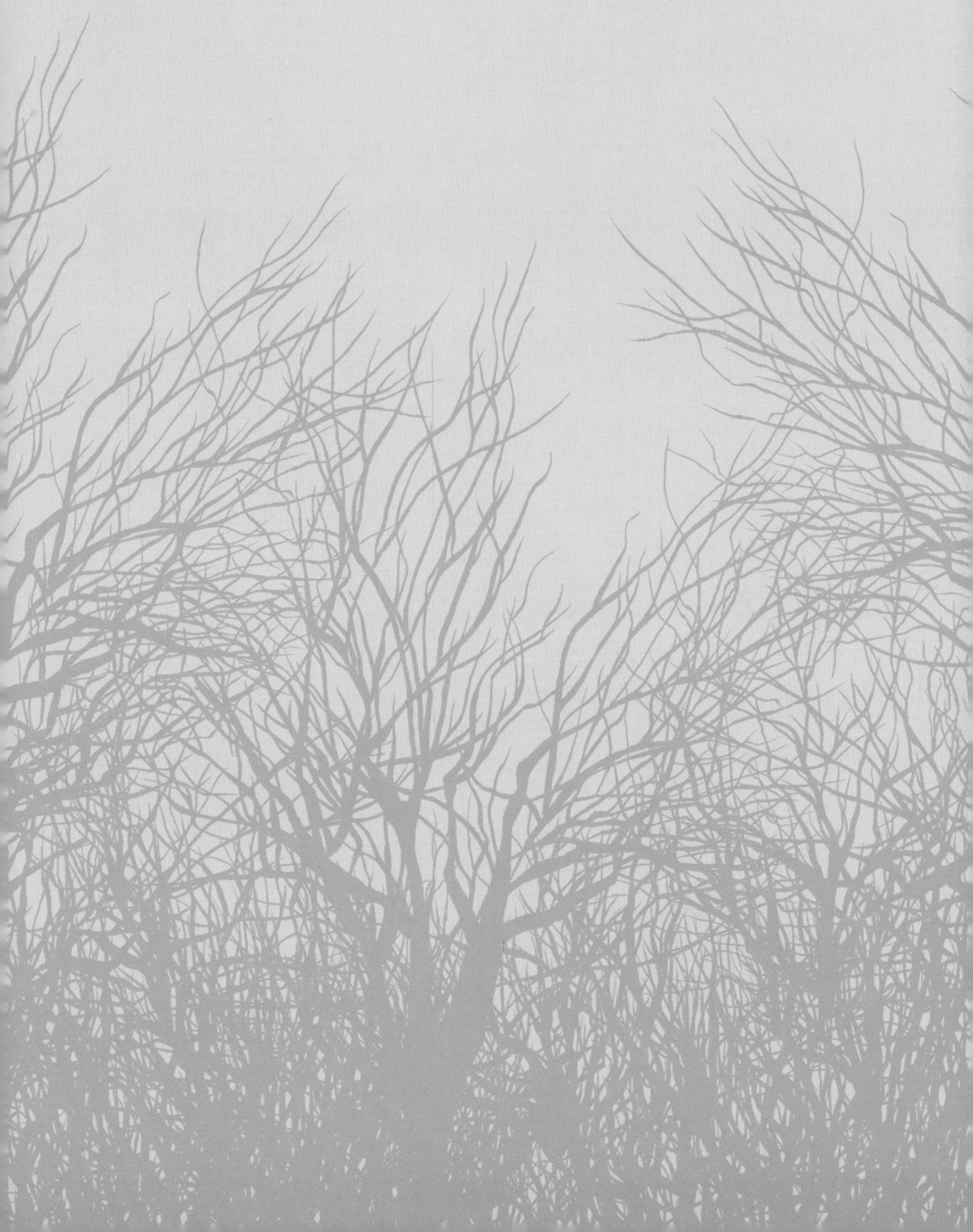

CHAPTER

THIRTY-FOUR

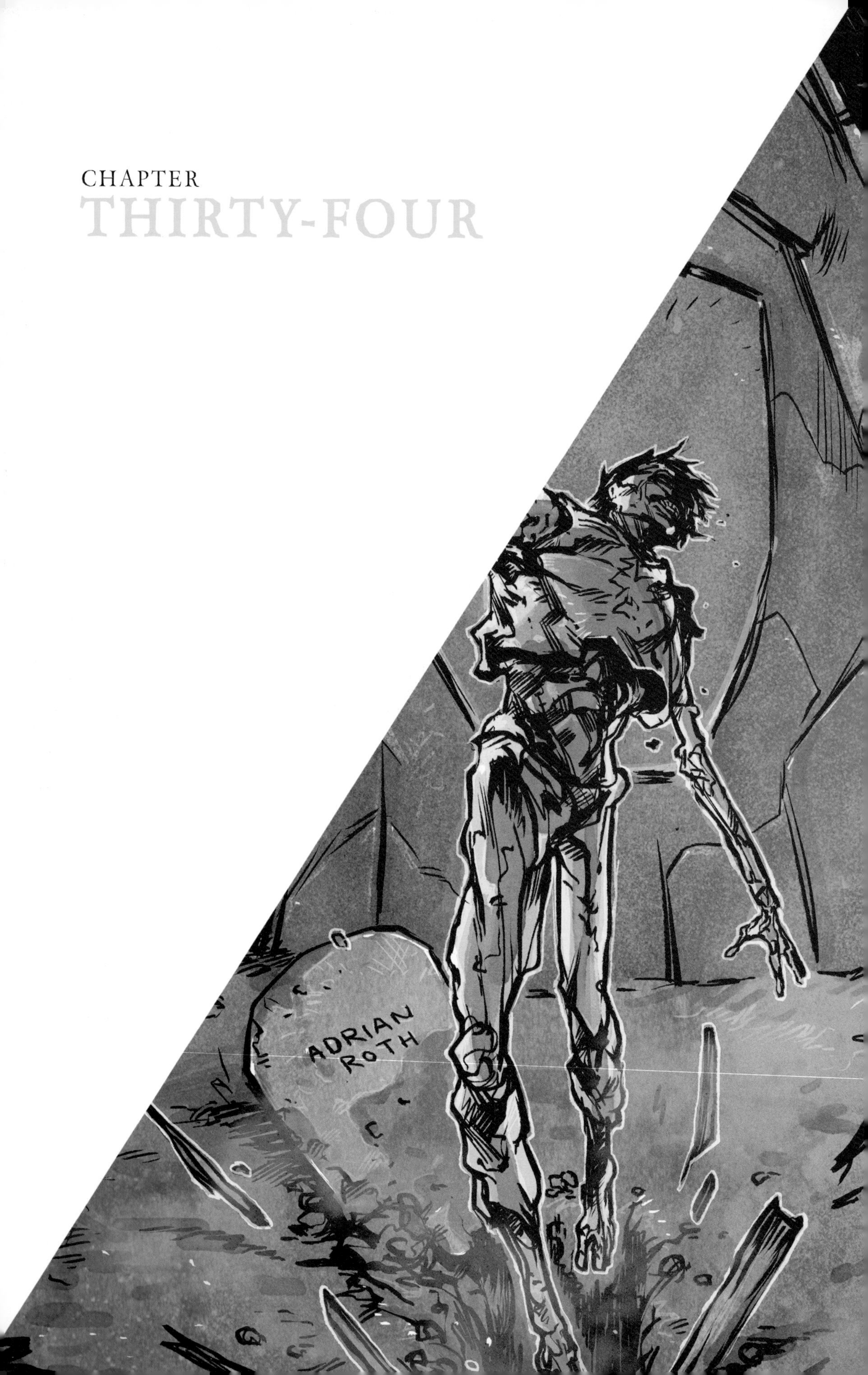
ADRIAN ROTH

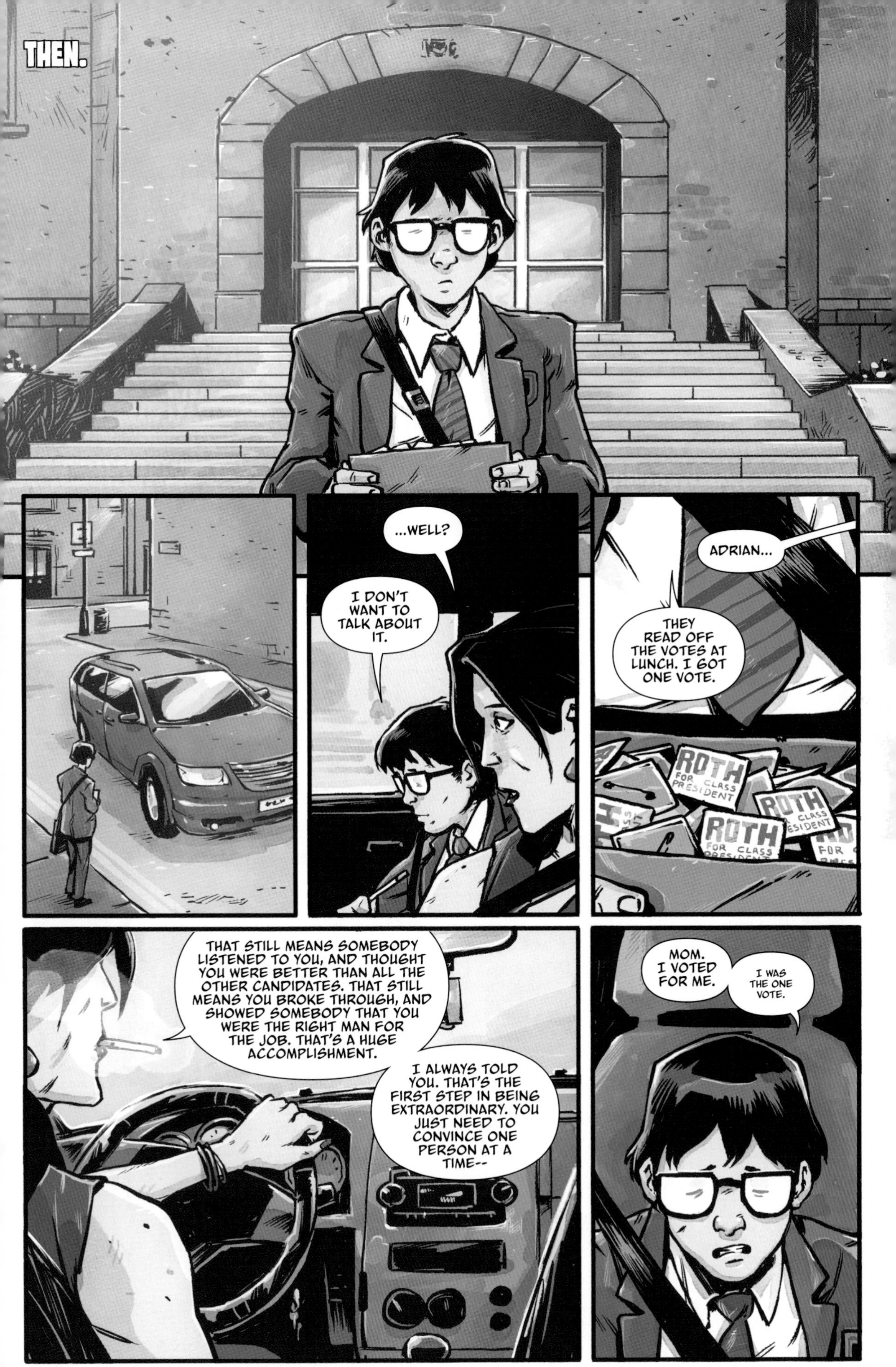
THEN.
...WELL?
I DON'T WANT TO TALK ABOUT IT.
ADRIAN...
THEY READ OFF THE VOTES AT LUNCH. I GOT ONE VOTE.
ROTH FOR CLASS PRESIDENT
THAT STILL MEANS SOMEBODY LISTENED TO YOU, AND THOUGHT YOU WERE BETTER THAN ALL THE OTHER CANDIDATES. THAT STILL MEANS YOU BROKE THROUGH, AND SHOWED SOMEBODY THAT YOU WERE THE RIGHT MAN FOR THE JOB. THAT'S A HUGE ACCOMPLISHMENT.
I ALWAYS TOLD YOU. THAT'S THE FIRST STEP IN BEING EXTRAORDINARY. YOU JUST NEED TO CONVINCE ONE PERSON AT A TIME--
MOM. I VOTED FOR ME.
I WAS THE ONE VOTE.

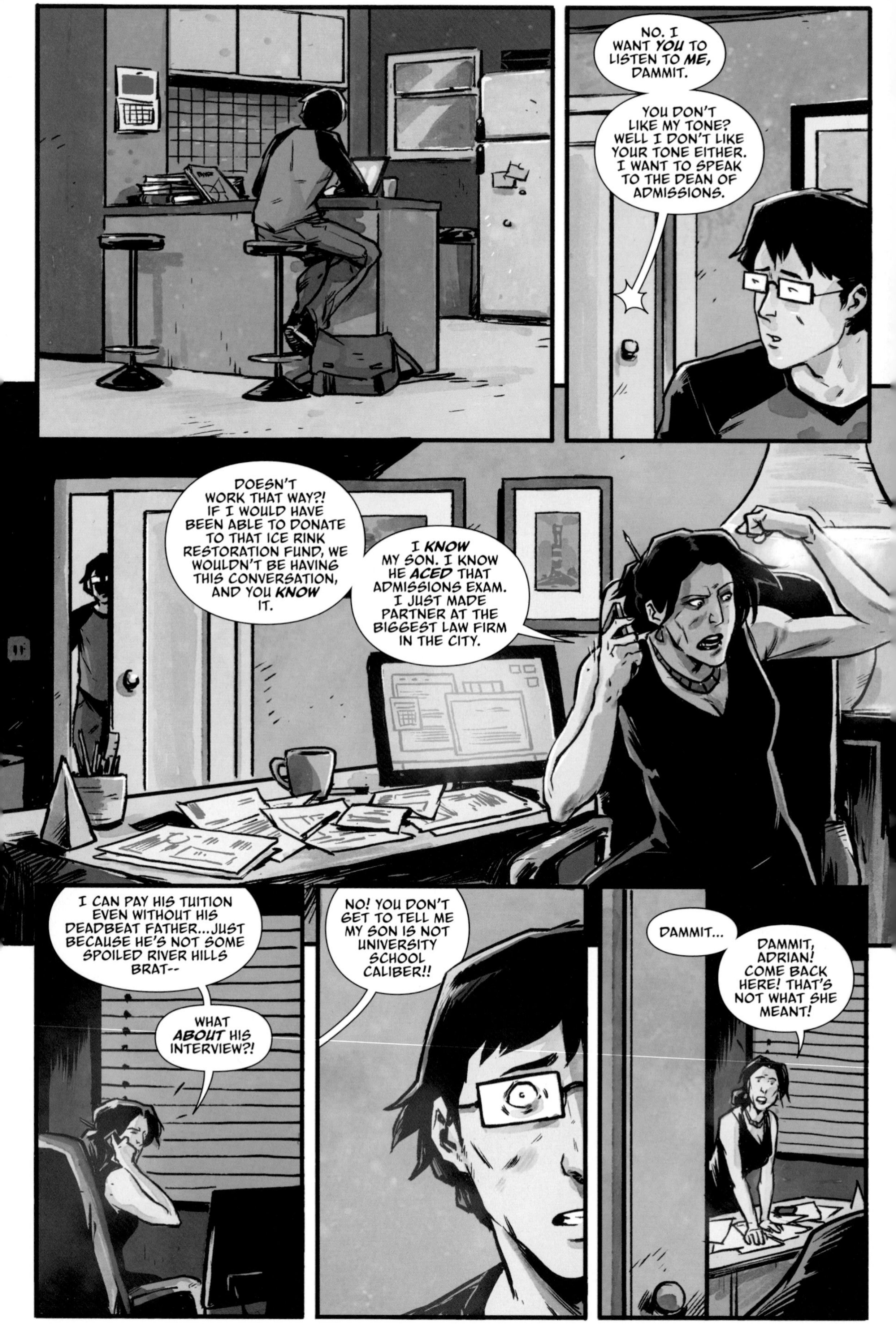
NO. I WANT YOU TO LISTEN TO ME, DAMMIT.
YOU DON'T LIKE MY TONE? WELL I DON'T LIKE YOUR TONE EITHER. I WANT TO SPEAK TO THE DEAN OF ADMISSIONS.
DOESN'T WORK THAT WAY?! IF I WOULD HAVE BEEN ABLE TO DONATE TO THAT ICE RINK RESTORATION FUND, WE WOULDN'T BE HAVING THIS CONVERSATION, AND YOU KNOW IT.
I KNOW MY SON. I KNOW HE ACED THAT ADMISSIONS EXAM. I JUST MADE PARTNER AT THE BIGGEST LAW FIRM IN THE CITY.
I CAN PAY HIS TUITION EVEN WITHOUT HIS DEADBEAT FATHER...JUST BECAUSE HE'S NOT SOME SPOILED RIVER HILLS BRAT--
WHAT ABOUT HIS INTERVIEW?!
NO! YOU DON'T GET TO TELL ME MY SON IS NOT UNIVERSITY SCHOOL CALIBER!!
DAMMIT...
DAMMIT, ADRIAN! COME BACK HERE! THAT'S NOT WHAT SHE MEANT!

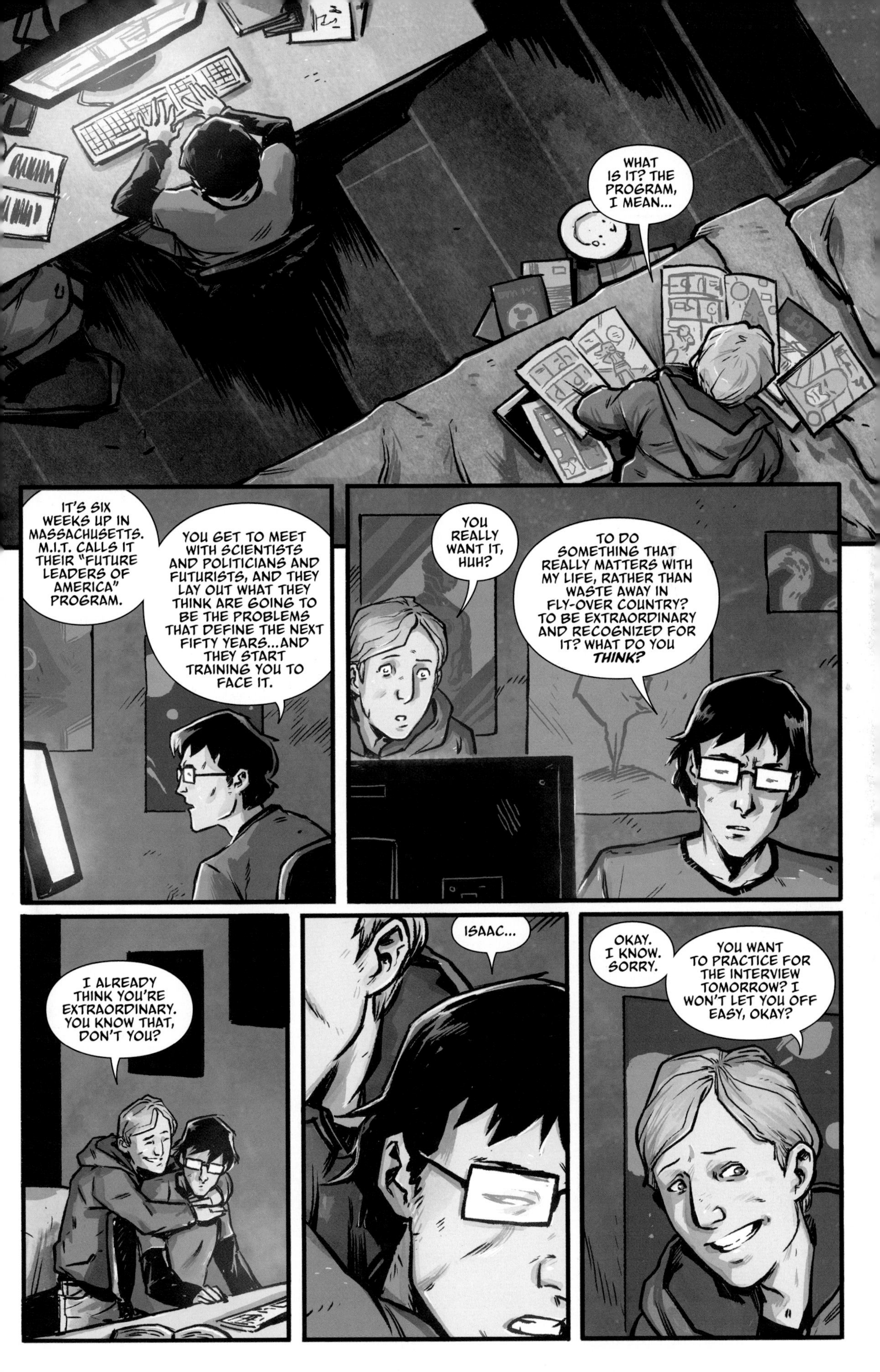
WHAT IS IT? THE PROGRAM, I MEAN...
IT'S SIX WEEKS UP IN MASSACHUSETTS. M.I.T. CALLS IT THEIR "FUTURE LEADERS OF AMERICA" PROGRAM.
YOU GET TO MEET WITH SCIENTISTS AND POLITICIANS AND FUTURISTS, AND THEY LAY OUT WHAT THEY THINK ARE GOING TO BE THE PROBLEMS THAT DEFINE THE NEXT FIFTY YEARS...AND THEY START TRAINING YOU TO FACE IT.
YOU REALLY WANT IT, HUH?
TO DO SOMETHING THAT REALLY MATTERS WITH MY LIFE, RATHER THAN WASTE AWAY IN FLY-OVER COUNTRY? TO BE EXTRAORDINARY AND RECOGNIZED FOR IT? WHAT DO YOU *THINK?*
I ALREADY THINK YOU'RE EXTRAORDINARY. YOU KNOW THAT, DON'T YOU?
ISAAC...
OKAY. I KNOW. SORRY.
YOU WANT TO PRACTICE FOR THE INTERVIEW TOMORROW? I WON'T LET YOU OFF EASY, OKAY?

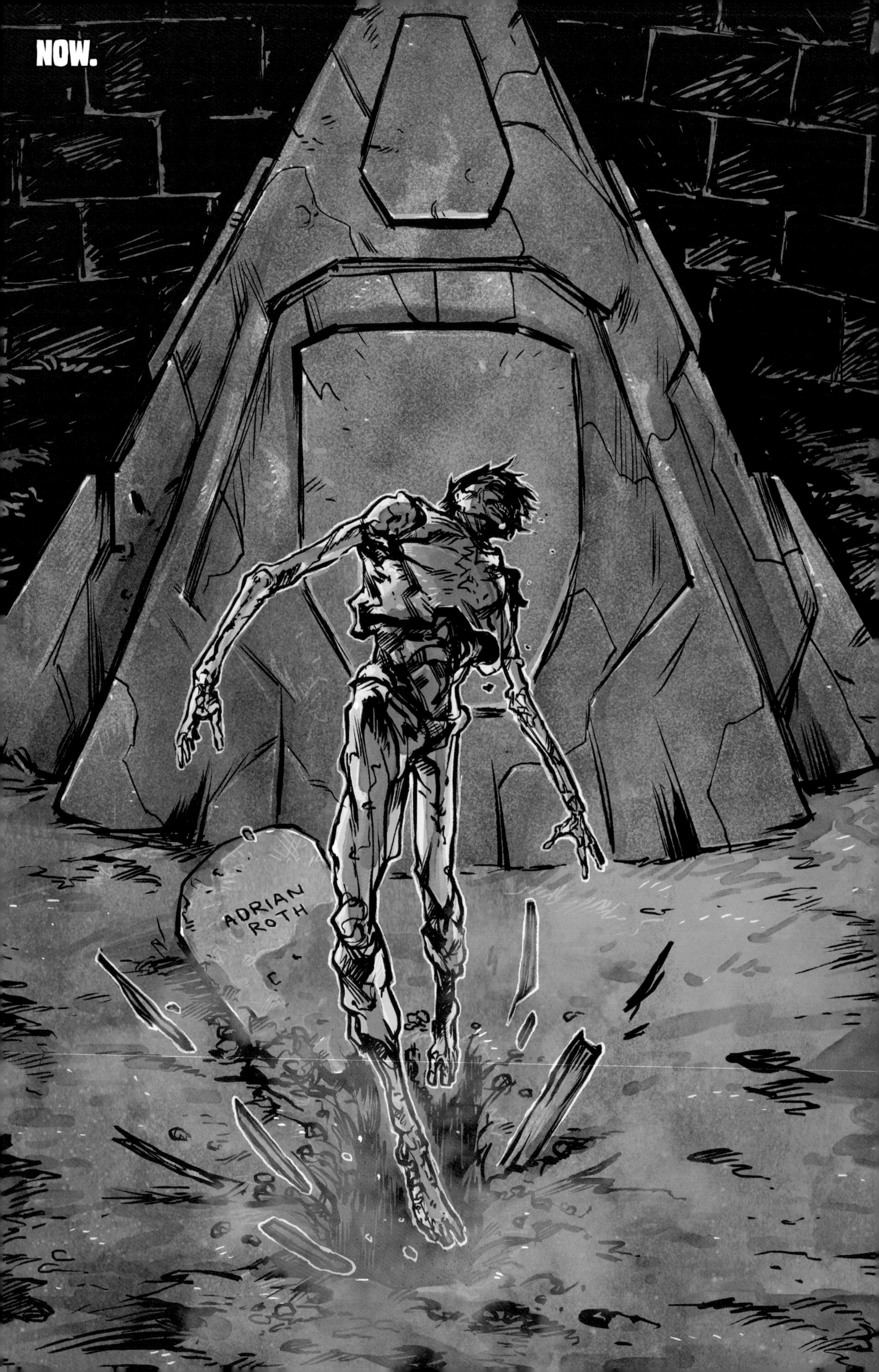
NOW.
ADRIAN ROTH

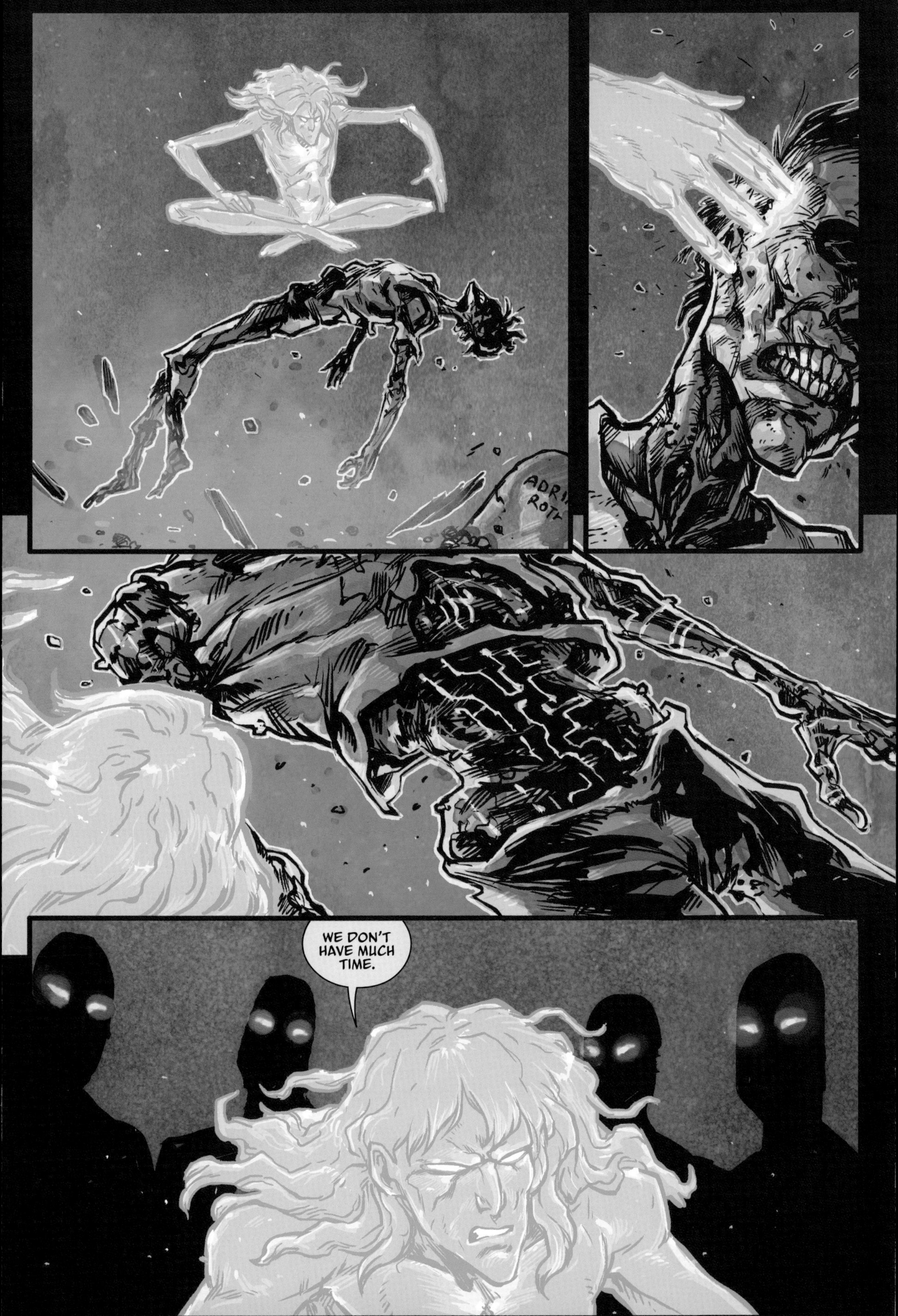
WE DON'T HAVE MUCH TIME.

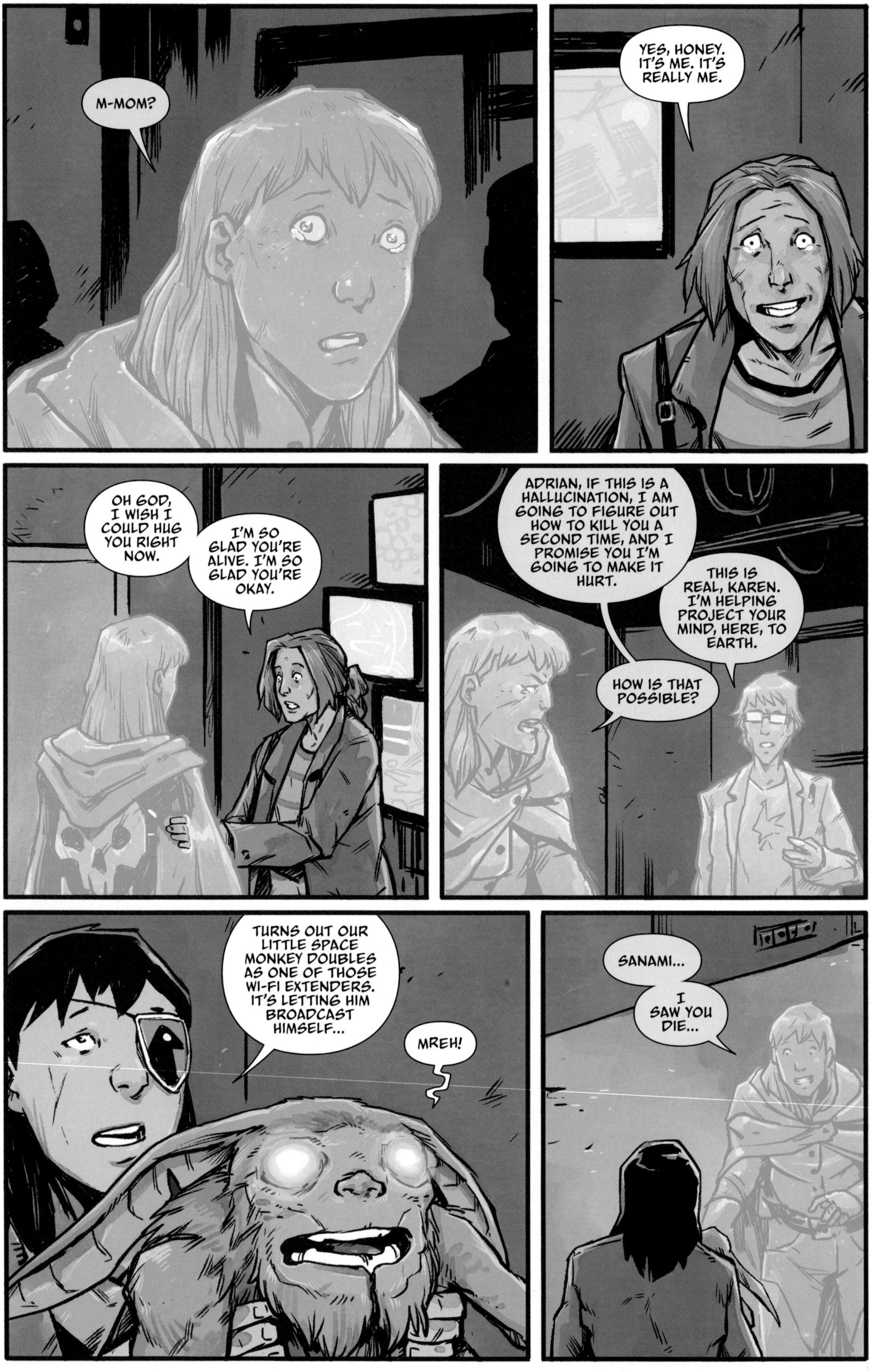
M-MOM?
YES, HONEY. IT'S ME. IT'S REALLY ME.
OH GOD, I WISH I COULD HUG YOU RIGHT NOW.
I'M SO GLAD YOU'RE ALIVE. I'M SO GLAD YOU'RE OKAY.
ADRIAN, IF THIS IS A HALLUCINATION, I AM GOING TO FIGURE OUT HOW TO KILL YOU A SECOND TIME, AND I PROMISE YOU I'M GOING TO MAKE IT HURT.
THIS IS REAL, KAREN. I'M HELPING PROJECT YOUR MIND, HERE, TO EARTH.
HOW IS THAT POSSIBLE?
TURNS OUT OUR LITTLE SPACE MONKEY DOUBLES AS ONE OF THOSE WI-FI EXTENDERS. IT'S LETTING HIM BROADCAST HIMSELF...
MREH!
SANAMI...
I SAW YOU DIE...

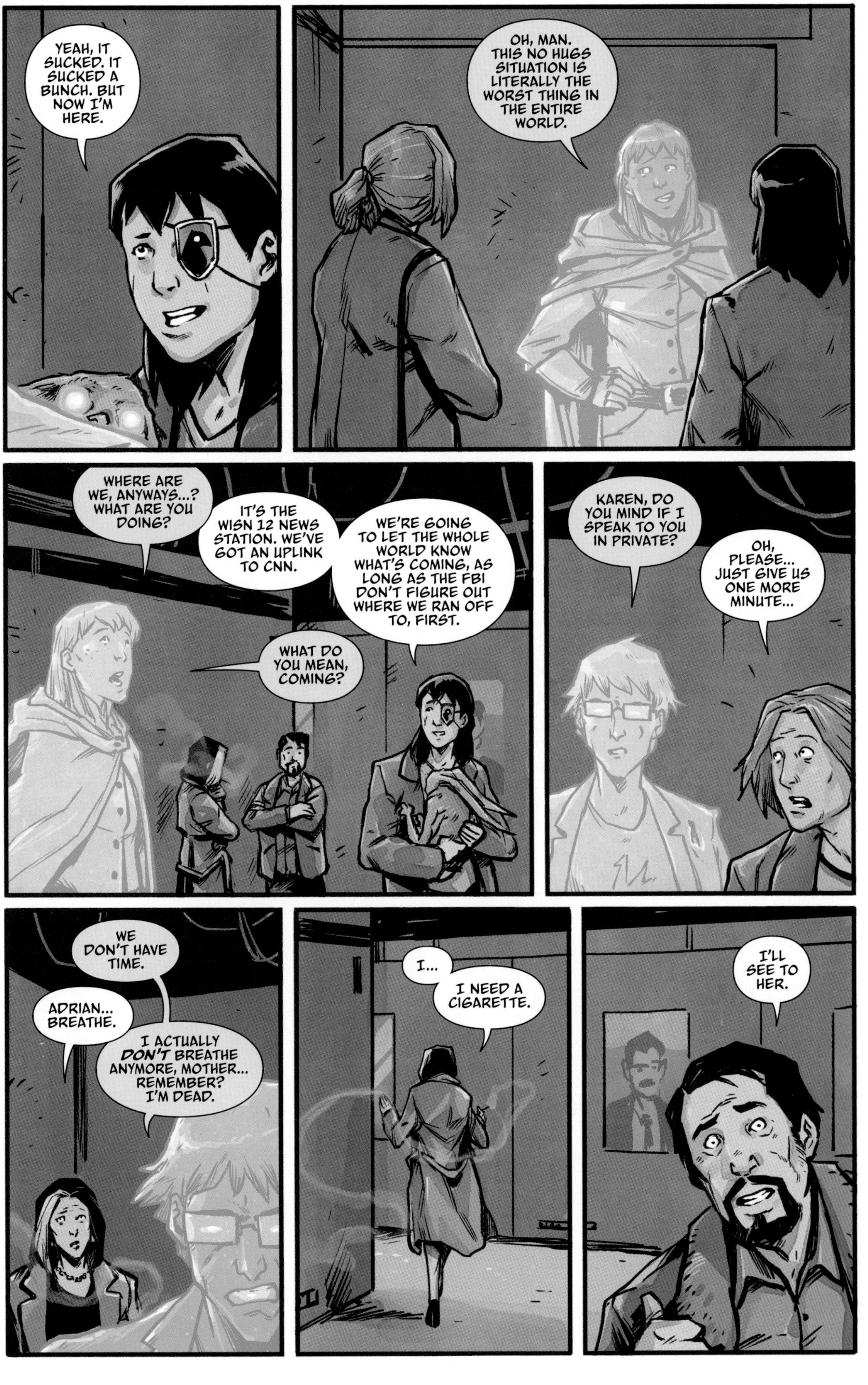

YEAH, IT SUCKED. IT SUCKED A BUNCH. BUT NOW I'M HERE.
OH, MAN. THIS NO HUGS SITUATION IS LITERALLY THE WORST THING IN THE ENTIRE WORLD.
WHERE ARE WE, ANYWAYS...? WHAT ARE YOU DOING?
IT'S THE WISN 12 NEWS STATION. WE'VE GOT AN UPLINK TO CNN.
WE'RE GOING TO LET THE WHOLE WORLD KNOW WHAT'S COMING, AS LONG AS THE FBI DON'T FIGURE OUT WHERE WE RAN OFF TO, FIRST.
WHAT DO YOU MEAN, COMING?
KAREN, DO YOU MIND IF I SPEAK TO YOU IN PRIVATE?
OH, PLEASE... JUST GIVE US ONE MORE MINUTE...
WE DON'T HAVE TIME.
ADRIAN... BREATHE.
I ACTUALLY DON'T BREATHE ANYMORE, MOTHER... REMEMBER? I'M DEAD.
I... I NEED A CIGARETTE.
I'LL SEE TO HER.

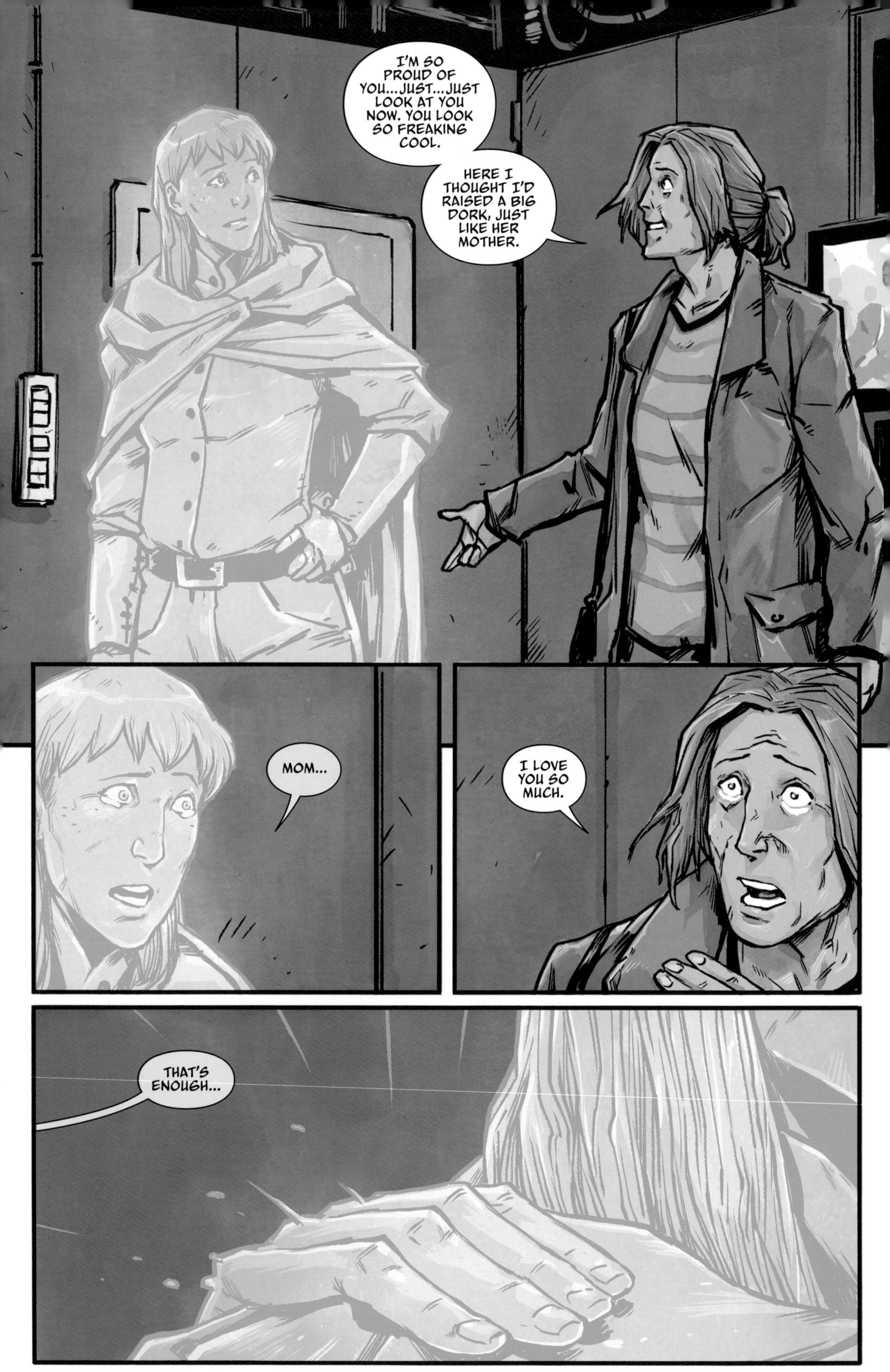

I'M SO PROUD OF YOU...JUST...JUST LOOK AT YOU NOW. YOU LOOK SO FREAKING COOL.
HERE I THOUGHT I'D RAISED A BIG DORK, JUST LIKE HER MOTHER.
MOM...
I LOVE YOU SO MUCH.
THAT'S ENOUGH...

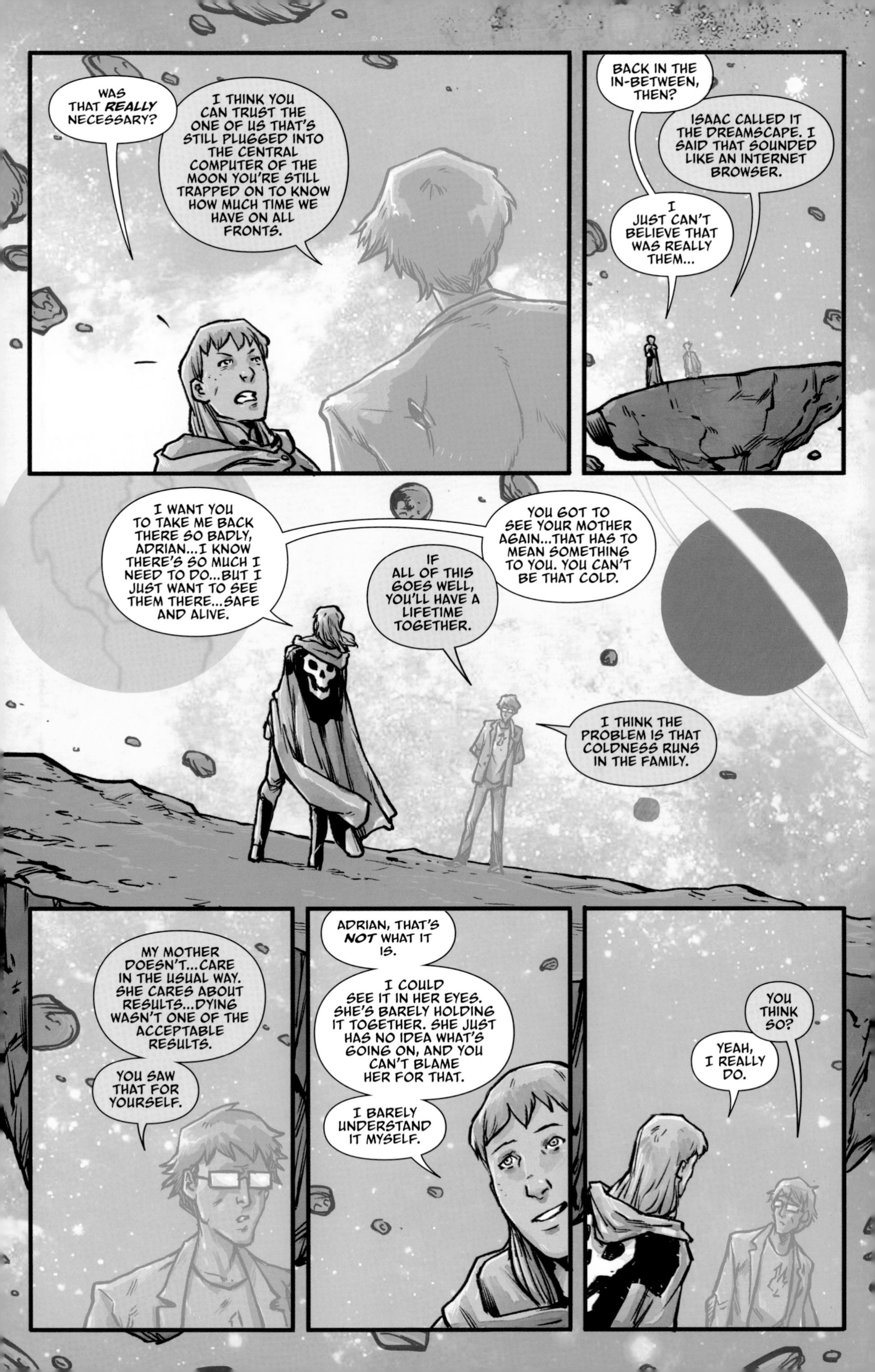
WAS THAT REALLY NECESSARY?
I THINK YOU CAN TRUST THE ONE OF US THAT'S STILL PLUGGED INTO THE CENTRAL COMPUTER OF THE MOON YOU'RE STILL TRAPPED ON TO KNOW HOW MUCH TIME WE HAVE ON ALL FRONTS.
BACK IN THE IN-BETWEEN, THEN?
ISAAC CALLED IT THE DREAMSCAPE. I SAID THAT SOUNDED LIKE AN INTERNET BROWSER.
I JUST CAN'T BELIEVE THAT WAS REALLY THEM...
I WANT YOU TO TAKE ME BACK THERE SO BADLY, ADRIAN...I KNOW THERE'S SO MUCH I NEED TO DO...BUT I JUST WANT TO SEE THEM THERE...SAFE AND ALIVE.
YOU GOT TO SEE YOUR MOTHER AGAIN...THAT HAS TO MEAN SOMETHING TO YOU. YOU CAN'T BE THAT COLD.
IF ALL OF THIS GOES WELL, YOU'LL HAVE A LIFETIME TOGETHER.
I THINK THE PROBLEM IS THAT COLDNESS RUNS IN THE FAMILY.
MY MOTHER DOESN'T...CARE IN THE USUAL WAY. SHE CARES ABOUT RESULTS...DYING WASN'T ONE OF THE ACCEPTABLE RESULTS.
YOU SAW THAT FOR YOURSELF.
ADRIAN, THAT'S NOT WHAT IT IS.
I COULD SEE IT IN HER EYES. SHE'S BARELY HOLDING IT TOGETHER. SHE JUST HAS NO IDEA WHAT'S GOING ON, AND YOU CAN'T BLAME HER FOR THAT.
I BARELY UNDERSTAND IT MYSELF.
YOU THINK SO?
YEAH, I REALLY DO.

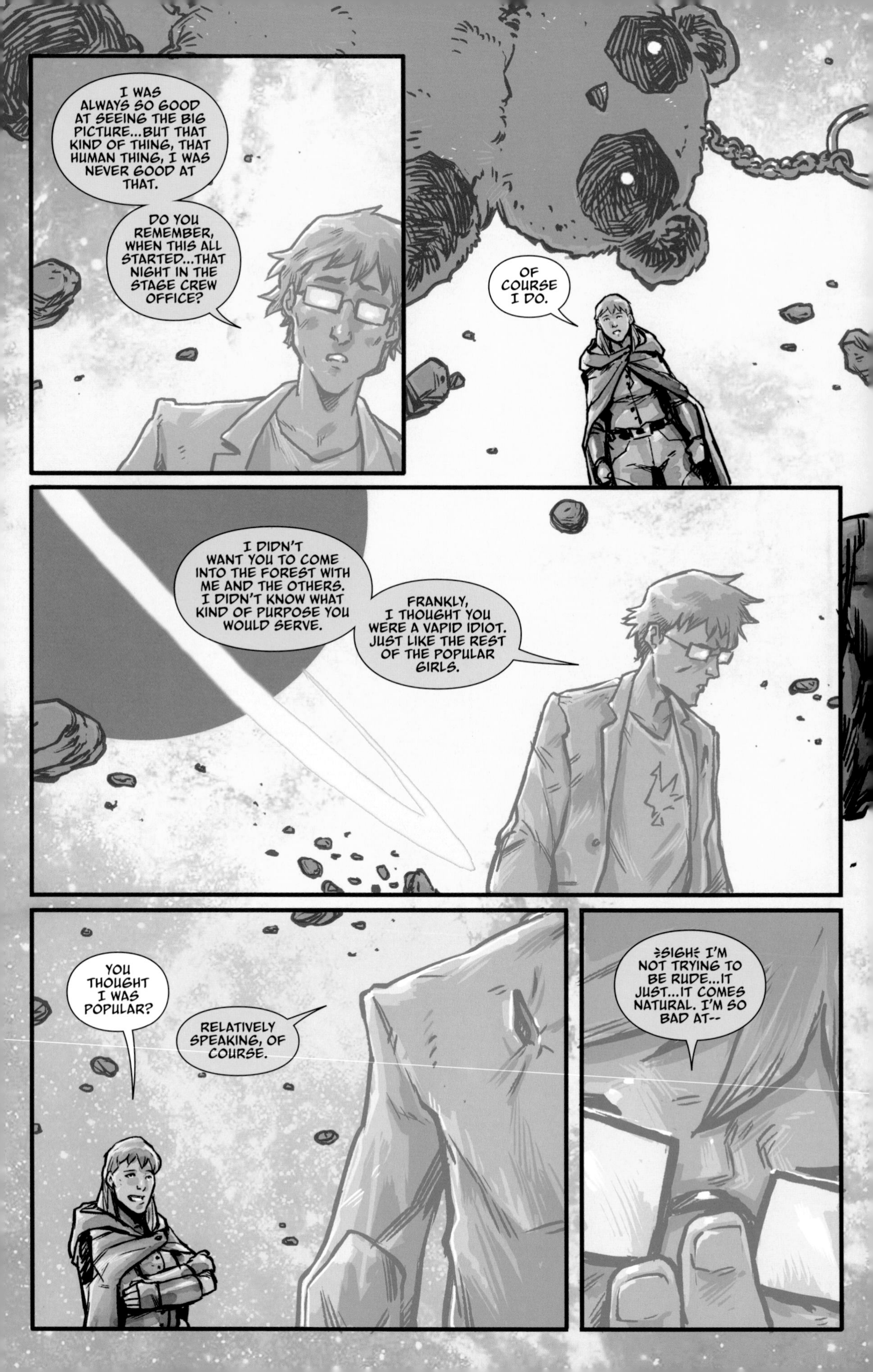
I WAS ALWAYS SO GOOD AT SEEING THE BIG PICTURE...BUT THAT KIND OF THING, THAT HUMAN THING, I WAS NEVER GOOD AT THAT.
DO YOU REMEMBER, WHEN THIS ALL STARTED...THAT NIGHT IN THE STAGE CREW OFFICE?
OF COURSE I DO.
I DIDN'T WANT YOU TO COME INTO THE FOREST WITH ME AND THE OTHERS. I DIDN'T KNOW WHAT KIND OF PURPOSE YOU WOULD SERVE.
FRANKLY, I THOUGHT YOU WERE A VAPID IDIOT. JUST LIKE THE REST OF THE POPULAR GIRLS.
YOU THOUGHT I WAS POPULAR?
RELATIVELY SPEAKING, OF COURSE.
SIGH I'M NOT TRYING TO BE RUDE...IT JUST...IT COMES NATURAL. I'M SO BAD AT--

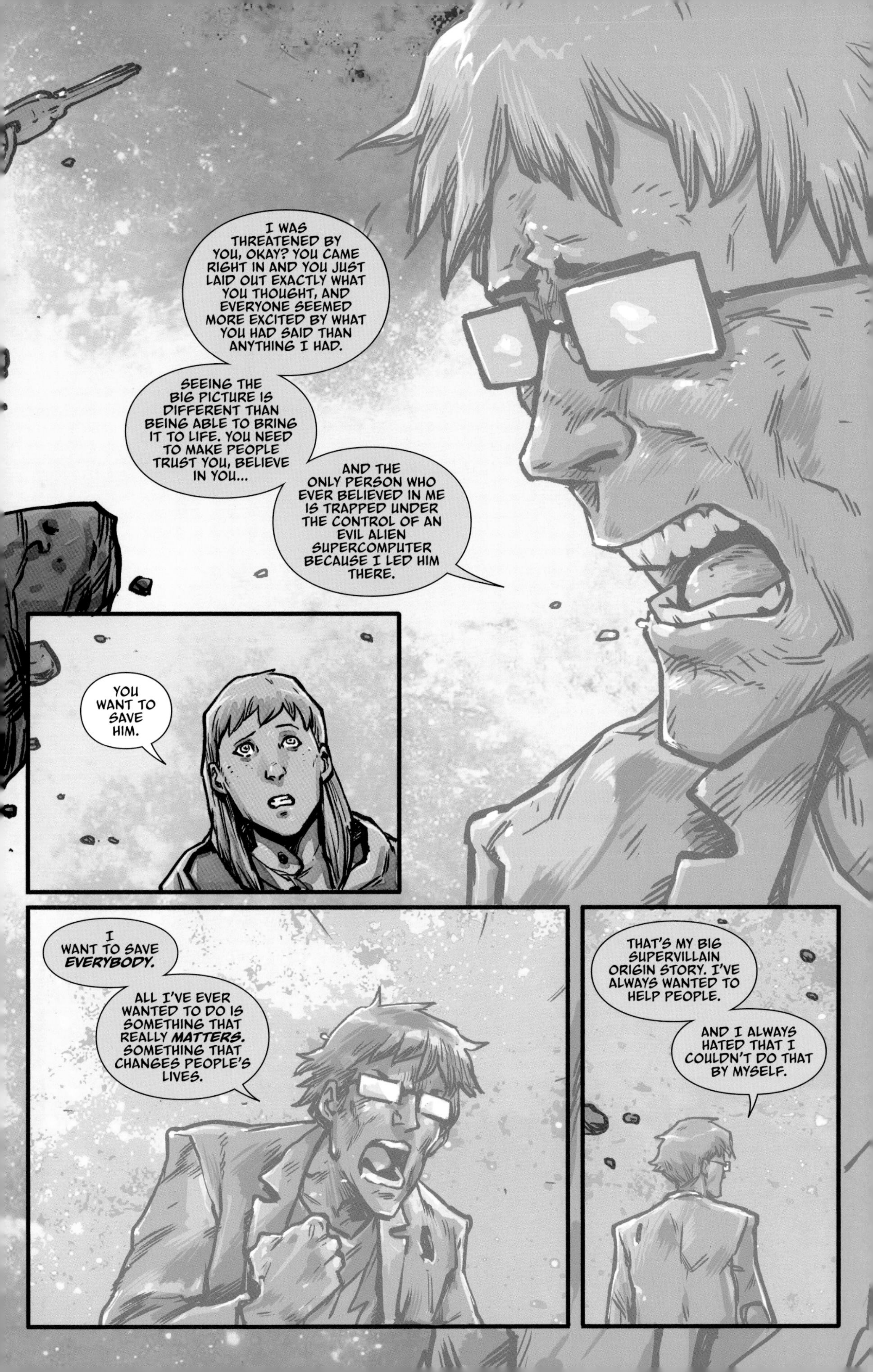
I WAS THREATENED BY YOU, OKAY? YOU CAME RIGHT IN AND YOU JUST LAID OUT EXACTLY WHAT YOU THOUGHT, AND EVERYONE SEEMED MORE EXCITED BY WHAT YOU HAD SAID THAN ANYTHING I HAD.
SEEING THE BIG PICTURE IS DIFFERENT THAN BEING ABLE TO BRING IT TO LIFE. YOU NEED TO MAKE PEOPLE TRUST YOU, BELIEVE IN YOU...
AND THE ONLY PERSON WHO EVER BELIEVED IN ME IS TRAPPED UNDER THE CONTROL OF AN EVIL ALIEN SUPERCOMPUTER BECAUSE I LED HIM THERE.
YOU WANT TO SAVE HIM.
I WANT TO SAVE ***EVERYBODY.***
ALL I'VE EVER WANTED TO DO IS SOMETHING THAT REALLY ***MATTERS.*** SOMETHING THAT CHANGES PEOPLE'S LIVES.
THAT'S MY BIG SUPERVILLAIN ORIGIN STORY. I'VE ALWAYS WANTED TO HELP PEOPLE.
AND I ALWAYS HATED THAT I COULDN'T DO THAT BY MYSELF.

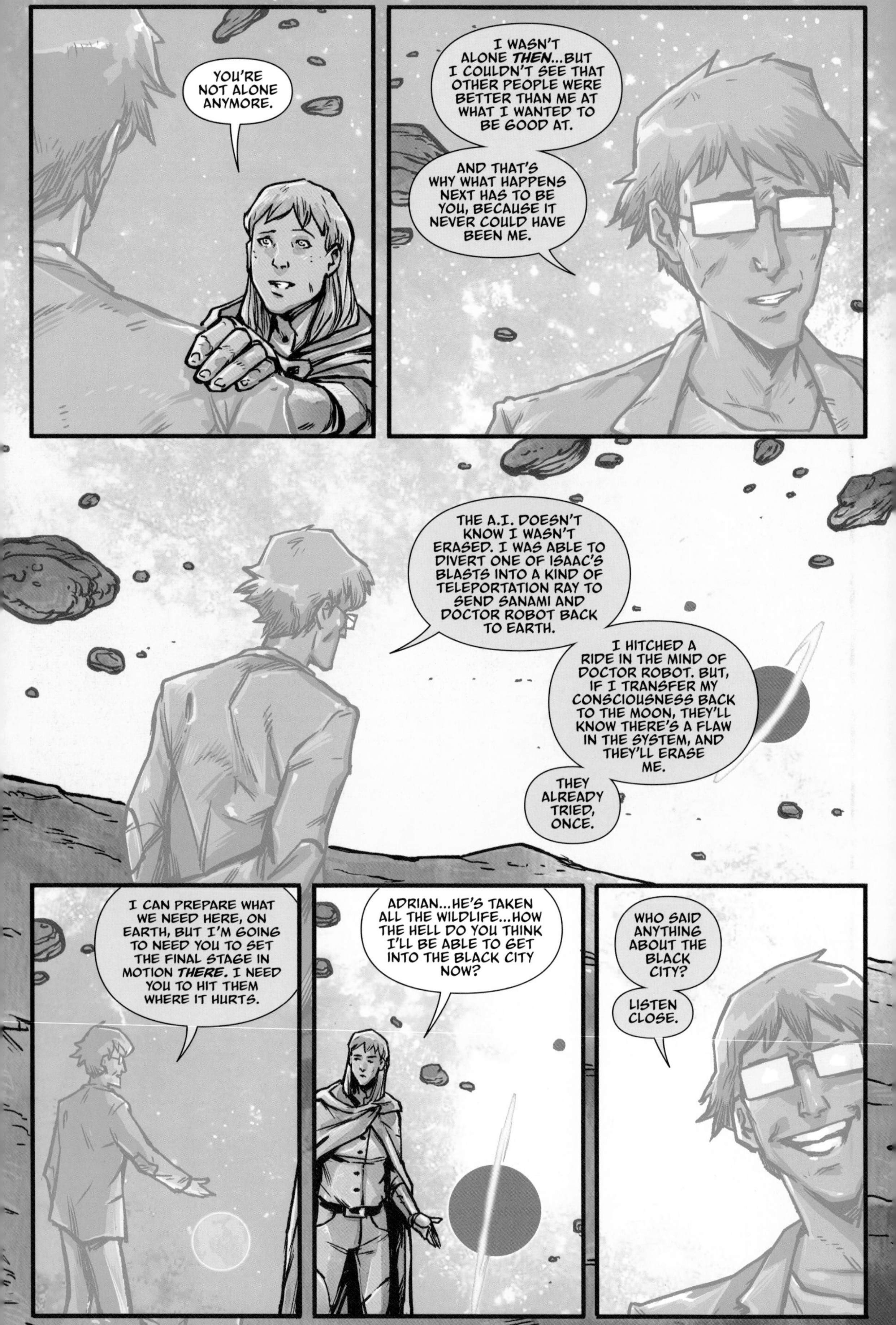
YOU'RE NOT ALONE ANYMORE.
I WASN'T ALONE THEN...BUT I COULDN'T SEE THAT OTHER PEOPLE WERE BETTER THAN ME AT WHAT I WANTED TO BE GOOD AT.
AND THAT'S WHY WHAT HAPPENS NEXT HAS TO BE YOU, BECAUSE IT NEVER COULD HAVE BEEN ME.
THE A.I. DOESN'T KNOW I WASN'T ERASED. I WAS ABLE TO DIVERT ONE OF ISAAC'S BLASTS INTO A KIND OF TELEPORTATION RAY TO SEND SANAMI AND DOCTOR ROBOT BACK TO EARTH.
I HITCHED A RIDE IN THE MIND OF DOCTOR ROBOT. BUT, IF I TRANSFER MY CONSCIOUSNESS BACK TO THE MOON, THEY'LL KNOW THERE'S A FLAW IN THE SYSTEM, AND THEY'LL ERASE ME.
THEY ALREADY TRIED, ONCE.
I CAN PREPARE WHAT WE NEED HERE, ON EARTH, BUT I'M GOING TO NEED YOU TO SET THE FINAL STAGE IN MOTION THERE. I NEED YOU TO HIT THEM WHERE IT HURTS.
ADRIAN...HE'S TAKEN ALL THE WILDLIFE...HOW THE HELL DO YOU THINK I'LL BE ABLE TO GET INTO THE BLACK CITY NOW?
WHO SAID ANYTHING ABOUT THE BLACK CITY?
LISTEN CLOSE.

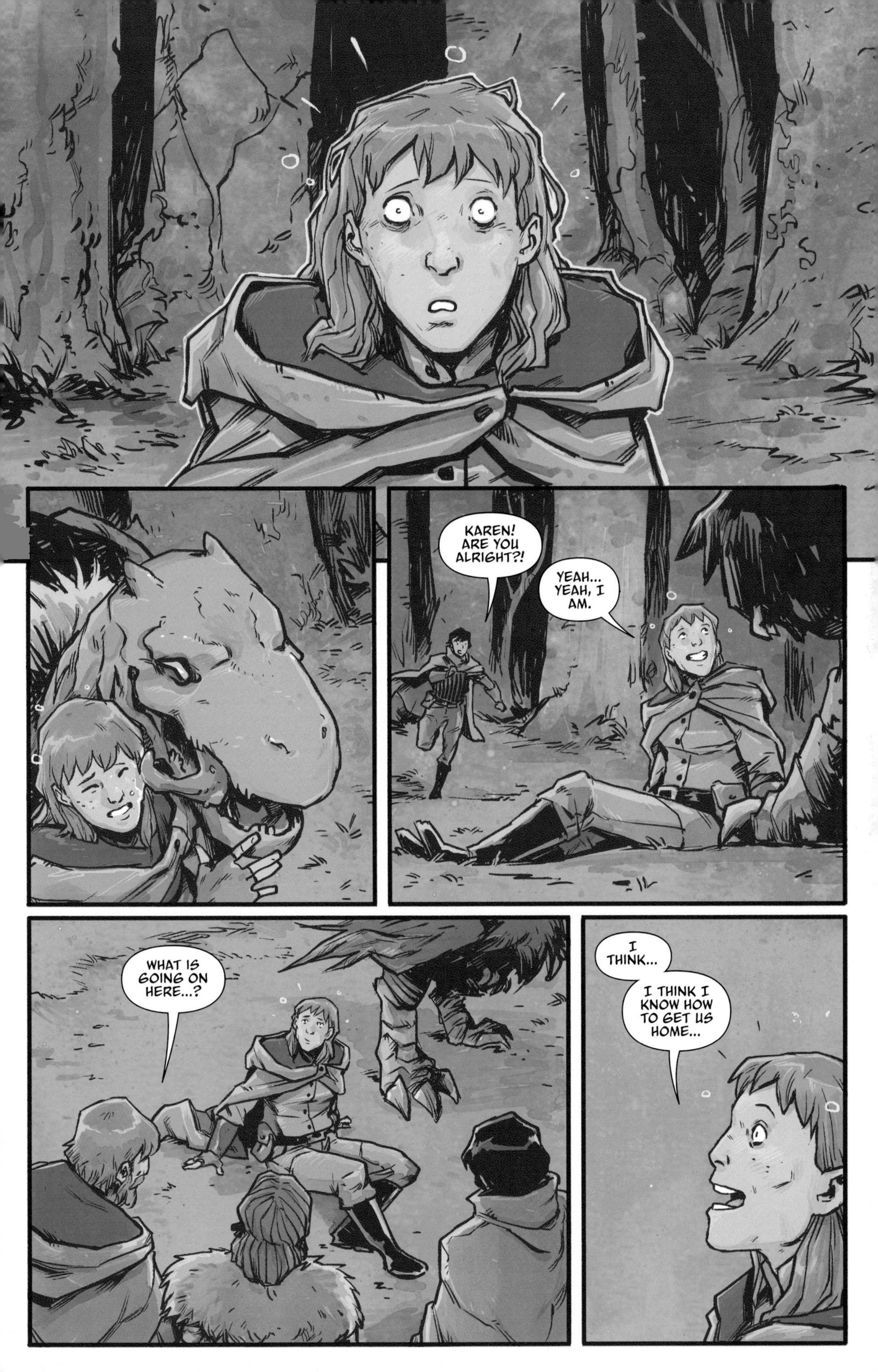
KAREN! ARE YOU ALRIGHT?!
YEAH... YEAH, I AM.
WHAT IS GOING ON HERE...?
I THINK...
I THINK I KNOW HOW TO GET US HOME...

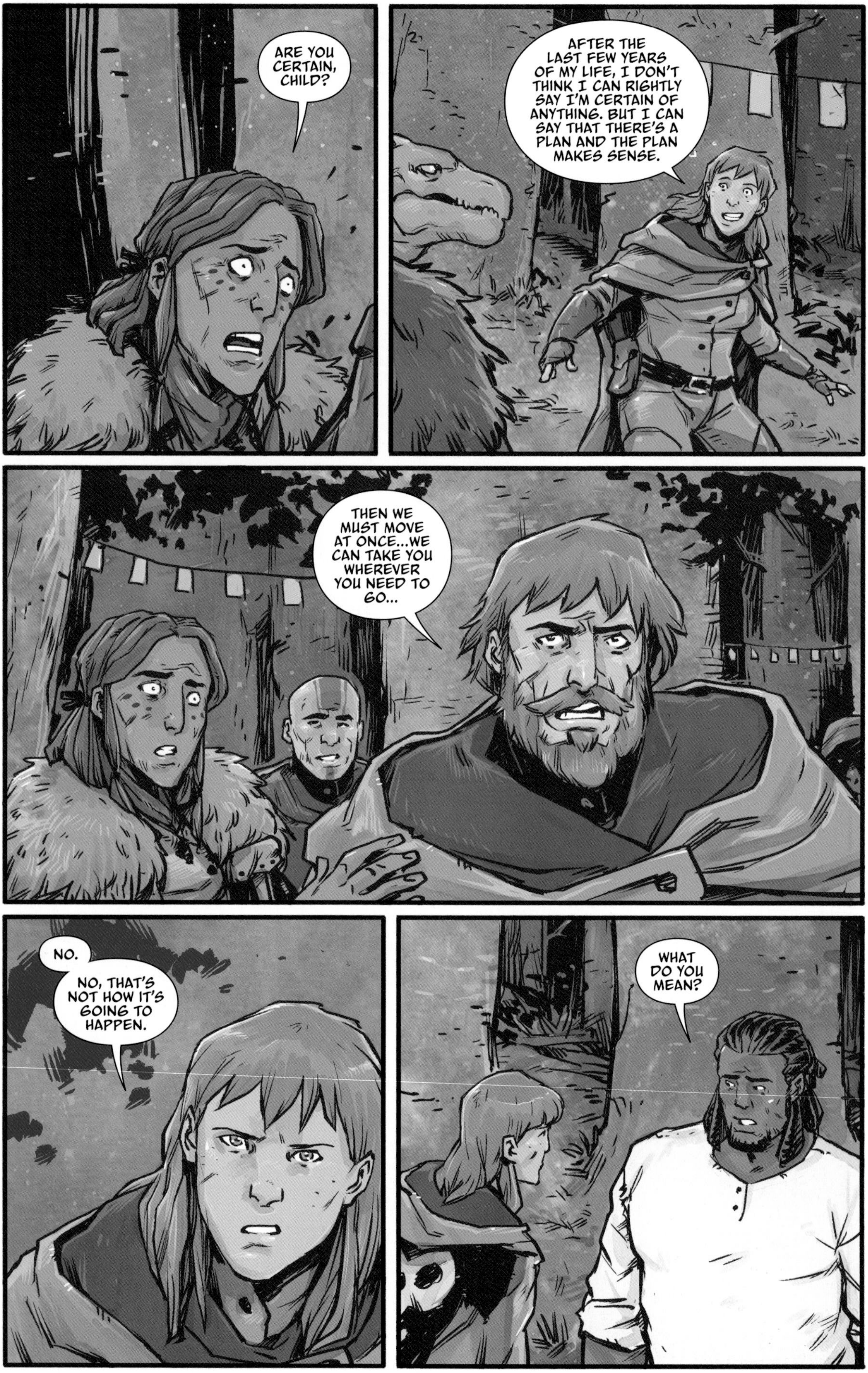
ARE YOU CERTAIN, CHILD?
AFTER THE LAST FEW YEARS OF MY LIFE, I DON'T THINK I CAN RIGHTLY SAY I'M CERTAIN OF ANYTHING. BUT I CAN SAY THAT THERE'S A PLAN AND THE PLAN MAKES SENSE.
THEN WE MUST MOVE AT ONCE...WE CAN TAKE YOU WHEREVER YOU NEED TO GO...
NO.
NO, THAT'S NOT HOW IT'S GOING TO HAPPEN.
WHAT DO YOU MEAN?

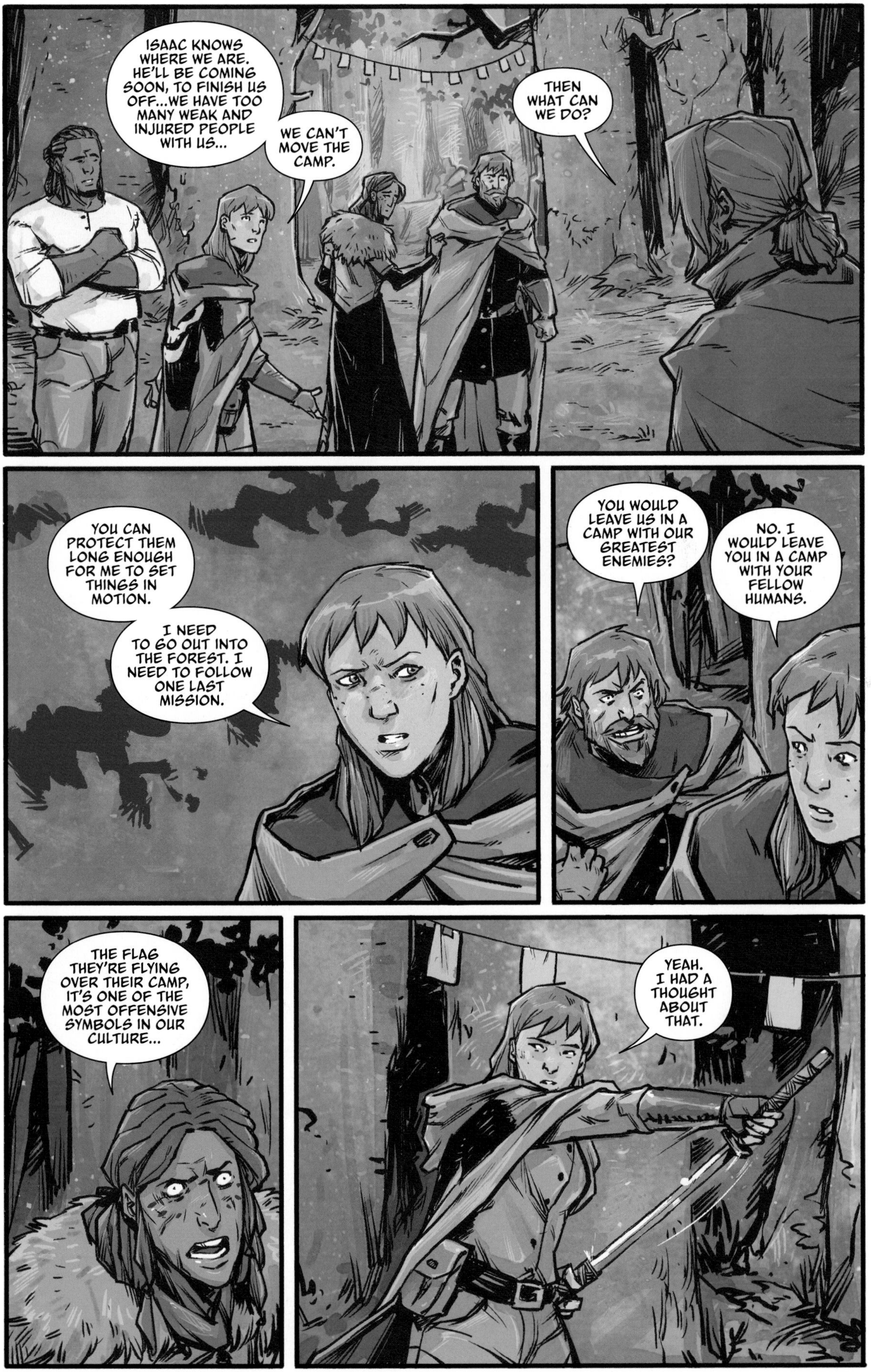
ISAAC KNOWS WHERE WE ARE. HE'LL BE COMING SOON, TO FINISH US OFF...WE HAVE TOO MANY WEAK AND INJURED PEOPLE WITH US...
WE CAN'T MOVE THE CAMP.
THEN WHAT CAN WE DO?
YOU CAN PROTECT THEM LONG ENOUGH FOR ME TO SET THINGS IN MOTION.
I NEED TO GO OUT INTO THE FOREST. I NEED TO FOLLOW ONE LAST MISSION.
YOU WOULD LEAVE US IN A CAMP WITH OUR GREATEST ENEMIES?
NO. I WOULD LEAVE YOU IN A CAMP WITH YOUR FELLOW HUMANS.
THE FLAG THEY'RE FLYING OVER THEIR CAMP, IT'S ONE OF THE MOST OFFENSIVE SYMBOLS IN OUR CULTURE...
YEAH. I HAD A THOUGHT ABOUT THAT.

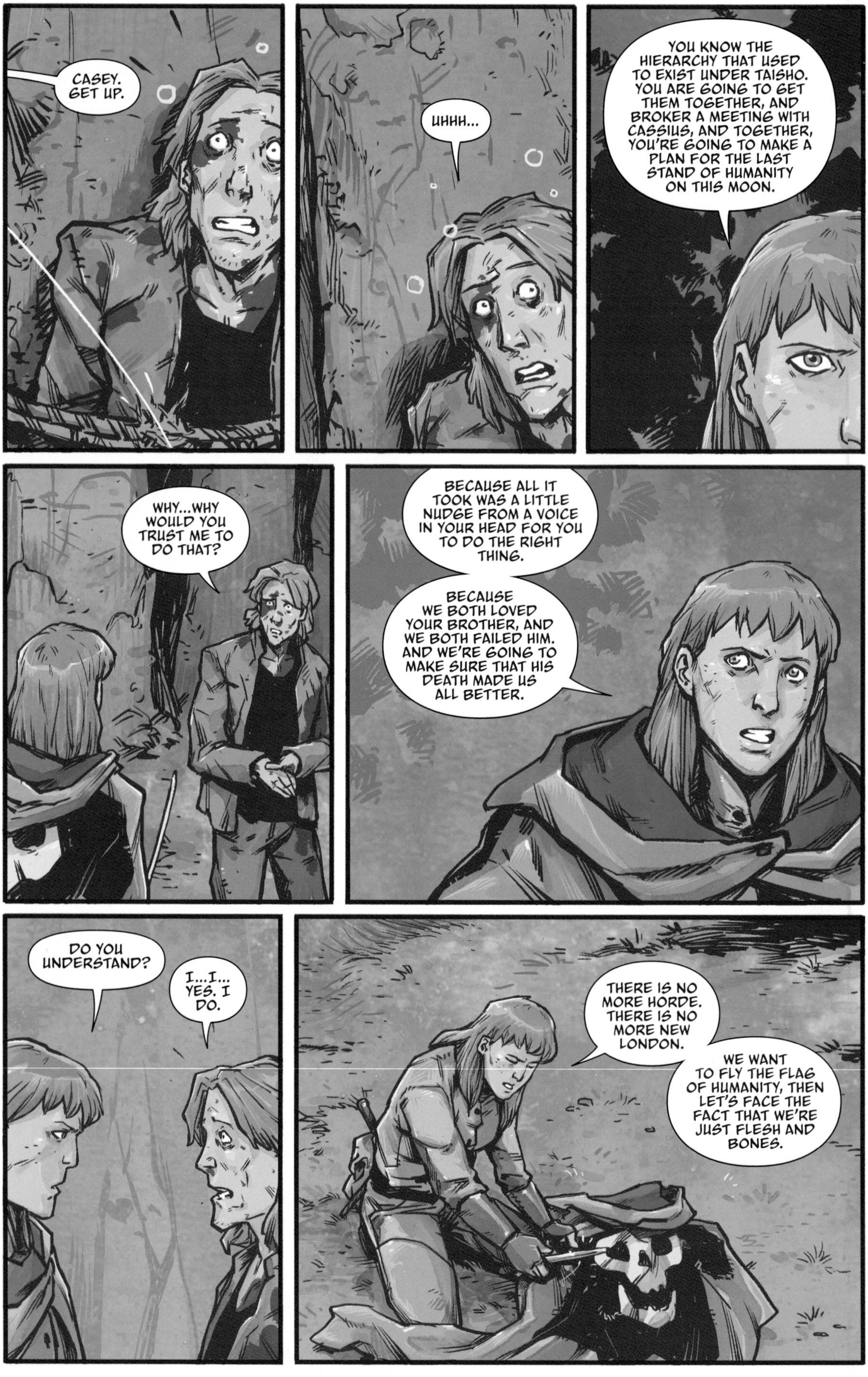
CASEY. GET UP.
UHHH...
YOU KNOW THE HIERARCHY THAT USED TO EXIST UNDER TAISHO. YOU ARE GOING TO GET THEM TOGETHER, AND BROKER A MEETING WITH CASSIUS, AND TOGETHER, YOU'RE GOING TO MAKE A PLAN FOR THE LAST STAND OF HUMANITY ON THIS MOON.
WHY...WHY WOULD YOU TRUST ME TO DO THAT?
BECAUSE ALL IT TOOK WAS A LITTLE NUDGE FROM A VOICE IN YOUR HEAD FOR YOU TO DO THE RIGHT THING.
BECAUSE WE BOTH LOVED YOUR BROTHER, AND WE BOTH FAILED HIM. AND WE'RE GOING TO MAKE SURE THAT HIS DEATH MADE US ALL BETTER.
DO YOU UNDERSTAND?
I...I... YES. I DO.
THERE IS NO MORE HORDE. THERE IS NO MORE NEW LONDON.
WE WANT TO FLY THE FLAG OF HUMANITY, THEN LET'S FACE THE FACT THAT WE'RE JUST FLESH AND BONES.

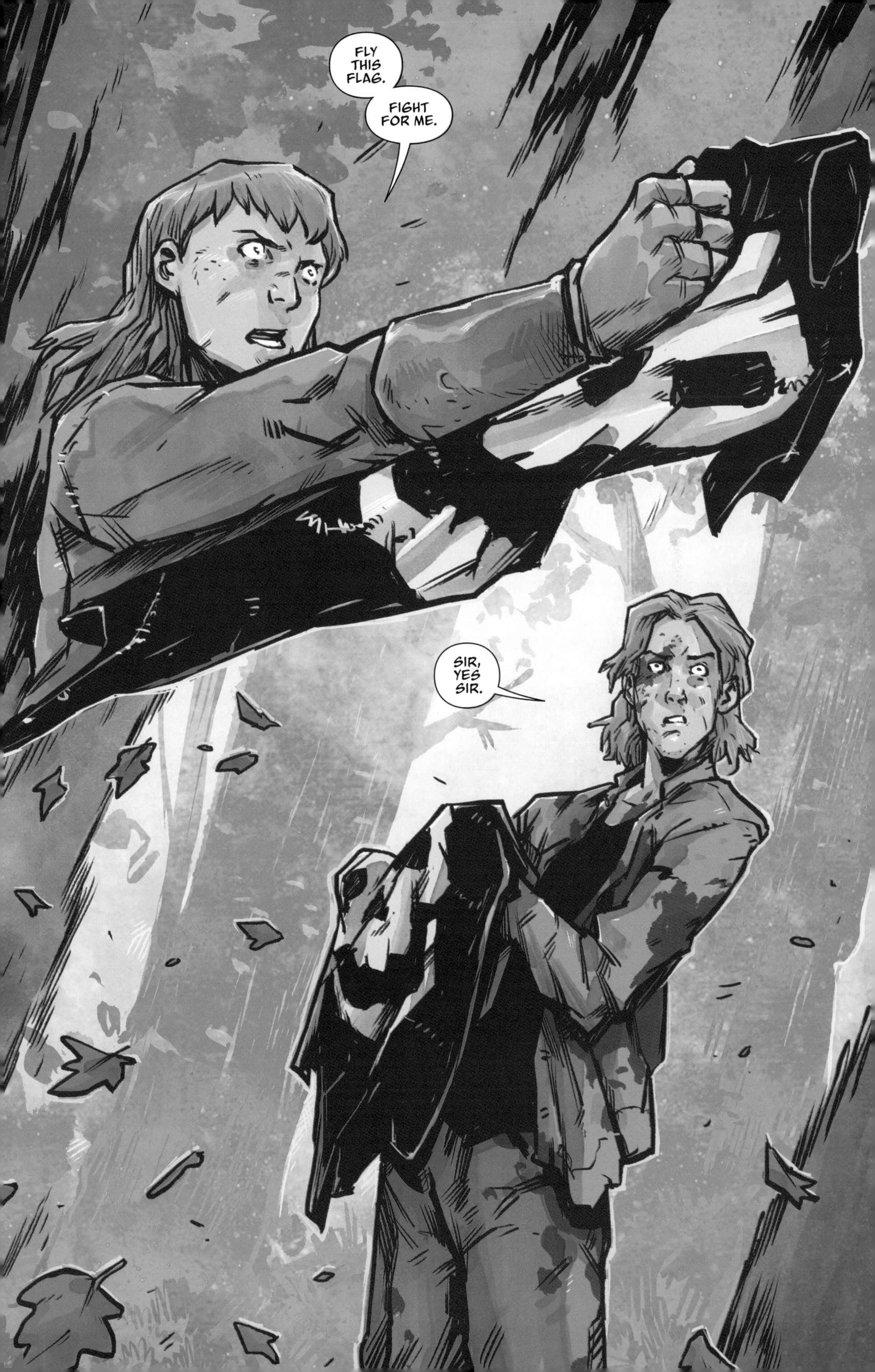
FLY THIS FLAG.
FIGHT FOR ME.
SIR, YES SIR.

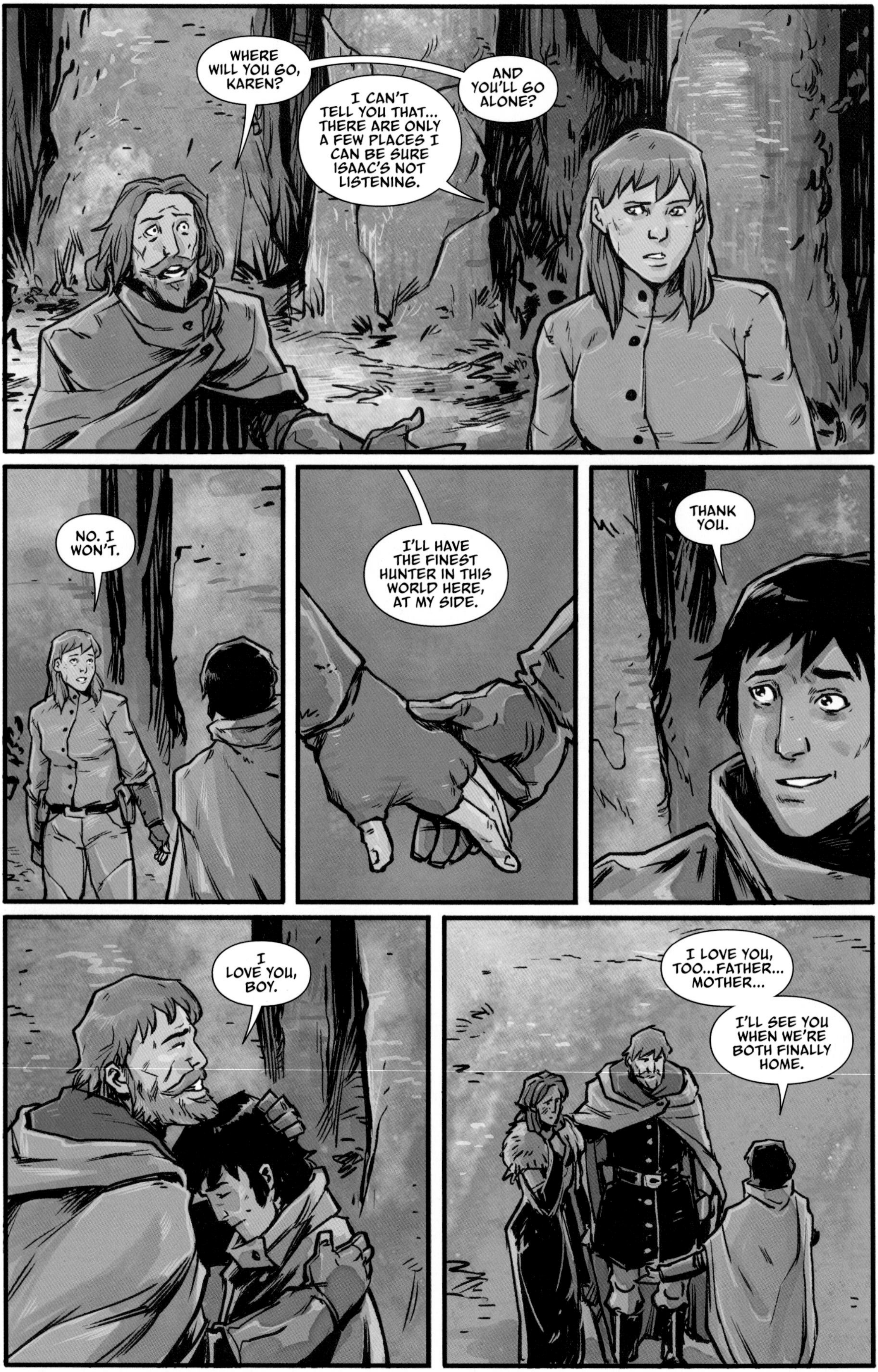
WHERE WILL YOU GO, KAREN?
AND YOU'LL GO ALONE?
I CAN'T TELL YOU THAT... THERE ARE ONLY A FEW PLACES I CAN BE SURE ISAAC'S NOT LISTENING.
NO. I WON'T.
I'LL HAVE THE FINEST HUNTER IN THIS WORLD HERE, AT MY SIDE.
THANK YOU.
I LOVE YOU, BOY.
I LOVE YOU, TOO...FATHER... MOTHER...
I'LL SEE YOU WHEN WE'RE BOTH FINALLY HOME.

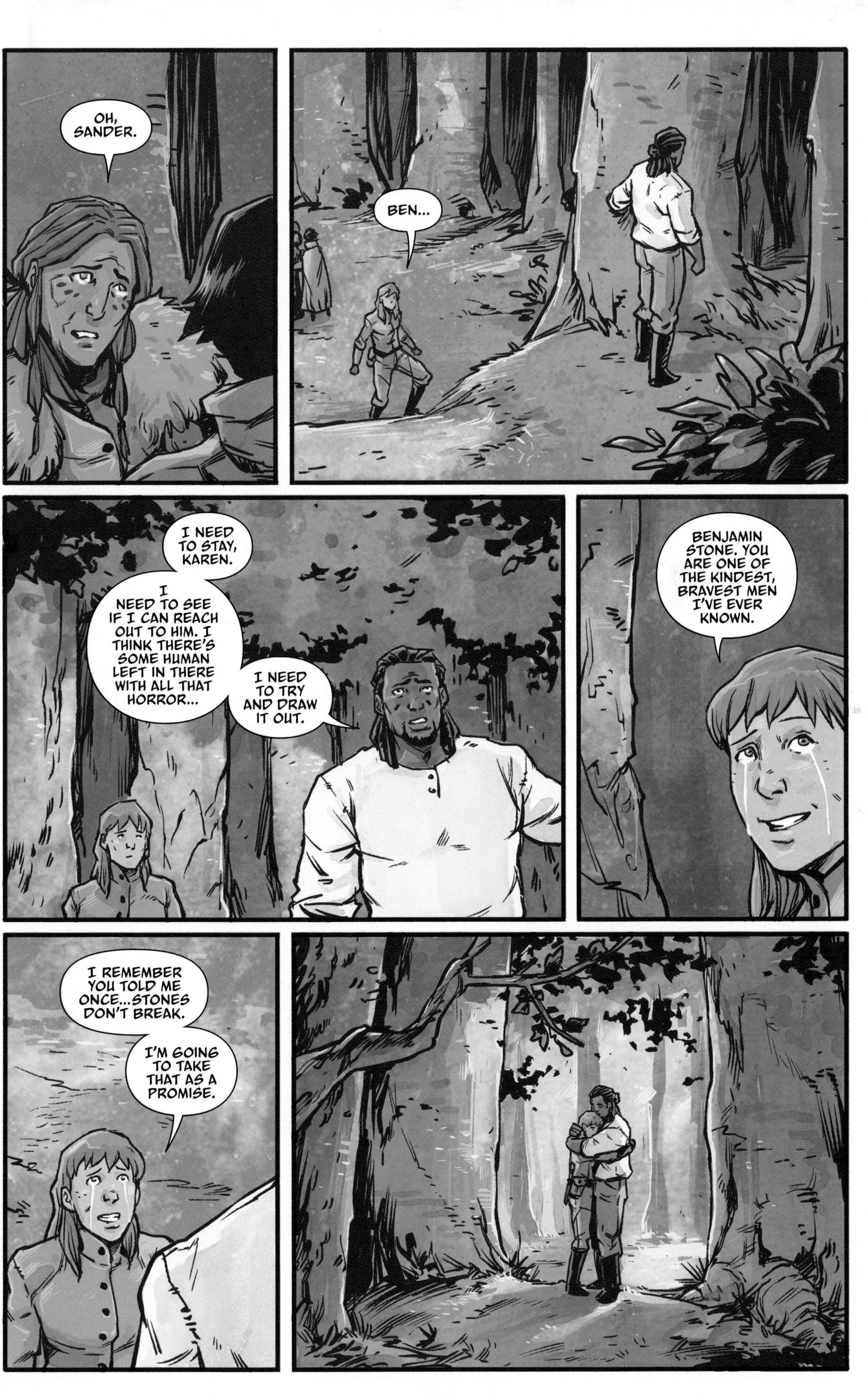
OH, SANDER.
BEN...
I NEED TO STAY, KAREN.
I NEED TO SEE IF I CAN REACH OUT TO HIM. I THINK THERE'S SOME HUMAN LEFT IN THERE WITH ALL THAT HORROR...
I NEED TO TRY AND DRAW IT OUT.
BENJAMIN STONE. YOU ARE ONE OF THE KINDEST, BRAVEST MEN I'VE EVER KNOWN.
I REMEMBER YOU TOLD ME ONCE...STONES DON'T BREAK.
I'M GOING TO TAKE THAT AS A PROMISE.

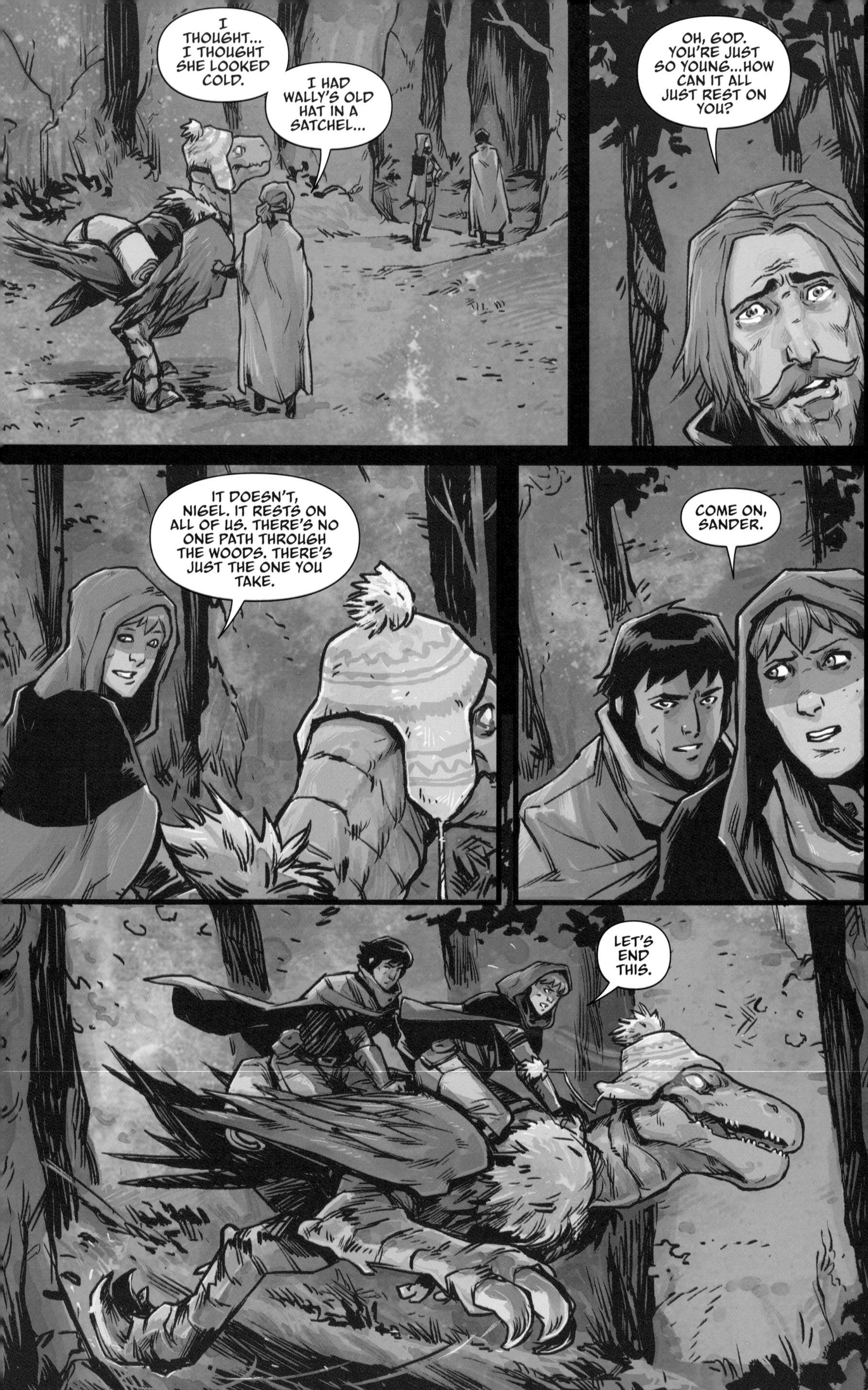
I THOUGHT... I THOUGHT SHE LOOKED COLD.
I HAD WALLY'S OLD HAT IN A SATCHEL...
OH, GOD. YOU'RE JUST SO YOUNG...HOW CAN IT ALL JUST REST ON YOU?
IT DOESN'T, NIGEL. IT RESTS ON ALL OF US. THERE'S NO ONE PATH THROUGH THE WOODS. THERE'S JUST THE ONE YOU TAKE.
COME ON, SANDER.
LET'S END THIS.

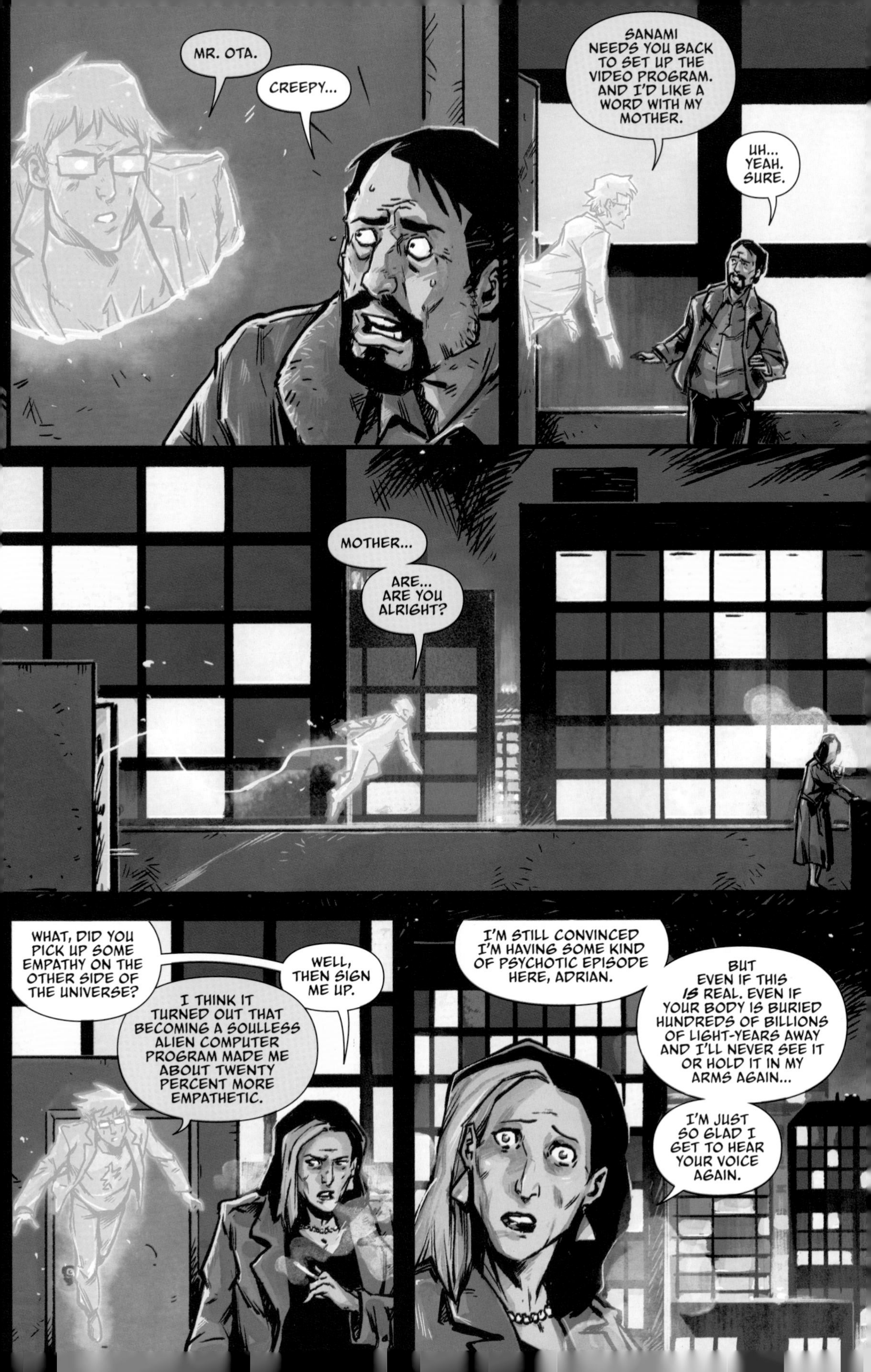

MR. OTA.
CREEPY...
SANAMI NEEDS YOU BACK TO SET UP THE VIDEO PROGRAM. AND I'D LIKE A WORD WITH MY MOTHER.
UH... YEAH. SURE.
MOTHER...
ARE... ARE YOU ALRIGHT?
WHAT, DID YOU PICK UP SOME EMPATHY ON THE OTHER SIDE OF THE UNIVERSE?
WELL, THEN SIGN ME UP.
I THINK IT TURNED OUT THAT BECOMING A SOULLESS ALIEN COMPUTER PROGRAM MADE ME ABOUT TWENTY PERCENT MORE EMPATHETIC.
I'M STILL CONVINCED I'M HAVING SOME KIND OF PSYCHOTIC EPISODE HERE, ADRIAN.
BUT EVEN IF THIS IS REAL. EVEN IF YOUR BODY IS BURIED HUNDREDS OF BILLIONS OF LIGHT-YEARS AWAY AND I'LL NEVER SEE IT OR HOLD IT IN MY ARMS AGAIN...
I'M JUST SO GLAD I GET TO HEAR YOUR VOICE AGAIN.

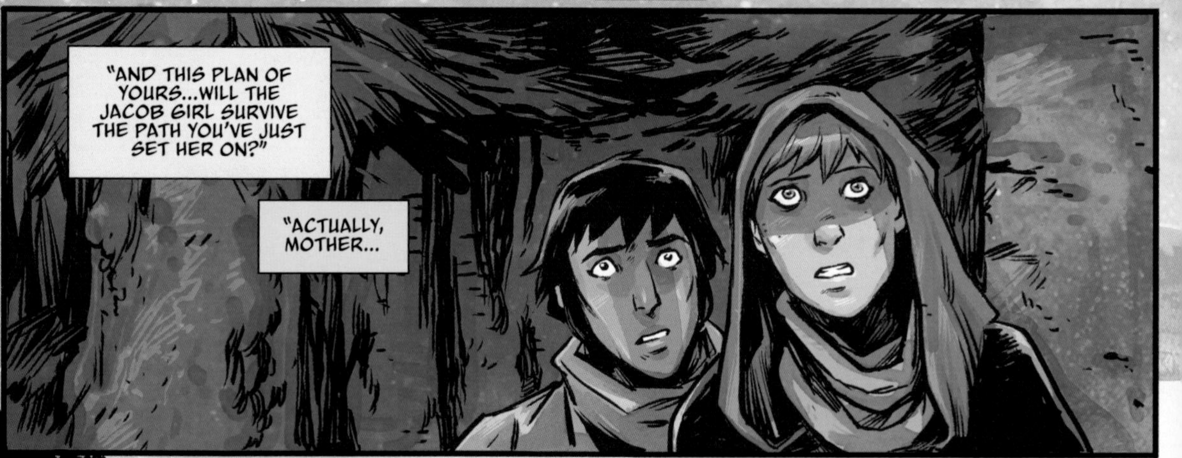
"AND THIS PLAN OF YOURS...WILL THE JACOB GIRL SURVIVE THE PATH YOU'VE JUST SET HER ON?"
"ACTUALLY, MOTHER...

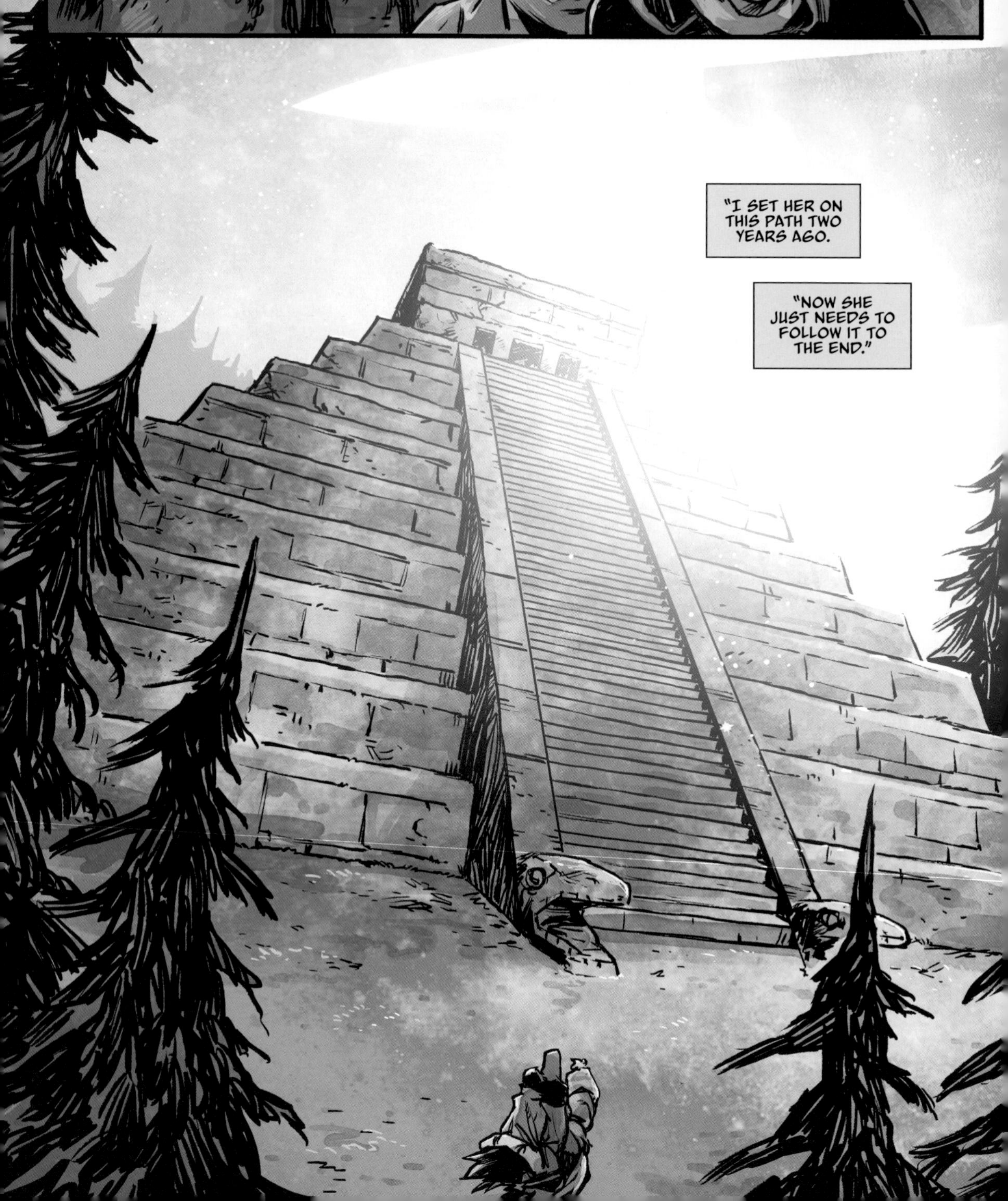
"I SET HER ON THIS PATH TWO YEARS AGO.
"NOW SHE JUST NEEDS TO FOLLOW IT TO THE END."

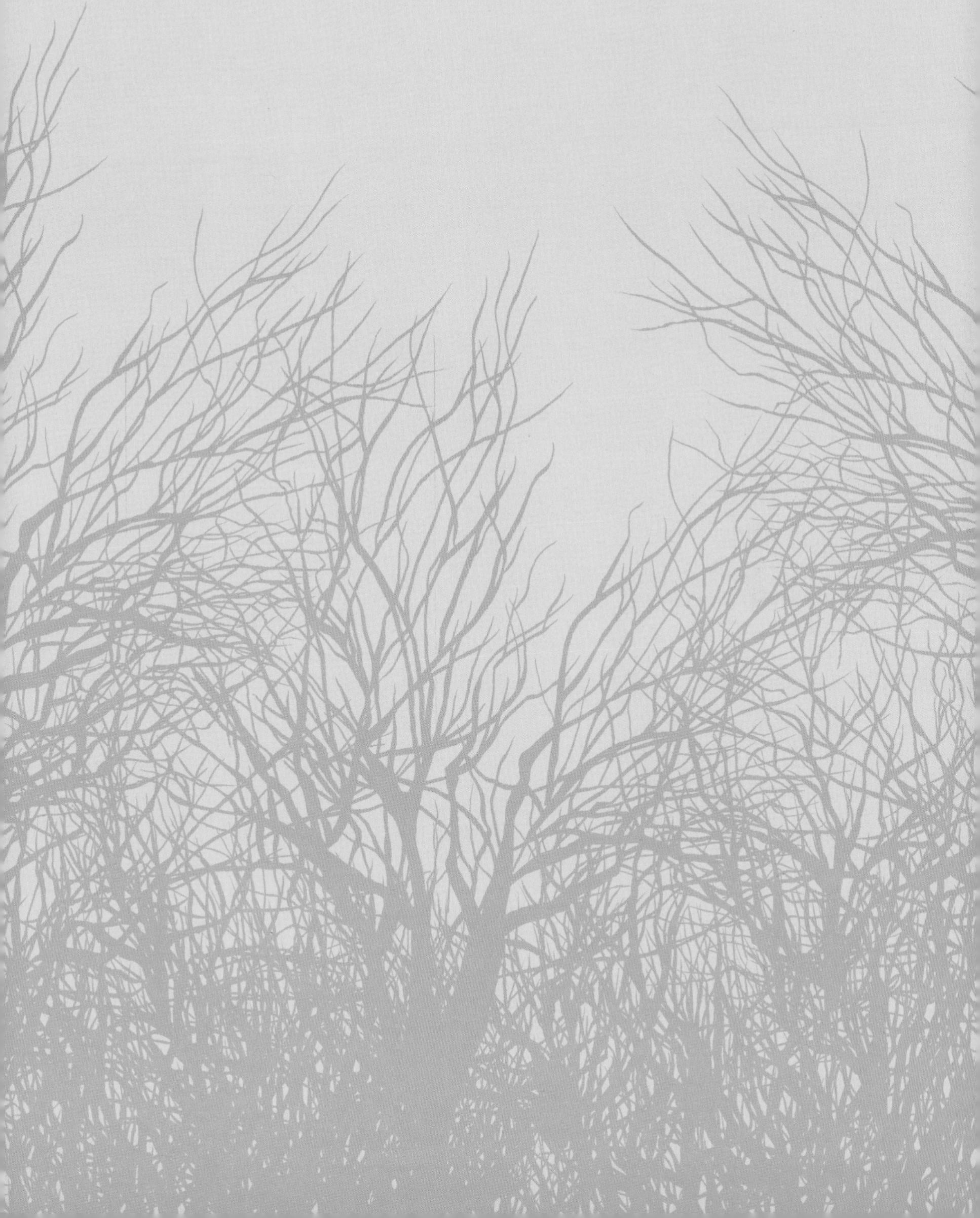

CHAPTER
THIRTY-FIVE

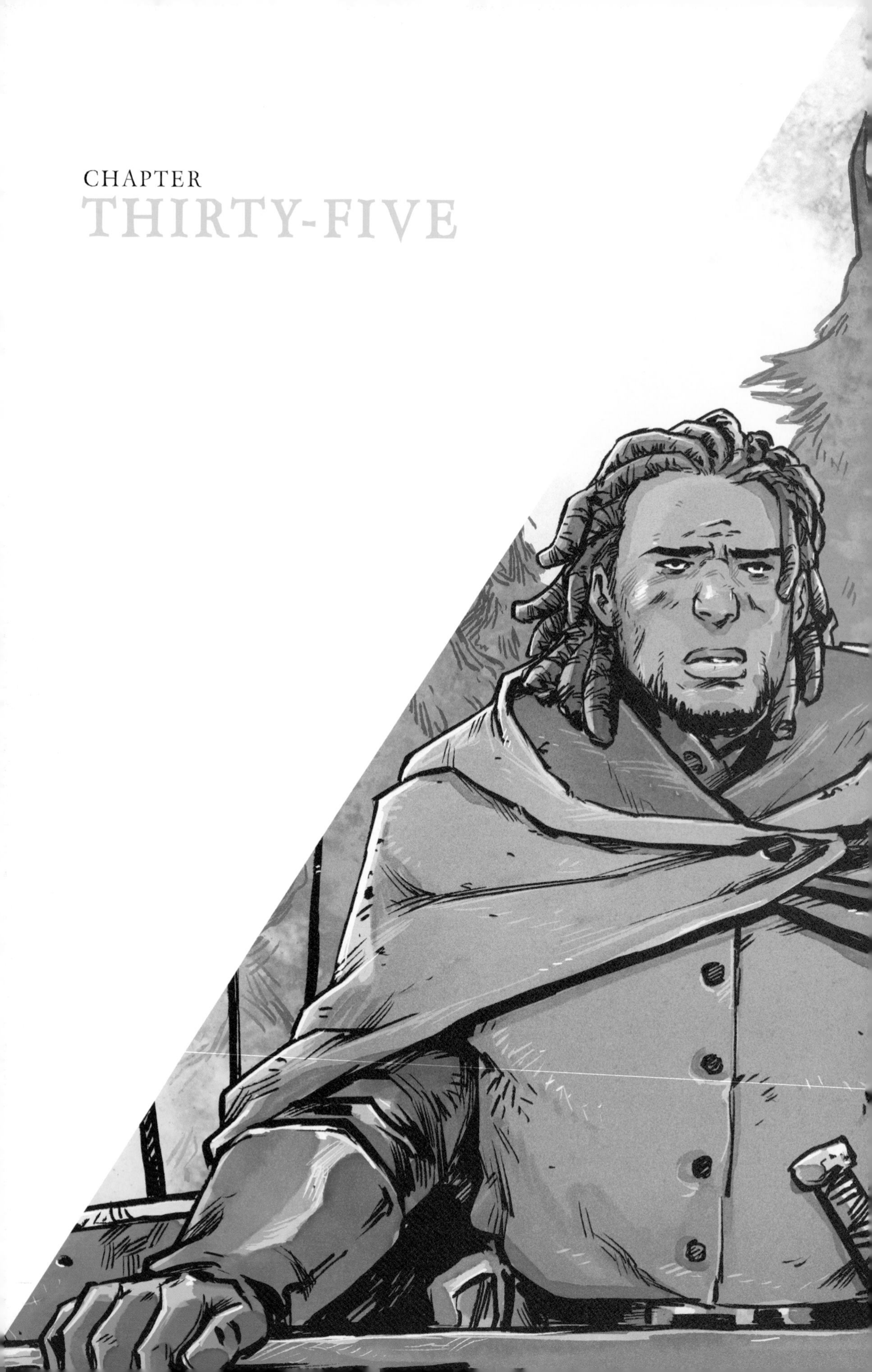

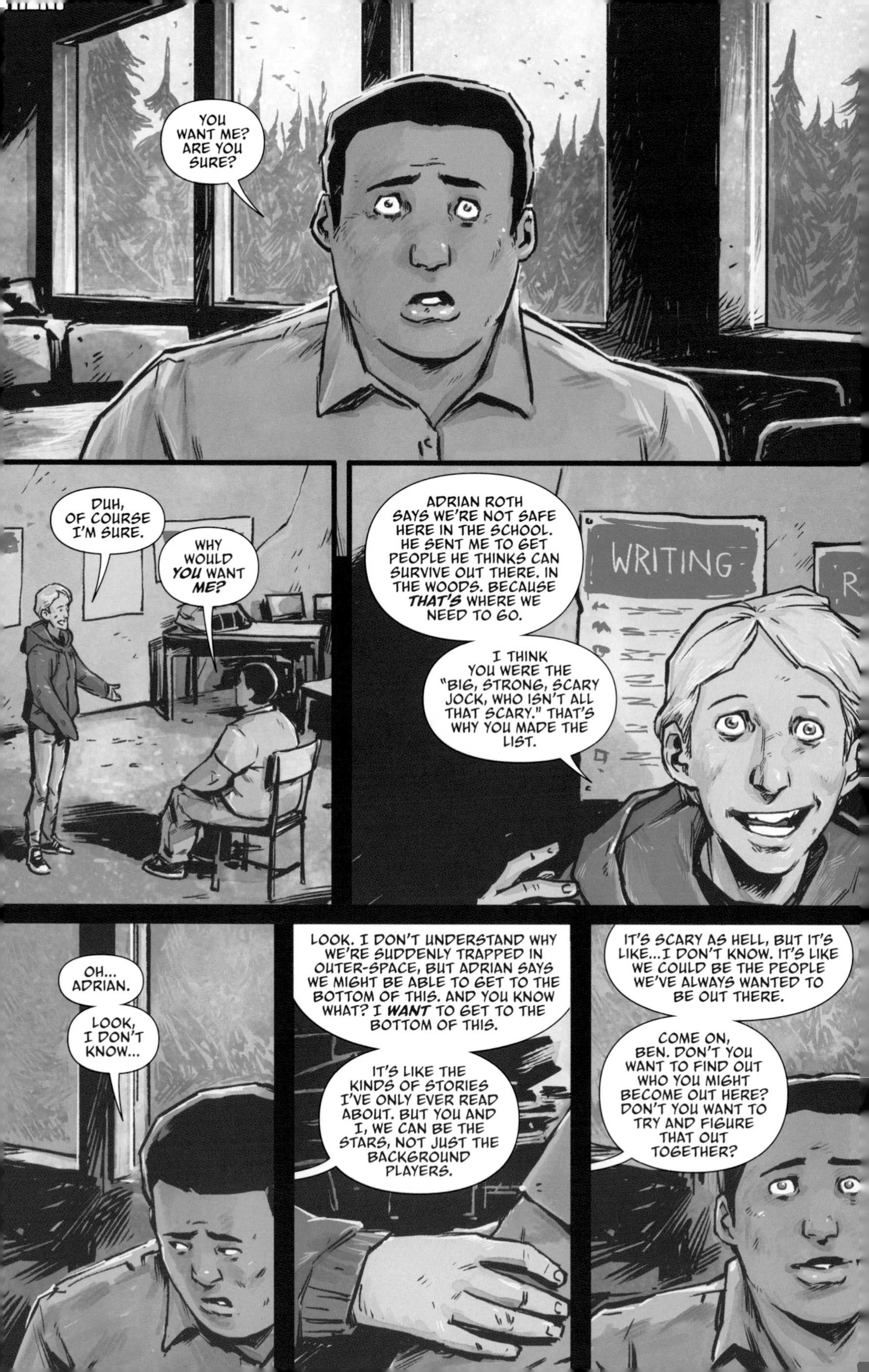

YOU WANT ME? ARE YOU SURE?
DUH, OF COURSE I'M SURE.
WHY WOULD *YOU* WANT *ME?*
ADRIAN ROTH SAYS WE'RE NOT SAFE HERE IN THE SCHOOL. HE SENT ME TO GET PEOPLE HE THINKS CAN SURVIVE OUT THERE. IN THE WOODS. BECAUSE *THAT'S* WHERE WE NEED TO GO.
WRITING
I THINK YOU WERE THE "BIG, STRONG, SCARY JOCK, WHO ISN'T ALL THAT SCARY." THAT'S WHY YOU MADE THE LIST.
OH... ADRIAN.
LOOK, I DON'T KNOW...
LOOK. I DON'T UNDERSTAND WHY WE'RE SUDDENLY TRAPPED IN OUTER-SPACE, BUT ADRIAN SAYS WE MIGHT BE ABLE TO GET TO THE BOTTOM OF THIS. AND YOU KNOW WHAT? I *WANT* TO GET TO THE BOTTOM OF THIS.
IT'S LIKE THE KINDS OF STORIES I'VE ONLY EVER READ ABOUT. BUT YOU AND I, WE CAN BE THE STARS, NOT JUST THE BACKGROUND PLAYERS.
IT'S SCARY AS HELL, BUT IT'S LIKE...I DON'T KNOW. IT'S LIKE WE COULD BE THE PEOPLE WE'VE ALWAYS WANTED TO BE OUT THERE.
COME ON, BEN. DON'T YOU WANT TO FIND OUT WHO YOU MIGHT BECOME OUT HERE? DON'T YOU WANT TO TRY AND FIGURE THAT OUT TOGETHER?

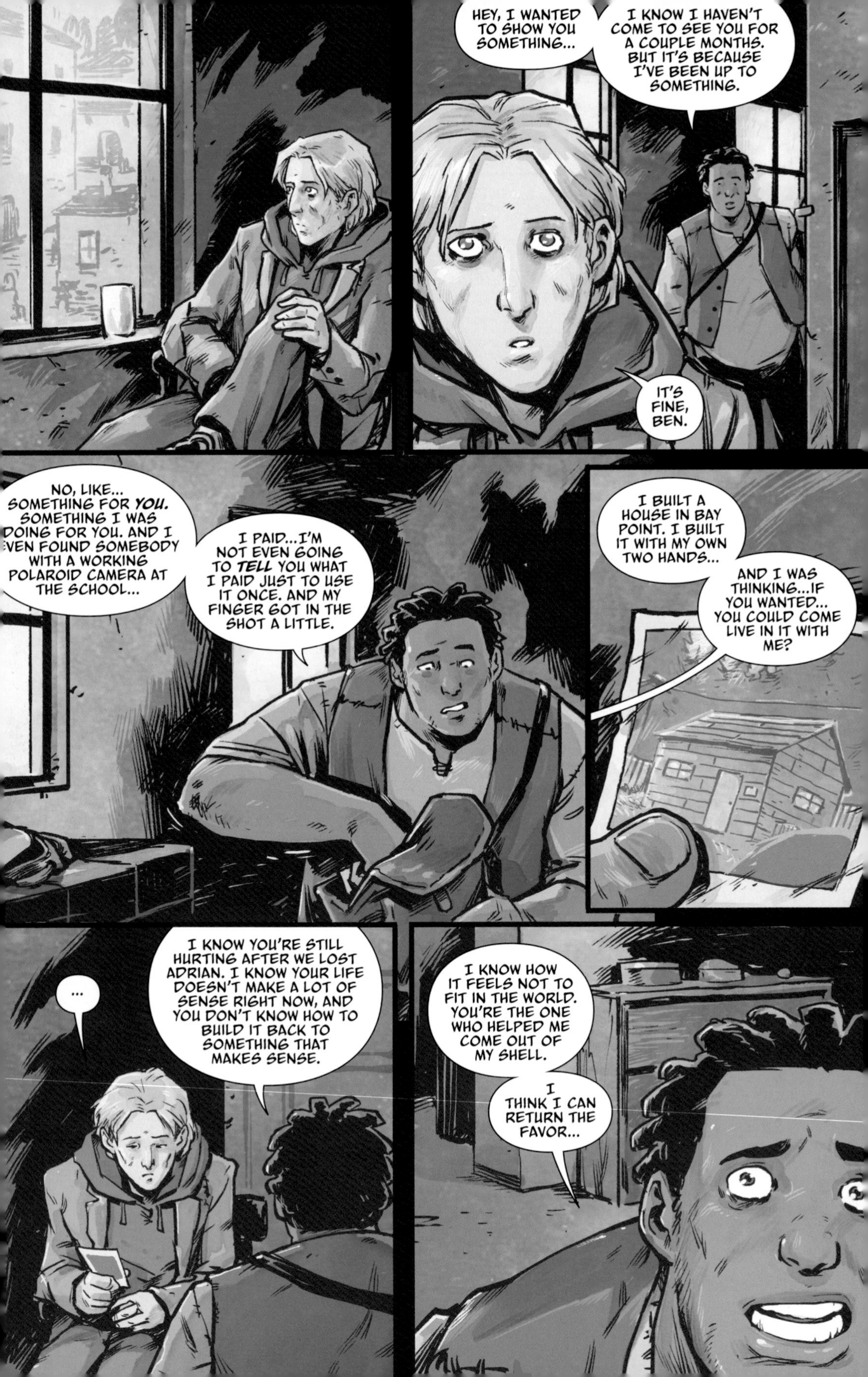
HEY, I WANTED TO SHOW YOU SOMETHING...
I KNOW I HAVEN'T COME TO SEE YOU FOR A COUPLE MONTHS. BUT IT'S BECAUSE I'VE BEEN UP TO SOMETHING.
IT'S FINE, BEN.
NO, LIKE... SOMETHING FOR *YOU.* SOMETHING I WAS DOING FOR YOU. AND I EVEN FOUND SOMEBODY WITH A WORKING POLAROID CAMERA AT THE SCHOOL...
I PAID...I'M NOT EVEN GOING TO *TELL* YOU WHAT I PAID JUST TO USE IT ONCE. AND MY FINGER GOT IN THE SHOT A LITTLE.
I BUILT A HOUSE IN BAY POINT. I BUILT IT WITH MY OWN TWO HANDS...
AND I WAS THINKING...IF YOU WANTED... YOU COULD COME LIVE IN IT WITH ME?
...
I KNOW YOU'RE STILL HURTING AFTER WE LOST ADRIAN. I KNOW YOUR LIFE DOESN'T MAKE A LOT OF SENSE RIGHT NOW, AND YOU DON'T KNOW HOW TO BUILD IT BACK TO SOMETHING THAT MAKES SENSE.
I KNOW HOW IT FEELS NOT TO FIT IN THE WORLD. YOU'RE THE ONE WHO HELPED ME COME OUT OF MY SHELL.
I THINK I CAN RETURN THE FAVOR...

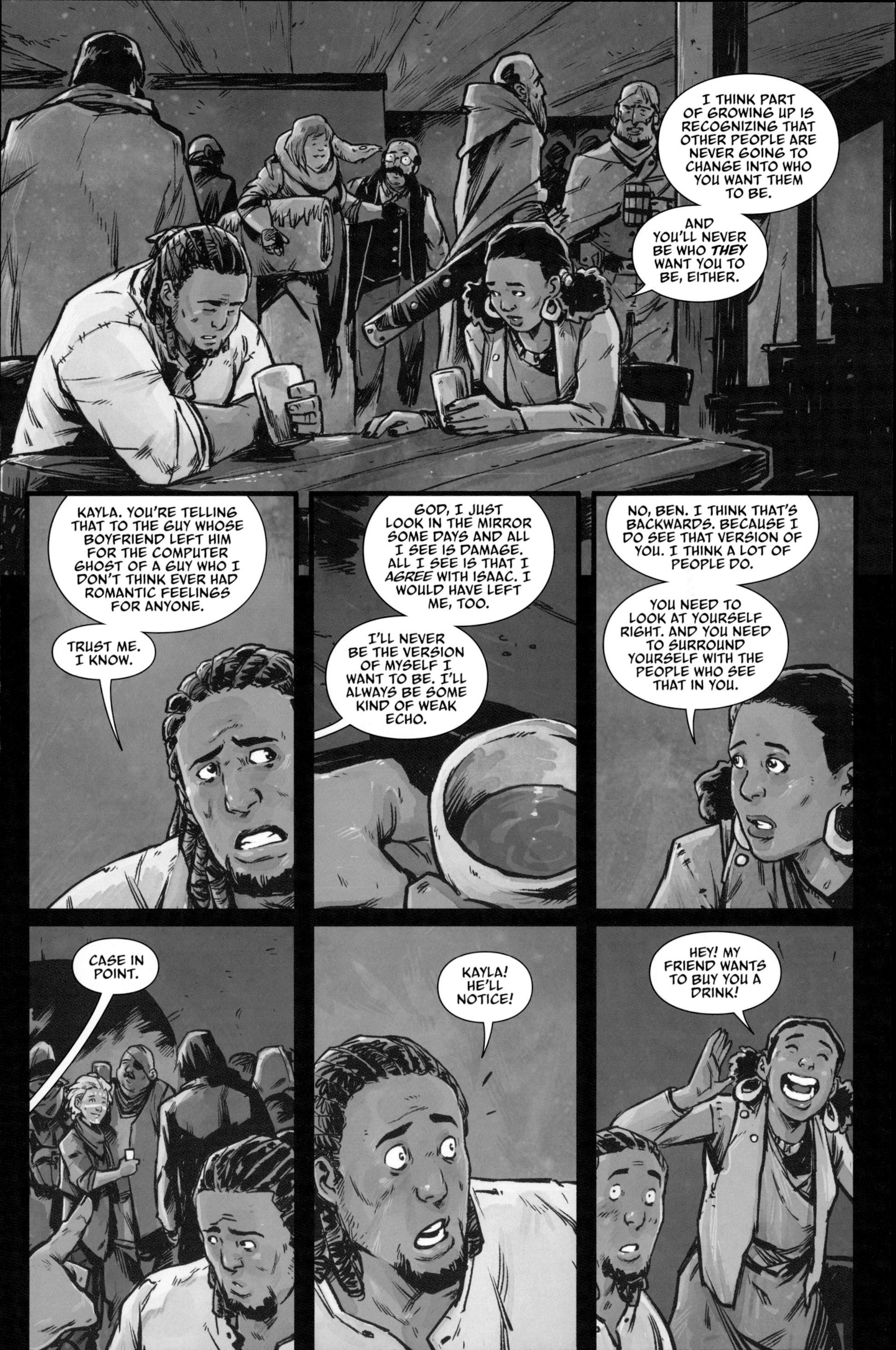
I THINK PART OF GROWING UP IS RECOGNIZING THAT OTHER PEOPLE ARE NEVER GOING TO CHANGE INTO WHO YOU WANT THEM TO BE.
AND YOU'LL NEVER BE WHO *THEY* WANT YOU TO BE, EITHER.
KAYLA. YOU'RE TELLING THAT TO THE GUY WHOSE BOYFRIEND LEFT HIM FOR THE COMPUTER GHOST OF A GUY WHO I DON'T THINK EVER HAD ROMANTIC FEELINGS FOR ANYONE.
TRUST ME. I KNOW.
GOD, I JUST LOOK IN THE MIRROR SOME DAYS AND ALL I SEE IS DAMAGE. ALL I SEE IS THAT I *AGREE* WITH ISAAC. I WOULD HAVE LEFT ME, TOO.
I'LL NEVER BE THE VERSION OF MYSELF I WANT TO BE. I'LL ALWAYS BE SOME KIND OF WEAK ECHO.
NO, BEN. I THINK THAT'S BACKWARDS. BECAUSE I DO SEE THAT VERSION OF YOU. I THINK A LOT OF PEOPLE DO.
YOU NEED TO LOOK AT YOURSELF RIGHT. AND YOU NEED TO SURROUND YOURSELF WITH THE PEOPLE WHO SEE THAT IN YOU.
CASE IN POINT.
KAYLA! HE'LL NOTICE!
HEY! MY FRIEND WANTS TO BUY YOU A DRINK!

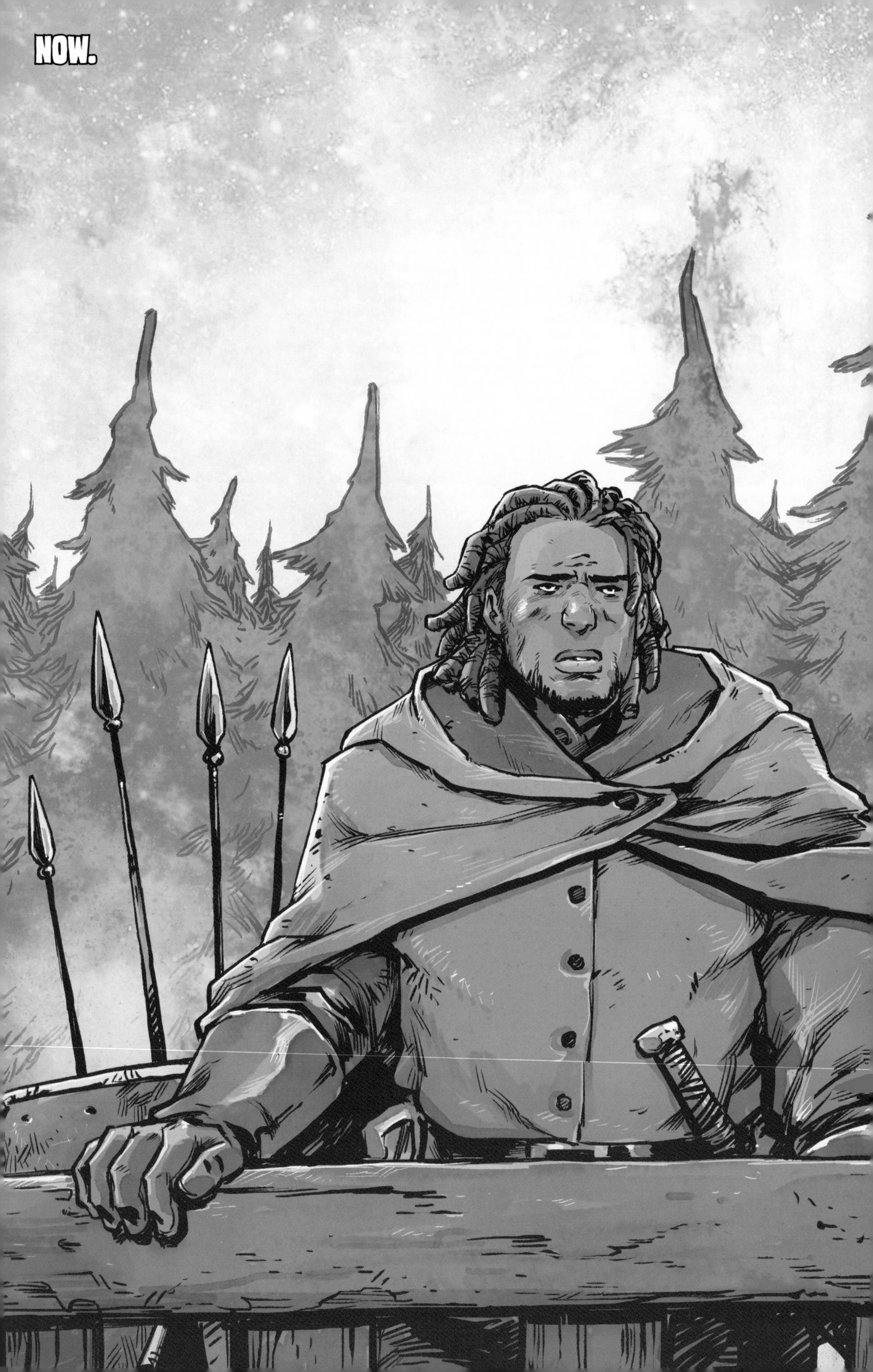
NOW.

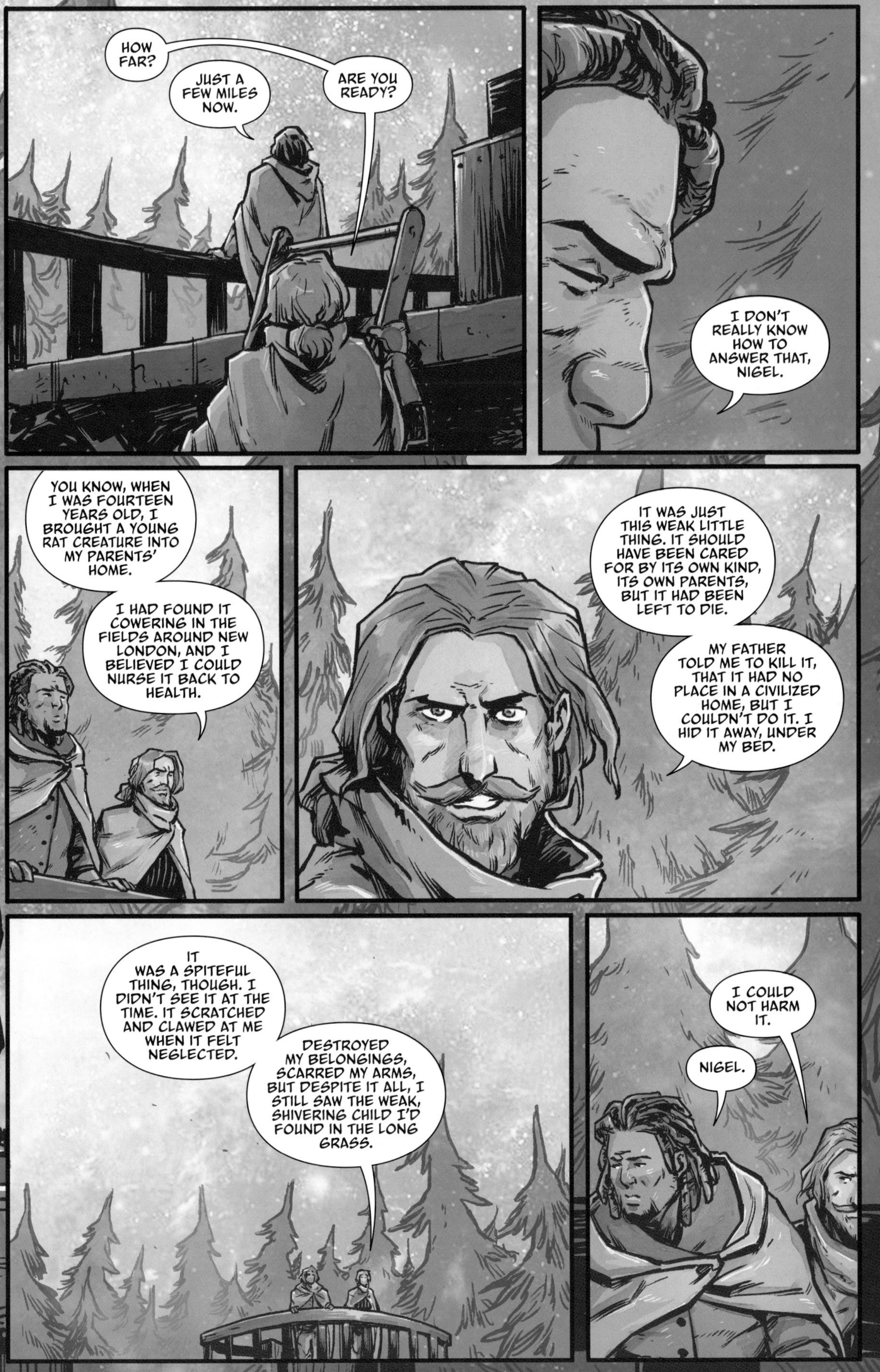
HOW FAR?
JUST A FEW MILES NOW.
ARE YOU READY?
I DON'T REALLY KNOW HOW TO ANSWER THAT, NIGEL.
YOU KNOW, WHEN I WAS FOURTEEN YEARS OLD, I BROUGHT A YOUNG RAT CREATURE INTO MY PARENTS' HOME.
I HAD FOUND IT COWERING IN THE FIELDS AROUND NEW LONDON, AND I BELIEVED I COULD NURSE IT BACK TO HEALTH.
IT WAS JUST THIS WEAK LITTLE THING. IT SHOULD HAVE BEEN CARED FOR BY ITS OWN KIND, ITS OWN PARENTS, BUT IT HAD BEEN LEFT TO DIE.
MY FATHER TOLD ME TO KILL IT, THAT IT HAD NO PLACE IN A CIVILIZED HOME, BUT I COULDN'T DO IT. I HID IT AWAY, UNDER MY BED.
IT WAS A SPITEFUL THING, THOUGH. I DIDN'T SEE IT AT THE TIME. IT SCRATCHED AND CLAWED AT ME WHEN IT FELT NEGLECTED.
DESTROYED MY BELONGINGS, SCARRED MY ARMS, BUT DESPITE IT ALL, I STILL SAW THE WEAK, SHIVERING CHILD I'D FOUND IN THE LONG GRASS.
I COULD NOT HARM IT.
NIGEL.

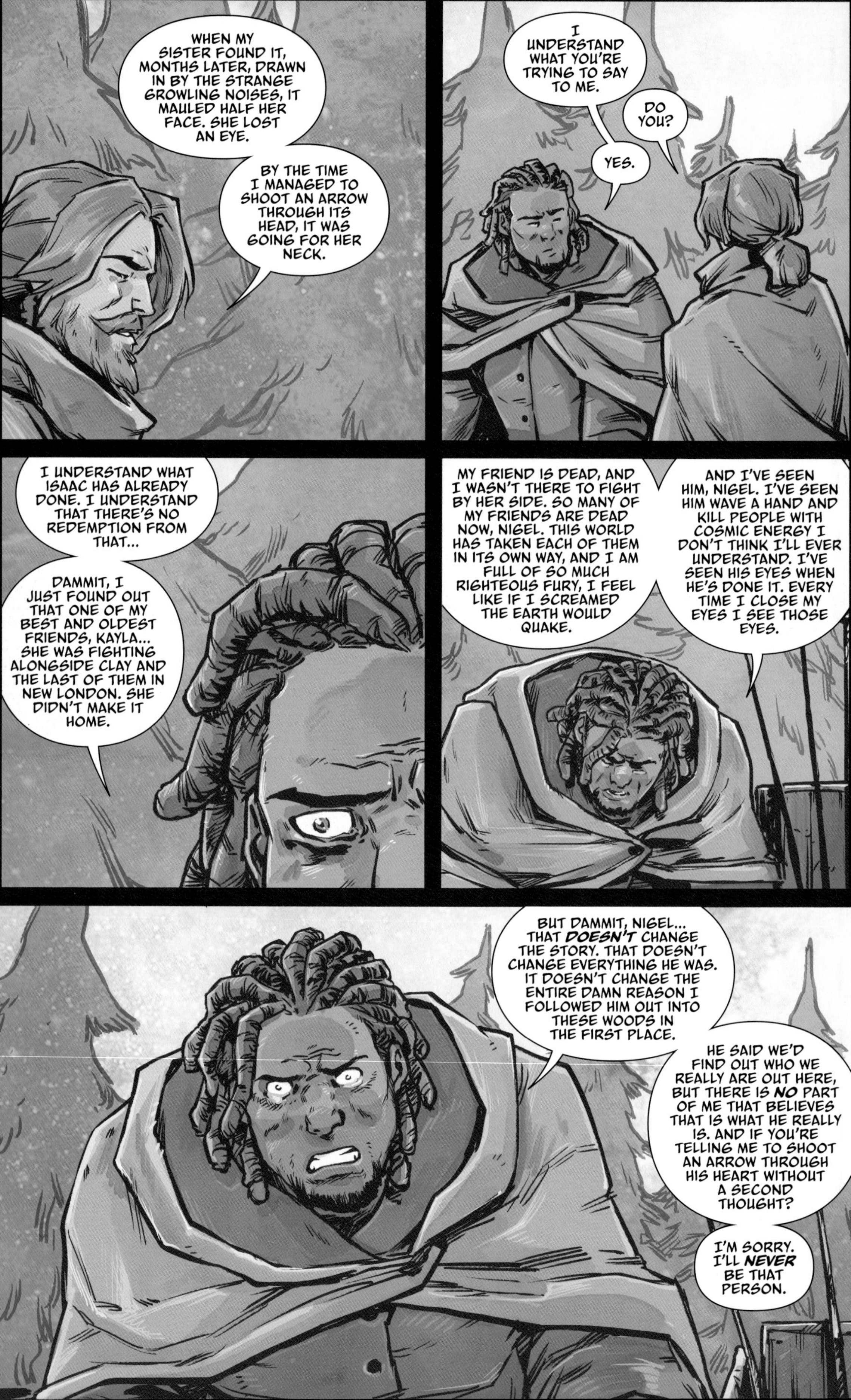
WHEN MY SISTER FOUND IT, MONTHS LATER, DRAWN IN BY THE STRANGE GROWLING NOISES, IT MAULED HALF HER FACE. SHE LOST AN EYE.
BY THE TIME I MANAGED TO SHOOT AN ARROW THROUGH ITS HEAD, IT WAS GOING FOR HER NECK.
I UNDERSTAND WHAT YOU'RE TRYING TO SAY TO ME.
DO YOU?
YES.
I UNDERSTAND WHAT ISAAC HAS ALREADY DONE. I UNDERSTAND THAT THERE'S NO REDEMPTION FROM THAT...
DAMMIT, I JUST FOUND OUT THAT ONE OF MY BEST AND OLDEST FRIENDS, KAYLA... SHE WAS FIGHTING ALONGSIDE CLAY AND THE LAST OF THEM IN NEW LONDON. SHE DIDN'T MAKE IT HOME.
MY FRIEND IS DEAD, AND I WASN'T THERE TO FIGHT BY HER SIDE. SO MANY OF MY FRIENDS ARE DEAD NOW, NIGEL. THIS WORLD HAS TAKEN EACH OF THEM IN ITS OWN WAY, AND I AM FULL OF SO MUCH RIGHTEOUS FURY, I FEEL LIKE IF I SCREAMED THE EARTH WOULD QUAKE.
AND I'VE SEEN HIM, NIGEL. I'VE SEEN HIM WAVE A HAND AND KILL PEOPLE WITH COSMIC ENERGY I DON'T THINK I'LL EVER UNDERSTAND. I'VE SEEN HIS EYES WHEN HE'S DONE IT. EVERY TIME I CLOSE MY EYES I SEE THOSE EYES.
BUT DAMMIT, NIGEL... THAT ***DOESN'T*** CHANGE THE STORY. THAT DOESN'T CHANGE EVERYTHING HE WAS. IT DOESN'T CHANGE THE ENTIRE DAMN REASON I FOLLOWED HIM OUT INTO THESE WOODS IN THE FIRST PLACE.
HE SAID WE'D FIND OUT WHO WE REALLY ARE OUT HERE, BUT THERE IS ***NO*** PART OF ME THAT BELIEVES THAT IS WHAT HE REALLY IS. AND IF YOU'RE TELLING ME TO SHOOT AN ARROW THROUGH HIS HEART WITHOUT A SECOND THOUGHT?
I'M SORRY. I'LL ***NEVER*** BE THAT PERSON.

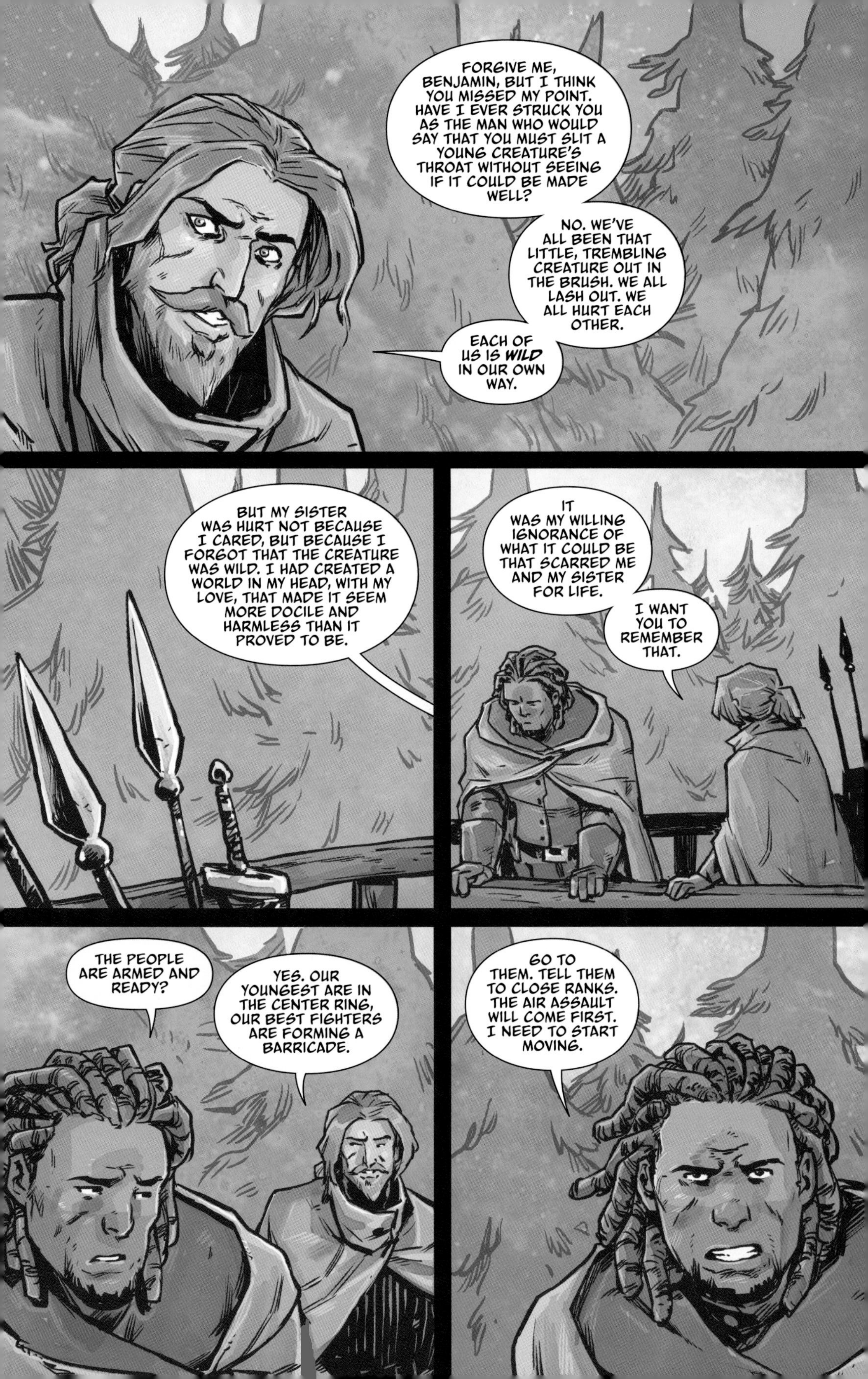
FORGIVE ME, BENJAMIN, BUT I THINK YOU MISSED MY POINT. HAVE I EVER STRUCK YOU AS THE MAN WHO WOULD SAY THAT YOU MUST SLIT A YOUNG CREATURE'S THROAT WITHOUT SEEING IF IT COULD BE MADE WELL?
NO. WE'VE ALL BEEN THAT LITTLE, TREMBLING CREATURE OUT IN THE BRUSH. WE ALL LASH OUT. WE ALL HURT EACH OTHER.
EACH OF US IS *WILD* IN OUR OWN WAY.
BUT MY SISTER WAS HURT NOT BECAUSE I CARED, BUT BECAUSE I FORGOT THAT THE CREATURE WAS WILD. I HAD CREATED A WORLD IN MY HEAD, WITH MY LOVE, THAT MADE IT SEEM MORE DOCILE AND HARMLESS THAN IT PROVED TO BE.
IT WAS MY WILLING IGNORANCE OF WHAT IT COULD BE THAT SCARRED ME AND MY SISTER FOR LIFE.
I WANT YOU TO REMEMBER THAT.
THE PEOPLE ARE ARMED AND READY?
YES. OUR YOUNGEST ARE IN THE CENTER RING, OUR BEST FIGHTERS ARE FORMING A BARRICADE.
GO TO THEM. TELL THEM TO CLOSE RANKS. THE AIR ASSAULT WILL COME FIRST. I NEED TO START MOVING.

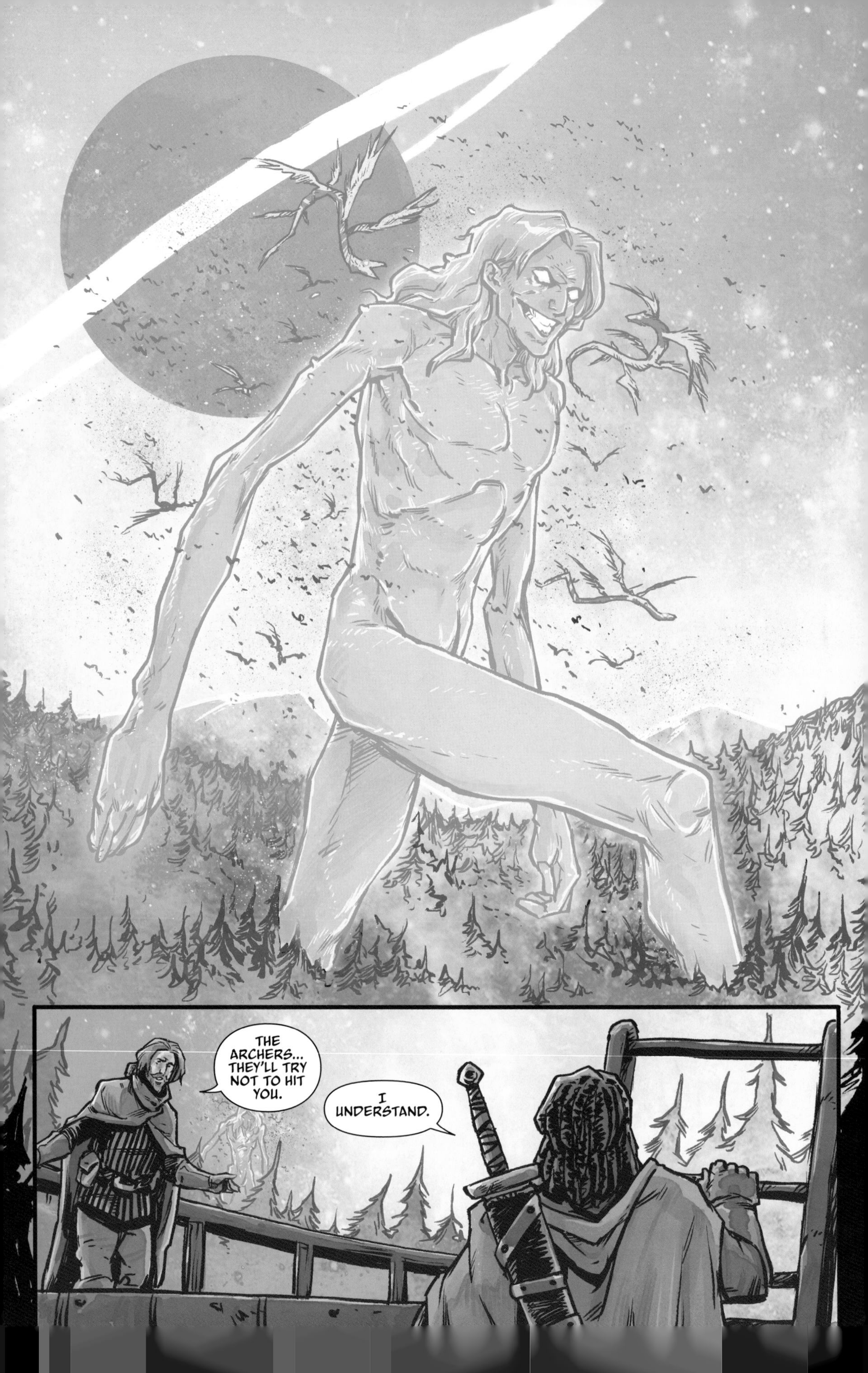
THE ARCHERS... THEY'LL TRY NOT TO HIT YOU.
I UNDERSTAND.

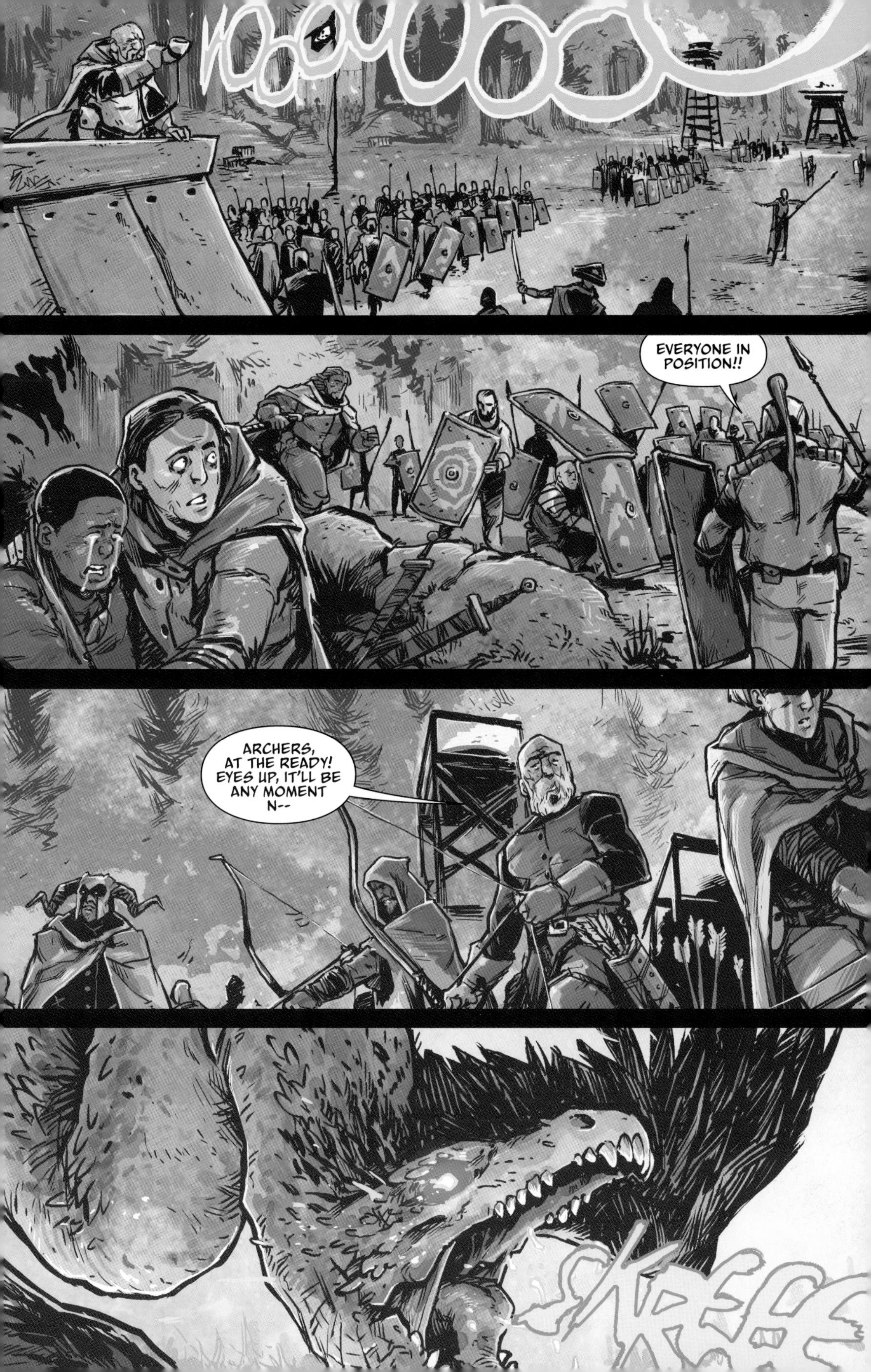
EVERYONE IN POSITION!!
ARCHERS, AT THE READY! EYES UP, IT'LL BE ANY MOMENT N--

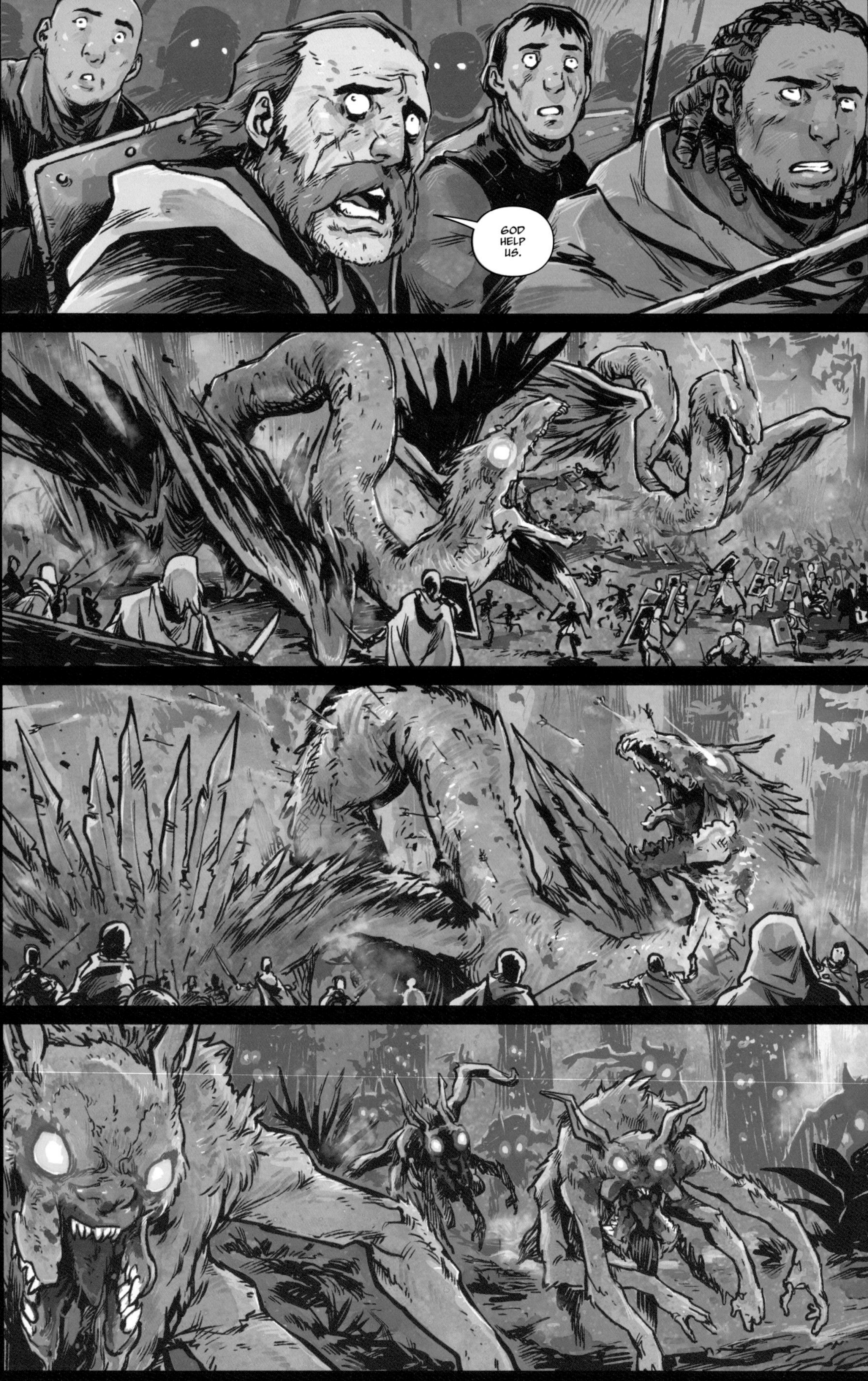
GOD HELP US.

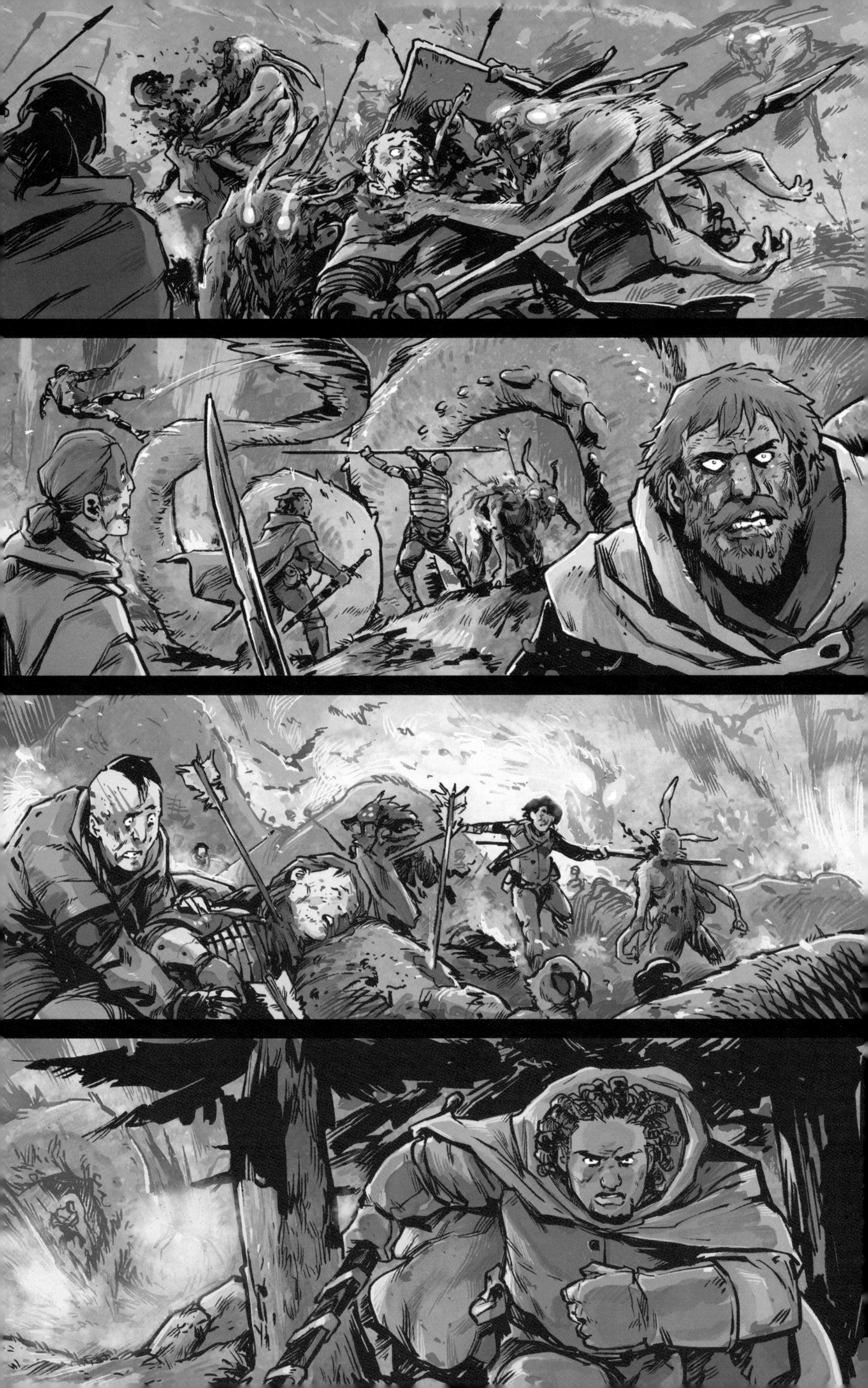

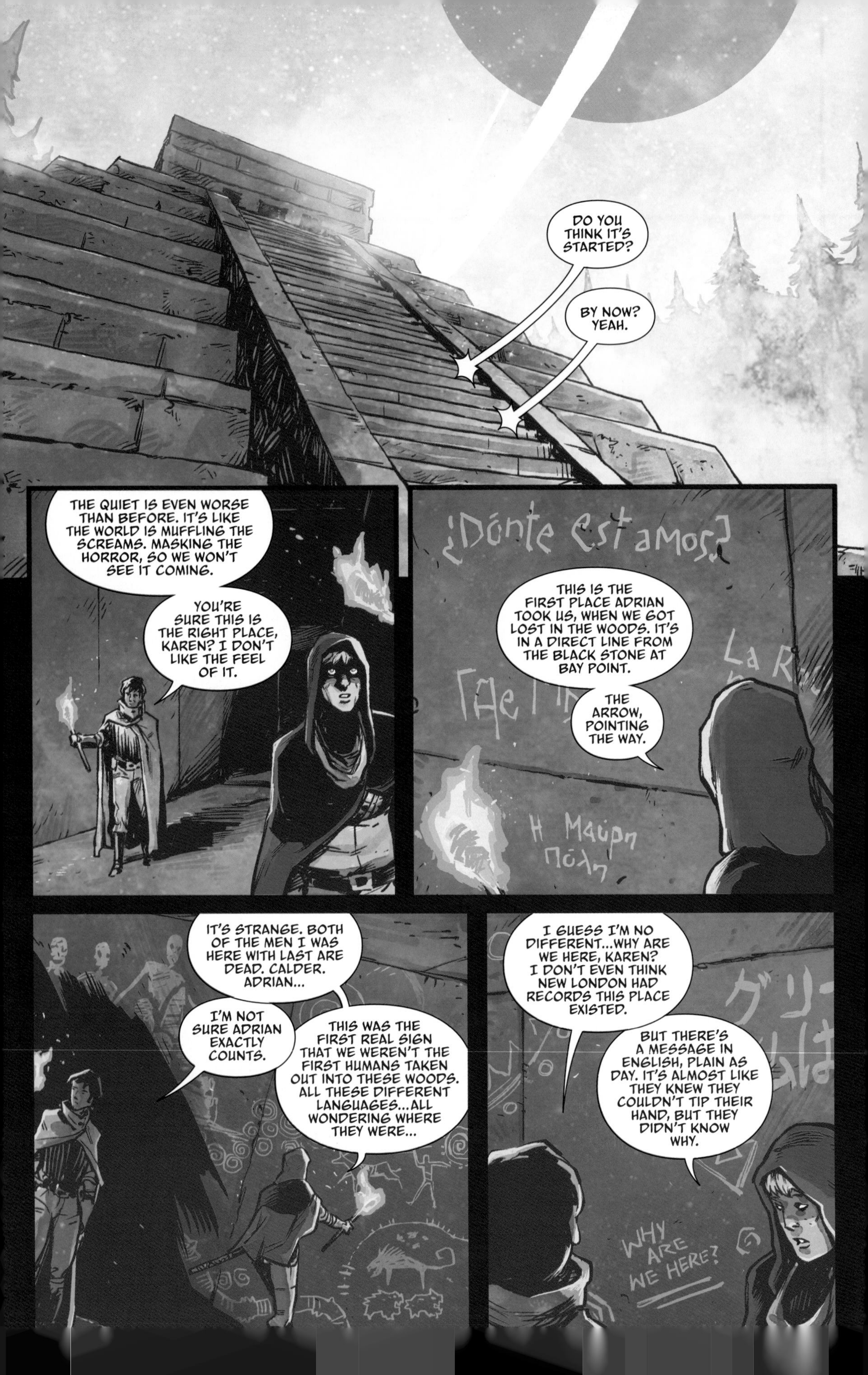
DO YOU THINK IT'S STARTED?
BY NOW? YEAH.
THE QUIET IS EVEN WORSE THAN BEFORE. IT'S LIKE THE WORLD IS MUFFLING THE SCREAMS. MASKING THE HORROR, SO WE WON'T SEE IT COMING.
YOU'RE SURE THIS IS THE RIGHT PLACE, KAREN? I DON'T LIKE THE FEEL OF IT.
¿Dónte estamos?
THIS IS THE FIRST PLACE ADRIAN TOOK US, WHEN WE GOT LOST IN THE WOODS. IT'S IN A DIRECT LINE FROM THE BLACK STONE AT BAY POINT.
THE ARROW, POINTING THE WAY.
Η Μαύρη
Πύλη
IT'S STRANGE. BOTH OF THE MEN I WAS HERE WITH LAST ARE DEAD. CALDER. ADRIAN...
I'M NOT SURE ADRIAN EXACTLY COUNTS.
THIS WAS THE FIRST REAL SIGN THAT WE WEREN'T THE FIRST HUMANS TAKEN OUT INTO THESE WOODS. ALL THESE DIFFERENT LANGUAGES...ALL WONDERING WHERE THEY WERE...
I GUESS I'M NO DIFFERENT...WHY ARE WE HERE, KAREN? I DON'T EVEN THINK NEW LONDON HAD RECORDS THIS PLACE EXISTED.
BUT THERE'S A MESSAGE IN ENGLISH, PLAIN AS DAY. IT'S ALMOST LIKE THEY KNEW THEY COULDN'T TIP THEIR HAND, BUT THEY DIDN'T KNOW WHY.
WHY ARE WE HERE?

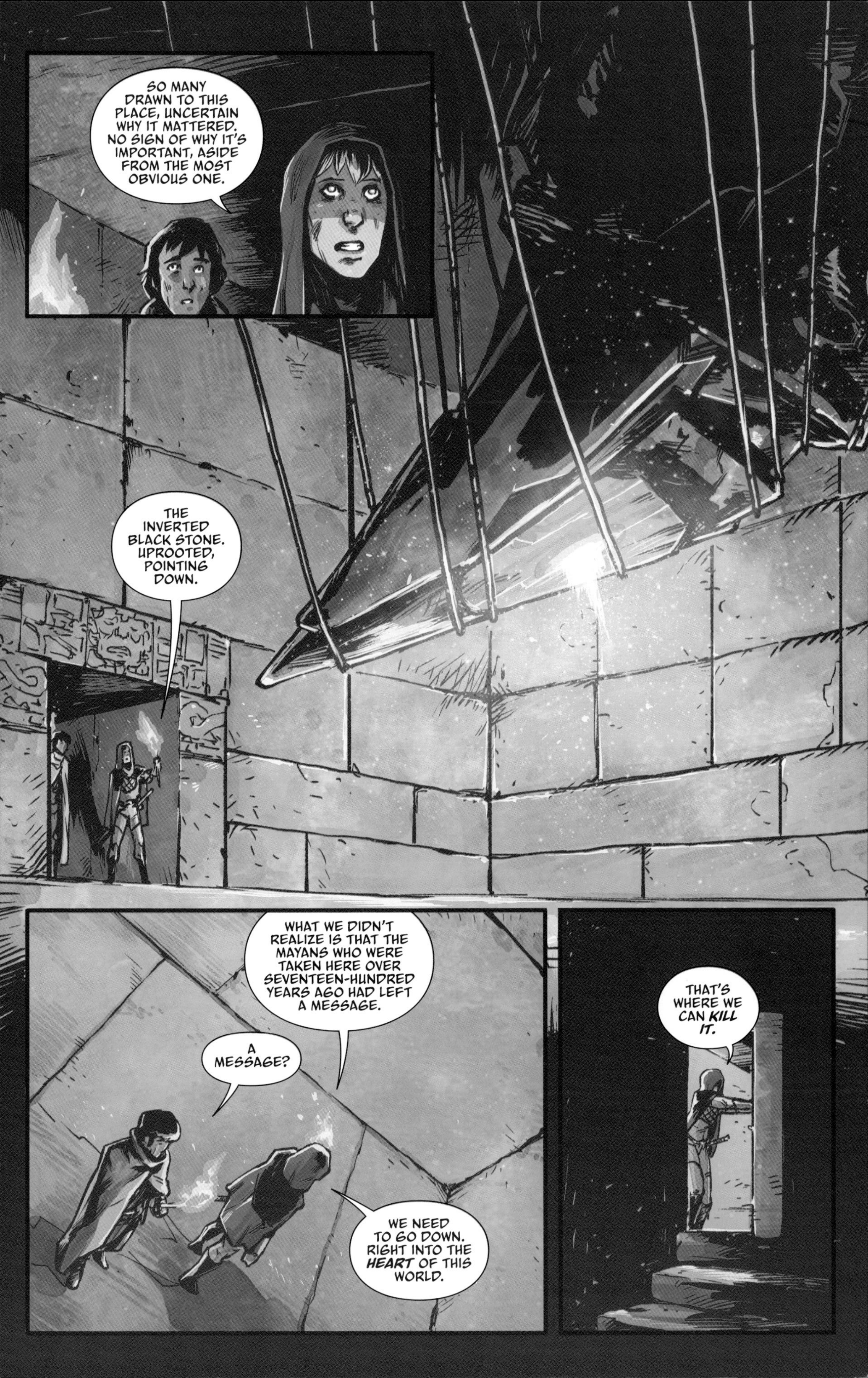
SO MANY DRAWN TO THIS PLACE, UNCERTAIN WHY IT MATTERED. NO SIGN OF WHY IT'S IMPORTANT, ASIDE FROM THE MOST OBVIOUS ONE.
THE INVERTED BLACK STONE. UPROOTED, POINTING DOWN.
WHAT WE DIDN'T REALIZE IS THAT THE MAYANS WHO WERE TAKEN HERE OVER SEVENTEEN-HUNDRED YEARS AGO HAD LEFT A MESSAGE.
A MESSAGE?
WE NEED TO GO DOWN. RIGHT INTO THE HEART OF THIS WORLD.
THAT'S WHERE WE CAN KILL IT.

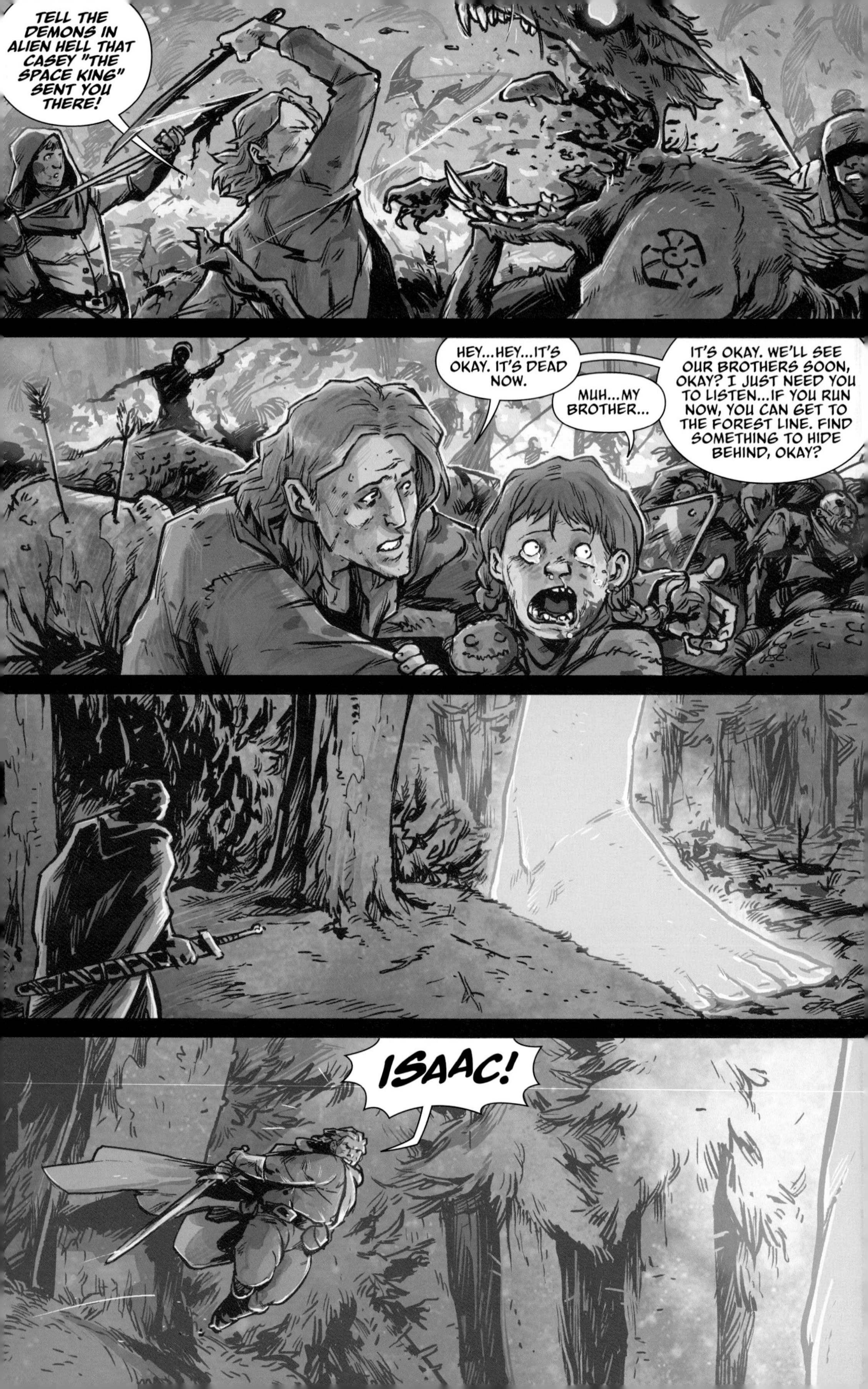
TELL THE DEMONS IN ALIEN HELL THAT CASEY "THE SPACE KING" SENT YOU THERE!
HEY...HEY...IT'S OKAY. IT'S DEAD NOW.
MUH...MY BROTHER...
IT'S OKAY. WE'LL SEE OUR BROTHERS SOON, OKAY? I JUST NEED YOU TO LISTEN...IF YOU RUN NOW, YOU CAN GET TO THE FOREST LINE. FIND SOMETHING TO HIDE BEHIND, OKAY?
ISAAC!

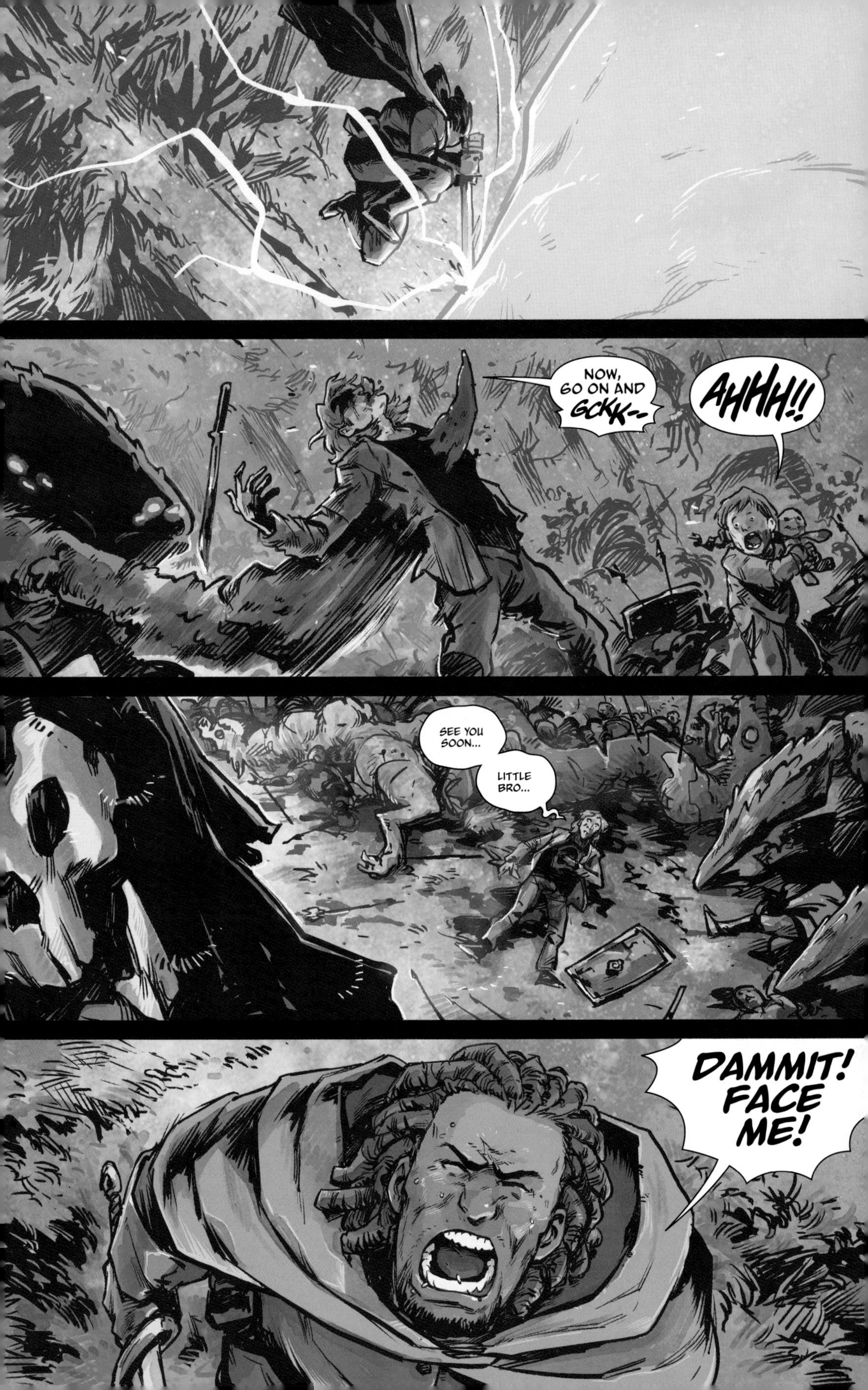
NOW, GO ON AND GCKK--
AHHH!!
SEE YOU SOON...
LITTLE BRO...
DAMMIT! FACE ME!

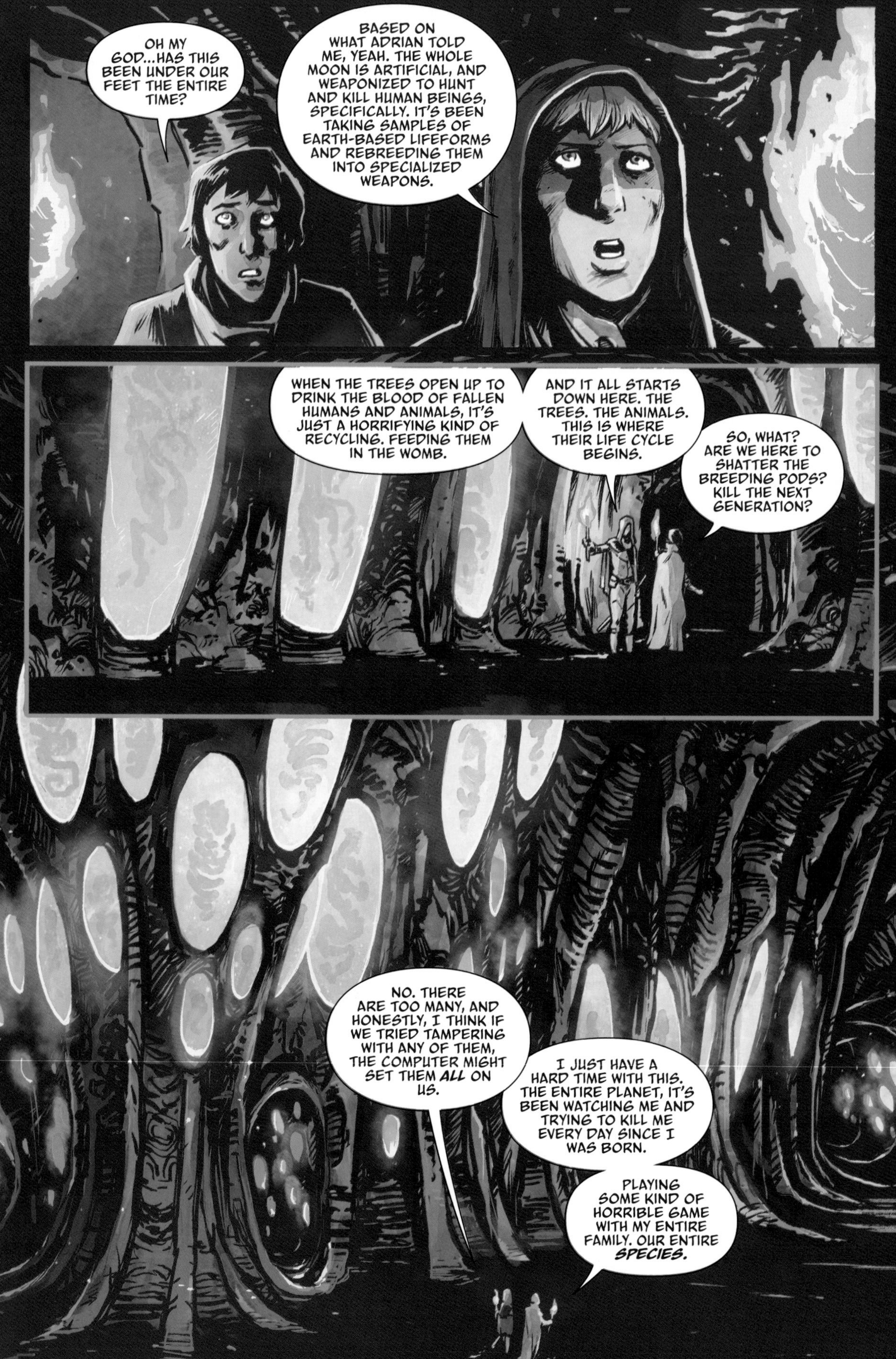
OH MY GOD...HAS THIS BEEN UNDER OUR FEET THE ENTIRE TIME?
BASED ON WHAT ADRIAN TOLD ME, YEAH. THE WHOLE MOON IS ARTIFICIAL, AND WEAPONIZED TO HUNT AND KILL HUMAN BEINGS, SPECIFICALLY. IT'S BEEN TAKING SAMPLES OF EARTH-BASED LIFEFORMS AND REBREEDING THEM INTO SPECIALIZED WEAPONS.
WHEN THE TREES OPEN UP TO DRINK THE BLOOD OF FALLEN HUMANS AND ANIMALS, IT'S JUST A HORRIFYING KIND OF RECYCLING. FEEDING THEM IN THE WOMB.
AND IT ALL STARTS DOWN HERE. THE TREES. THE ANIMALS. THIS IS WHERE THEIR LIFE CYCLE BEGINS.
SO, WHAT? ARE WE HERE TO SHATTER THE BREEDING PODS? KILL THE NEXT GENERATION?
NO. THERE ARE TOO MANY, AND HONESTLY, I THINK IF WE TRIED TAMPERING WITH ANY OF THEM, THE COMPUTER MIGHT SET THEM *ALL* ON US.
I JUST HAVE A HARD TIME WITH THIS. THE ENTIRE PLANET, IT'S BEEN WATCHING ME AND TRYING TO KILL ME EVERY DAY SINCE I WAS BORN.
PLAYING SOME KIND OF HORRIBLE GAME WITH MY ENTIRE FAMILY. OUR ENTIRE ***SPECIES.***

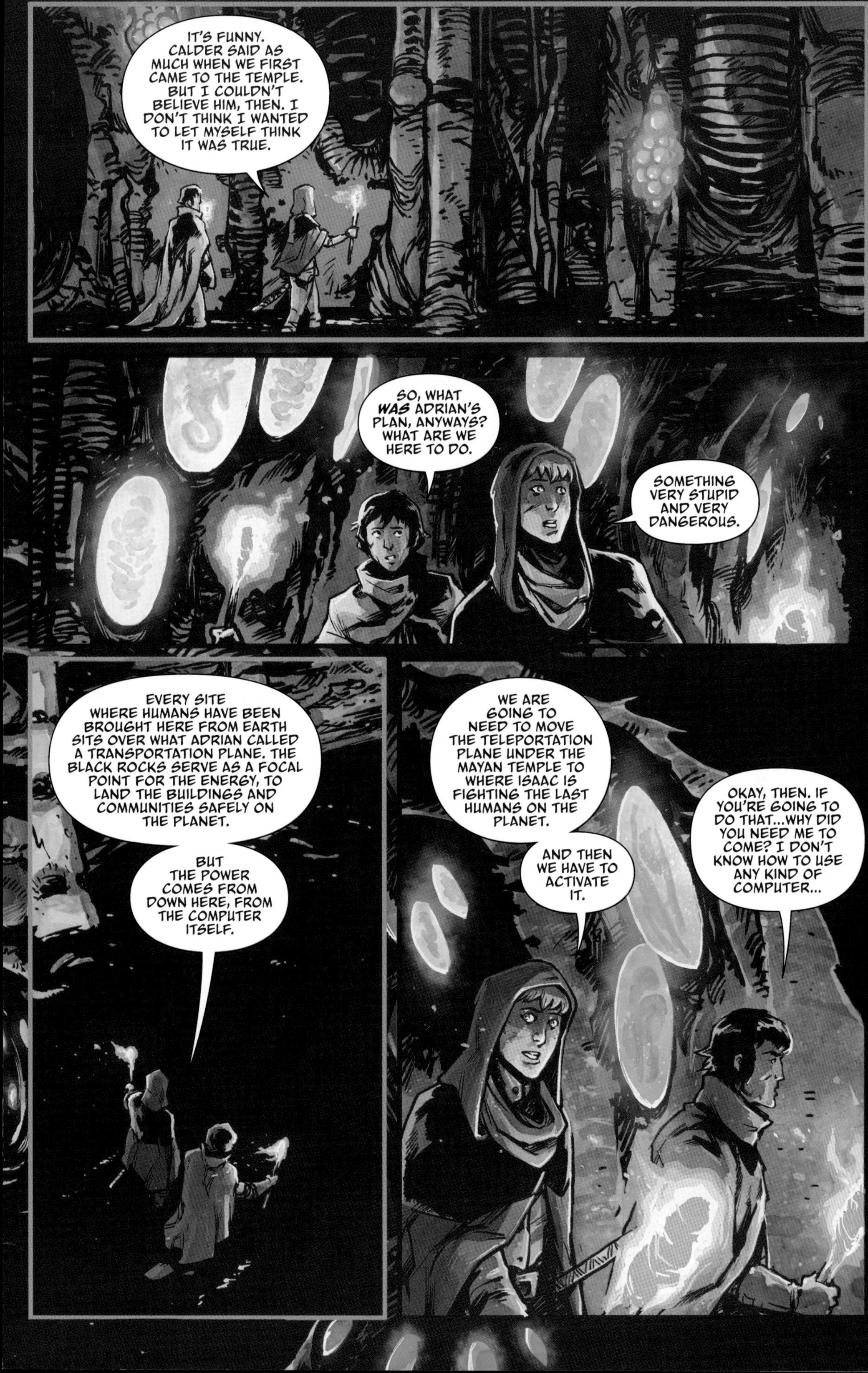
IT'S FUNNY. CALDER SAID AS MUCH WHEN WE FIRST CAME TO THE TEMPLE. BUT I COULDN'T BELIEVE HIM, THEN. I DON'T THINK I WANTED TO LET MYSELF THINK IT WAS TRUE.
SO, WHAT *WAS* ADRIAN'S PLAN, ANYWAYS? WHAT ARE WE HERE TO DO.
SOMETHING VERY STUPID AND VERY DANGEROUS.
EVERY SITE WHERE HUMANS HAVE BEEN BROUGHT HERE FROM EARTH SITS OVER WHAT ADRIAN CALLED A TRANSPORTATION PLANE. THE BLACK ROCKS SERVE AS A FOCAL POINT FOR THE ENERGY, TO LAND THE BUILDINGS AND COMMUNITIES SAFELY ON THE PLANET.
BUT THE POWER COMES FROM DOWN HERE, FROM THE COMPUTER ITSELF.
WE ARE GOING TO NEED TO MOVE THE TELEPORTATION PLANE UNDER THE MAYAN TEMPLE TO WHERE ISAAC IS FIGHTING THE LAST HUMANS ON THE PLANET.
AND THEN WE HAVE TO ACTIVATE IT.
OKAY, THEN. IF YOU'RE GOING TO DO THAT...WHY DID YOU NEED ME TO COME? I DON'T KNOW HOW TO USE ANY KIND OF COMPUTER...

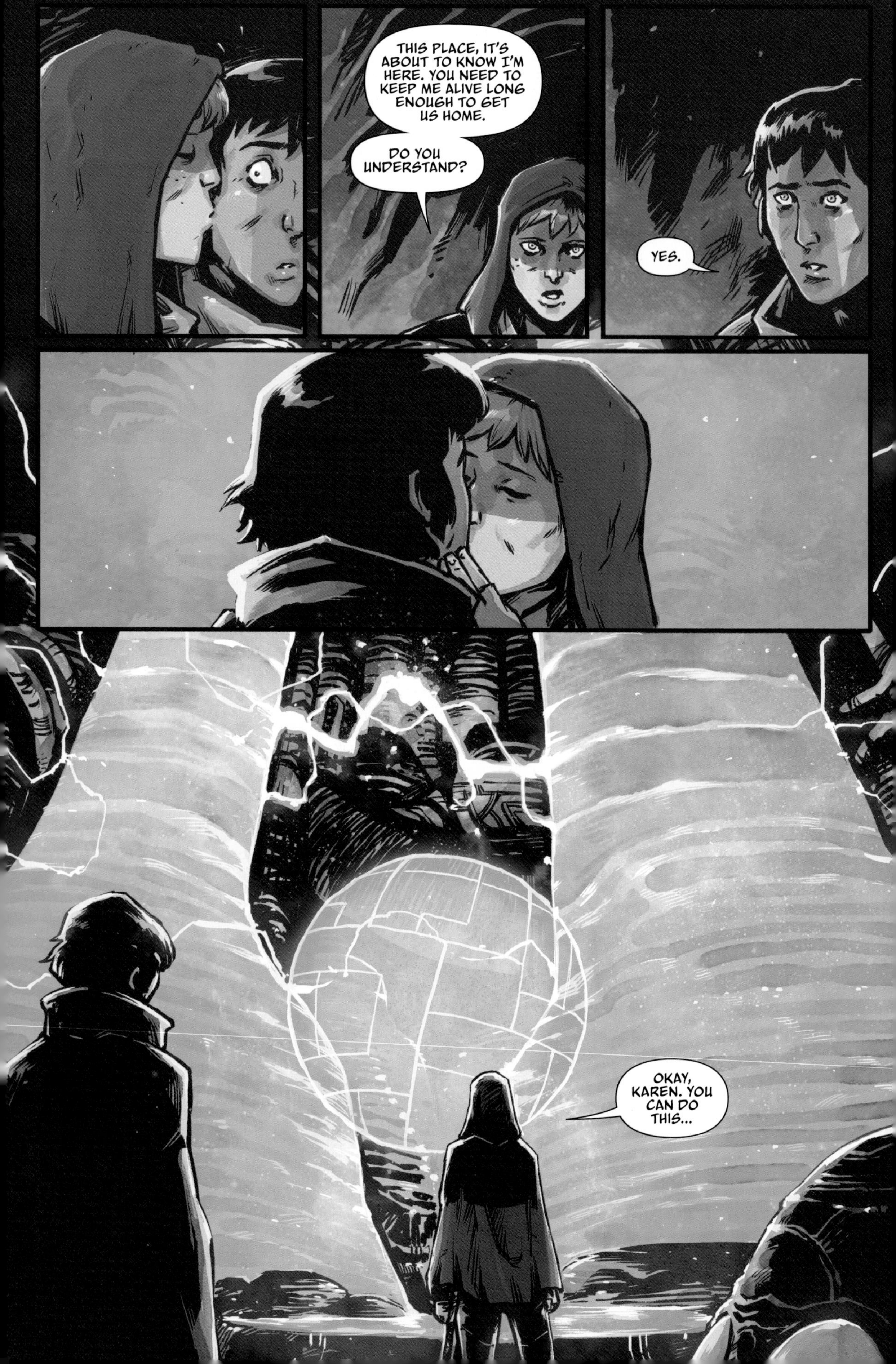
THIS PLACE, IT'S ABOUT TO KNOW I'M HERE. YOU NEED TO KEEP ME ALIVE LONG ENOUGH TO GET US HOME.
DO YOU UNDERSTAND?
YES.
OKAY, KAREN. YOU CAN DO THIS...

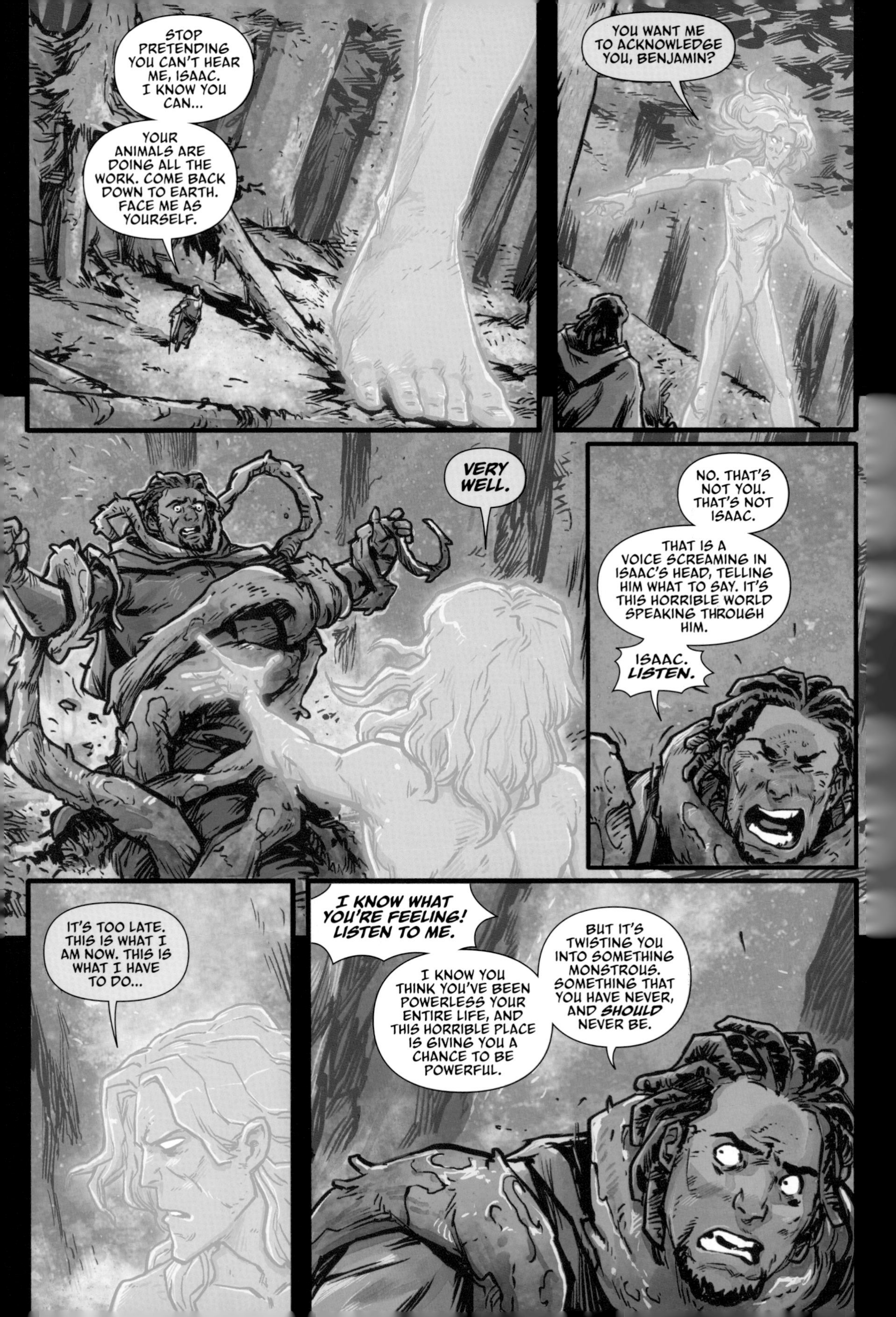
STOP PRETENDING YOU CAN'T HEAR ME, ISAAC. I KNOW YOU CAN...
YOUR ANIMALS ARE DOING ALL THE WORK. COME BACK DOWN TO EARTH. FACE ME AS YOURSELF.
YOU WANT ME TO ACKNOWLEDGE YOU, BENJAMIN?
VERY WELL.
NO. THAT'S NOT YOU. THAT'S NOT ISAAC.
THAT IS A VOICE SCREAMING IN ISAAC'S HEAD, TELLING HIM WHAT TO SAY. IT'S THIS HORRIBLE WORLD SPEAKING THROUGH HIM.
ISAAC. LISTEN.
IT'S TOO LATE. THIS IS WHAT I AM NOW. THIS IS WHAT I HAVE TO DO...
I KNOW WHAT YOU'RE FEELING! LISTEN TO ME.
I KNOW YOU THINK YOU'VE BEEN POWERLESS YOUR ENTIRE LIFE, AND THIS HORRIBLE PLACE IS GIVING YOU A CHANCE TO BE POWERFUL.
BUT IT'S TWISTING YOU INTO SOMETHING MONSTROUS. SOMETHING THAT YOU HAVE NEVER, AND SHOULD NEVER BE.

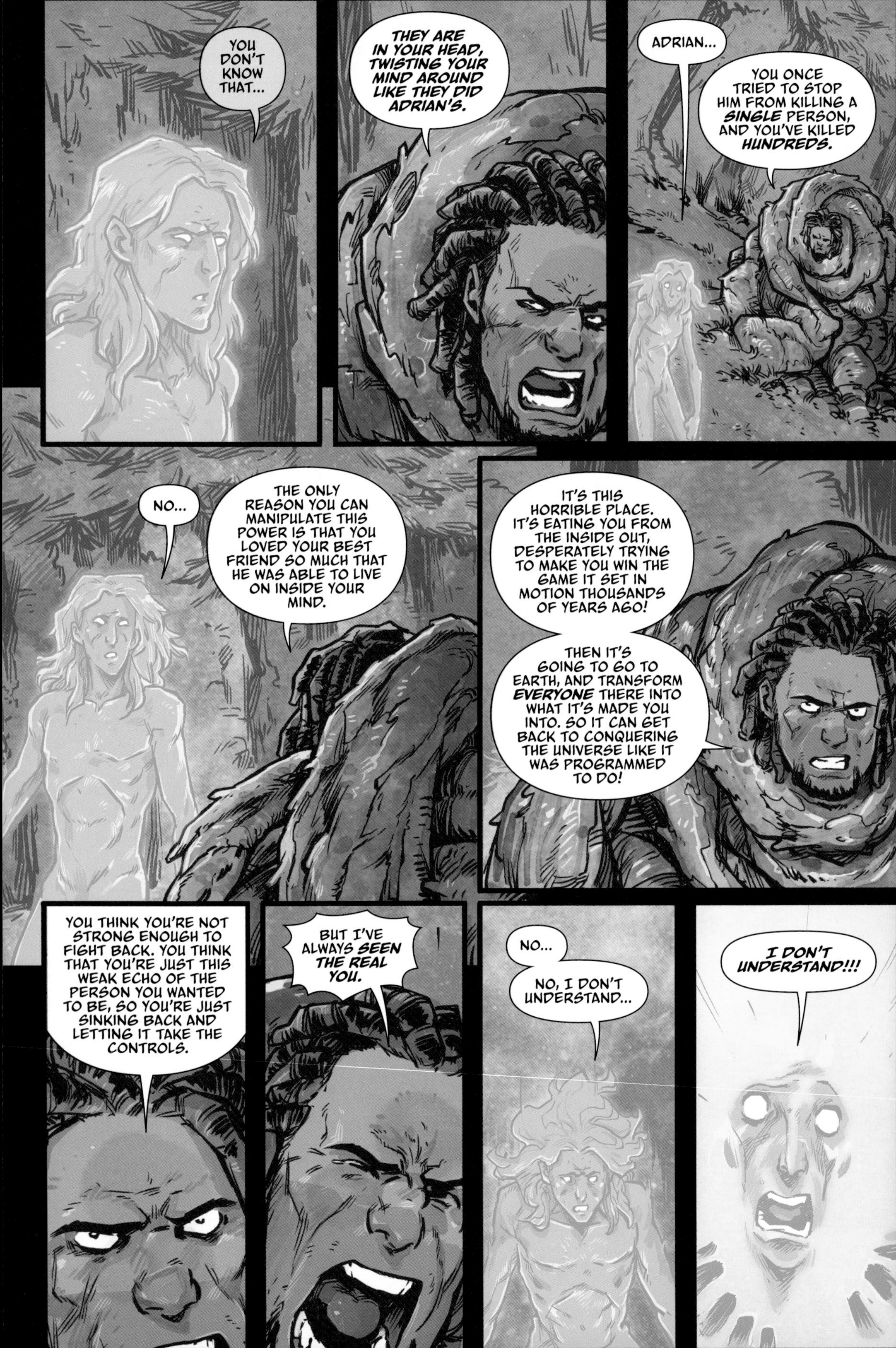

YOU DON'T KNOW THAT...
THEY ARE IN YOUR HEAD, TWISTING YOUR MIND AROUND LIKE THEY DID ADRIAN'S.
ADRIAN...
YOU ONCE TRIED TO STOP HIM FROM KILLING A SINGLE PERSON, AND YOU'VE KILLED HUNDREDS.
NO...
THE ONLY REASON YOU CAN MANIPULATE THIS POWER IS THAT YOU LOVED YOUR BEST FRIEND SO MUCH THAT HE WAS ABLE TO LIVE ON INSIDE YOUR MIND.
IT'S THIS HORRIBLE PLACE. IT'S EATING YOU FROM THE INSIDE OUT, DESPERATELY TRYING TO MAKE YOU WIN THE GAME IT SET IN MOTION THOUSANDS OF YEARS AGO!
THEN IT'S GOING TO GO TO EARTH, AND TRANSFORM EVERYONE THERE INTO WHAT IT'S MADE YOU INTO. SO IT CAN GET BACK TO CONQUERING THE UNIVERSE LIKE IT WAS PROGRAMMED TO DO!
YOU THINK YOU'RE NOT STRONG ENOUGH TO FIGHT BACK. YOU THINK THAT YOU'RE JUST THIS WEAK ECHO OF THE PERSON YOU WANTED TO BE, SO YOU'RE JUST SINKING BACK AND LETTING IT TAKE THE CONTROLS.
BUT I'VE ALWAYS SEEN THE REAL YOU.
NO...
NO, I DON'T UNDERSTAND...
I DON'T UNDERSTAND!!!

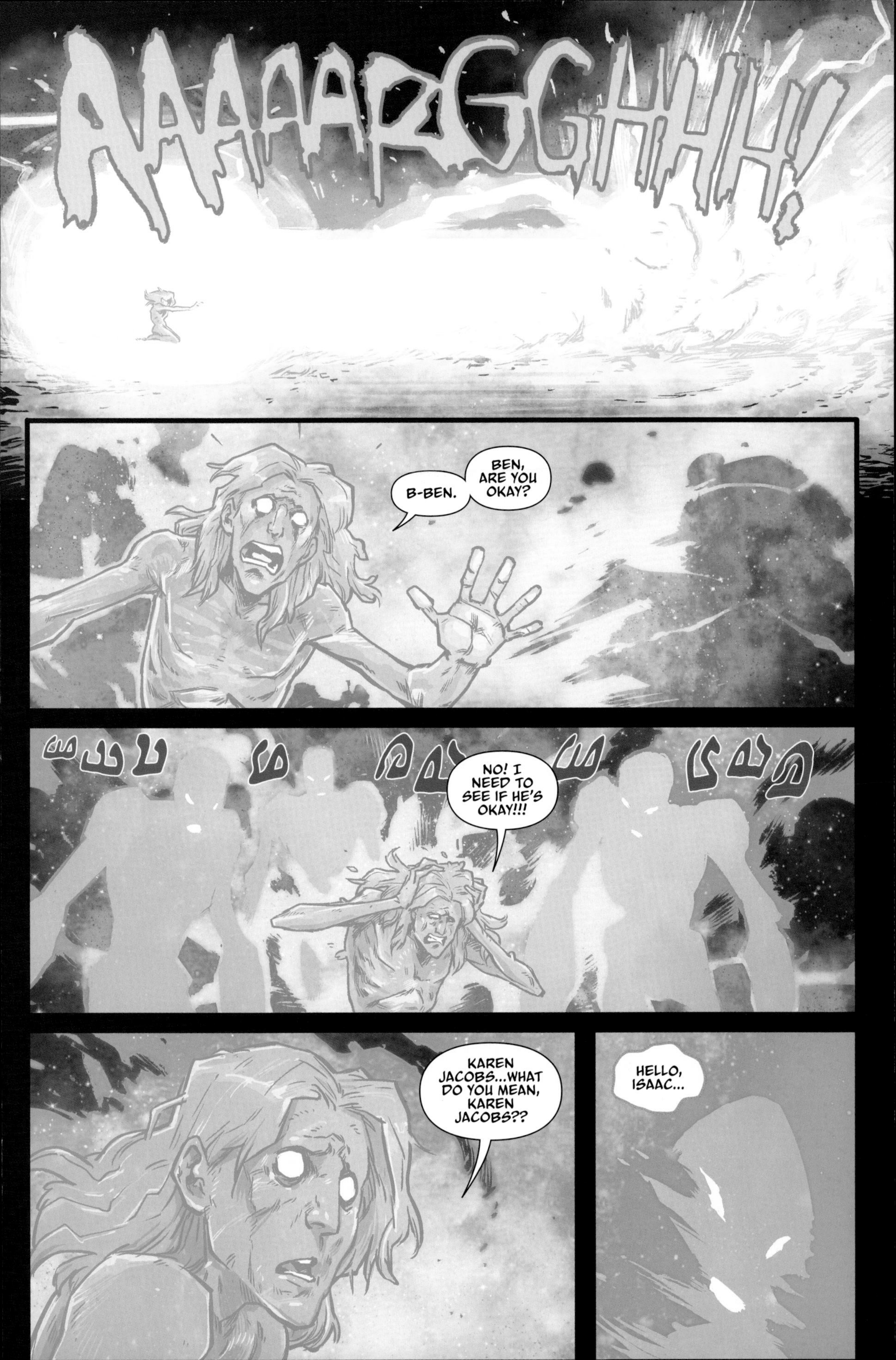
AAAAARGGHHH!
B-BEN.
BEN, ARE YOU OKAY?
NO! I NEED TO SEE IF HE'S OKAY!!!
KAREN JACOBS...WHAT DO YOU MEAN, KAREN JACOBS??
HELLO, ISAAC...

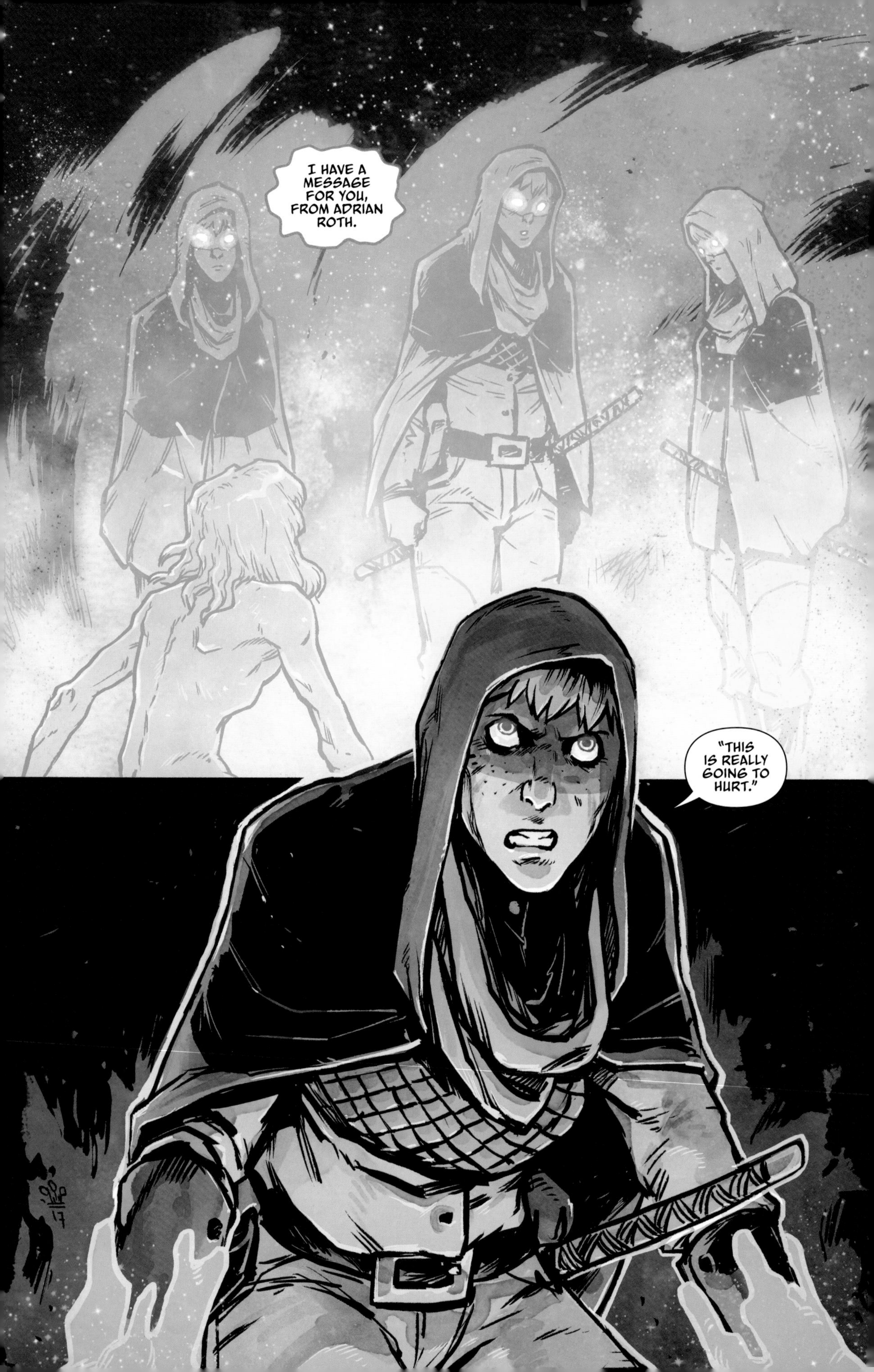
I HAVE A MESSAGE FOR YOU, FROM ADRIAN ROTH.
"THIS IS REALLY GOING TO HURT."

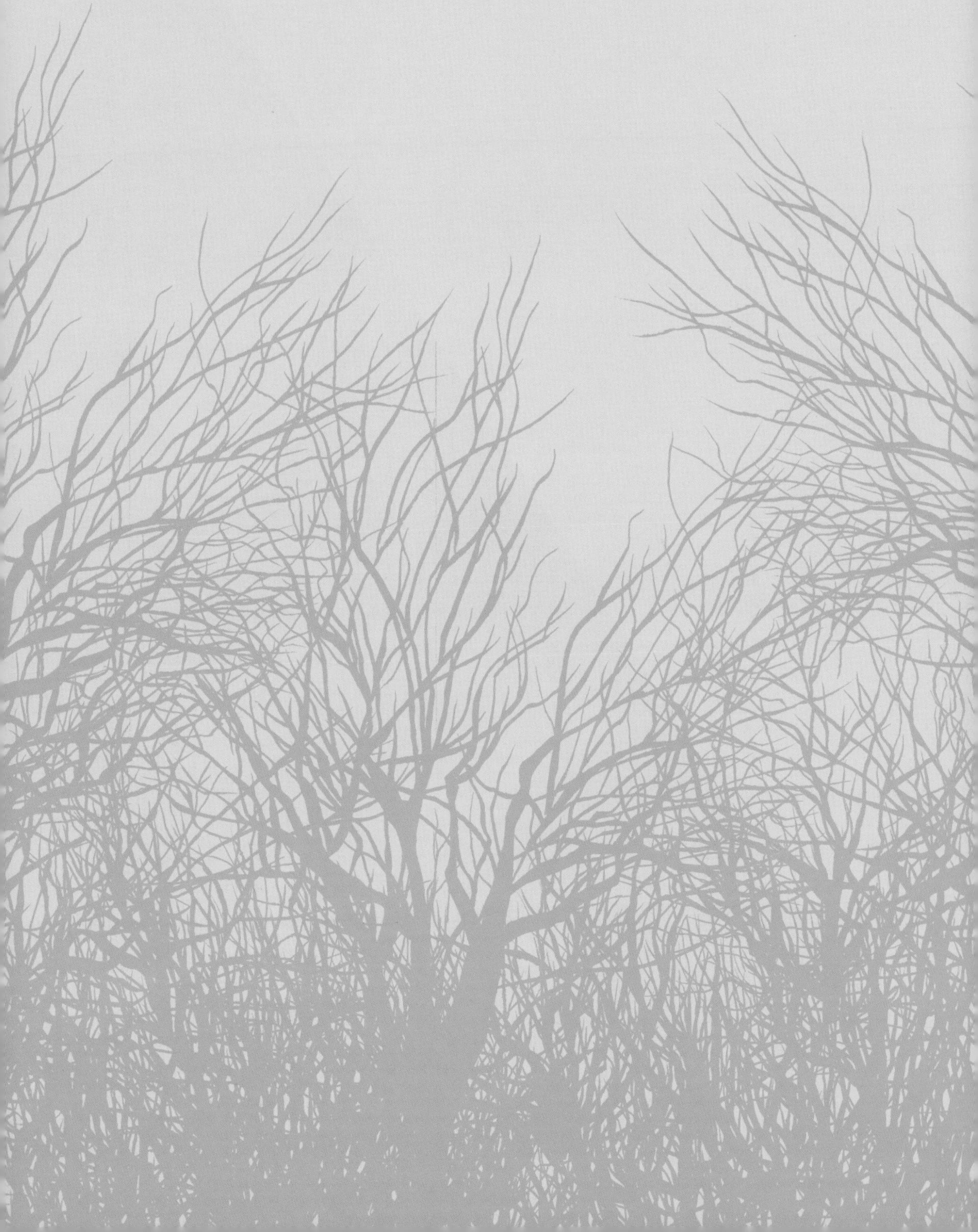

CHAPTER THIRTY-SIX

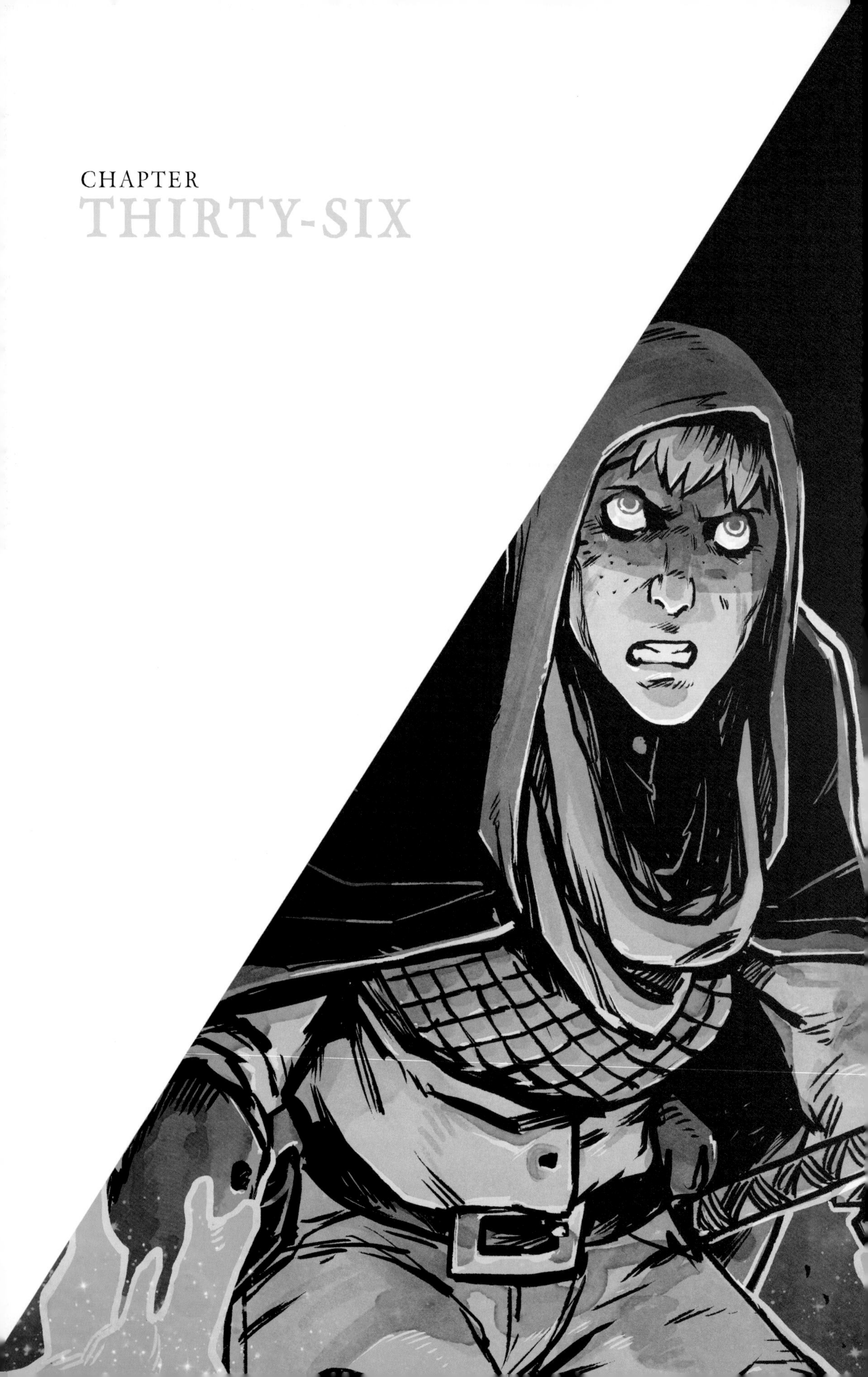

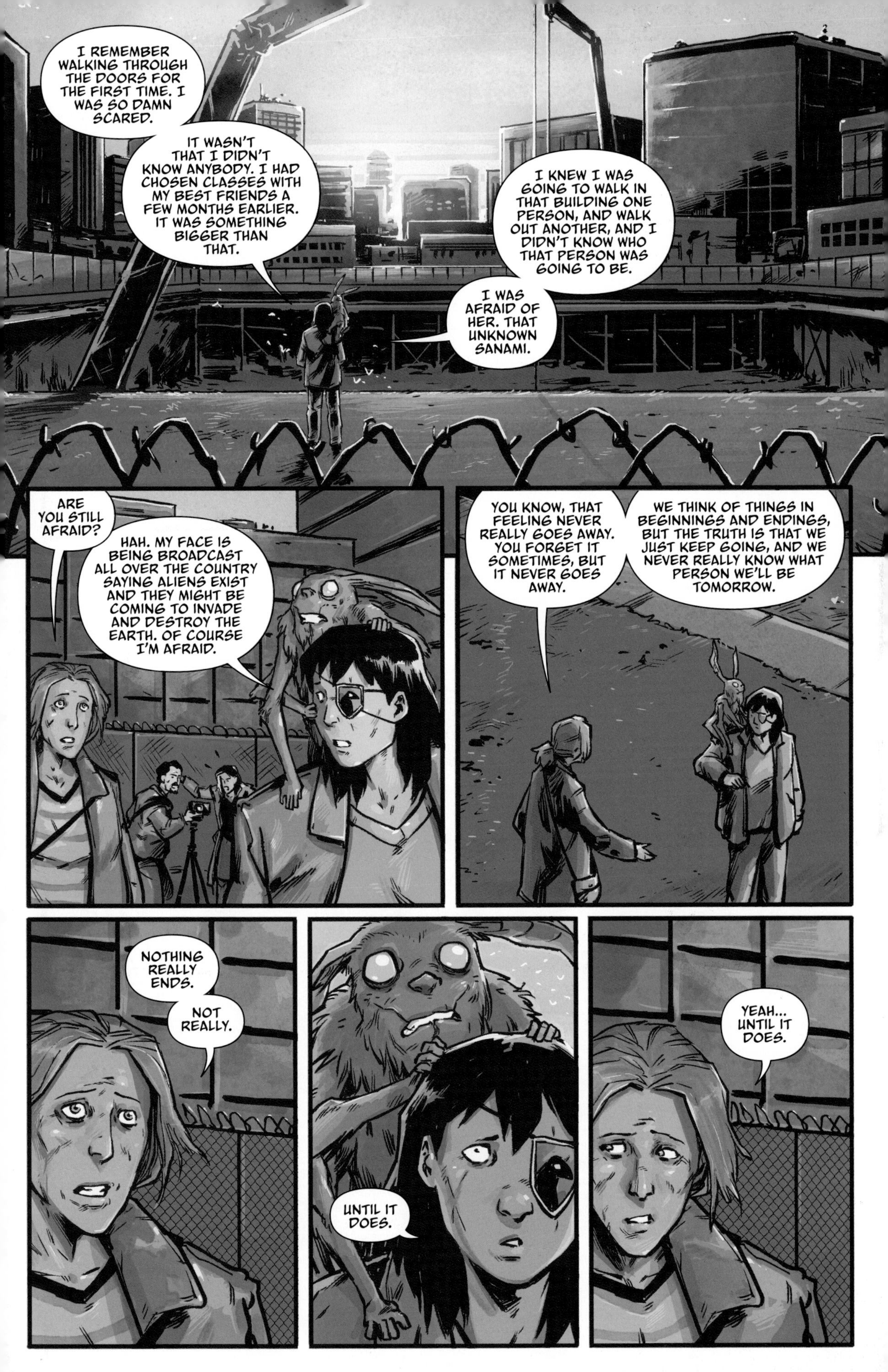
I REMEMBER WALKING THROUGH THE DOORS FOR THE FIRST TIME. I WAS SO DAMN SCARED.
IT WASN'T THAT I DIDN'T KNOW ANYBODY. I HAD CHOSEN CLASSES WITH MY BEST FRIENDS A FEW MONTHS EARLIER. IT WAS SOMETHING BIGGER THAN THAT.
I KNEW I WAS GOING TO WALK IN THAT BUILDING ONE PERSON, AND WALK OUT ANOTHER, AND I DIDN'T KNOW WHO THAT PERSON WAS GOING TO BE.
I WAS AFRAID OF HER. THAT UNKNOWN SANAMI.
ARE YOU STILL AFRAID?
HAH. MY FACE IS BEING BROADCAST ALL OVER THE COUNTRY SAYING ALIENS EXIST AND THEY MIGHT BE COMING TO INVADE AND DESTROY THE EARTH. OF COURSE I'M AFRAID.
YOU KNOW, THAT FEELING NEVER REALLY GOES AWAY. YOU FORGET IT SOMETIMES, BUT IT NEVER GOES AWAY.
WE THINK OF THINGS IN BEGINNINGS AND ENDINGS, BUT THE TRUTH IS THAT WE JUST KEEP GOING, AND WE NEVER REALLY KNOW WHAT PERSON WE'LL BE TOMORROW.
NOTHING REALLY ENDS.
NOT REALLY.
UNTIL IT DOES.
YEAH... UNTIL IT DOES.

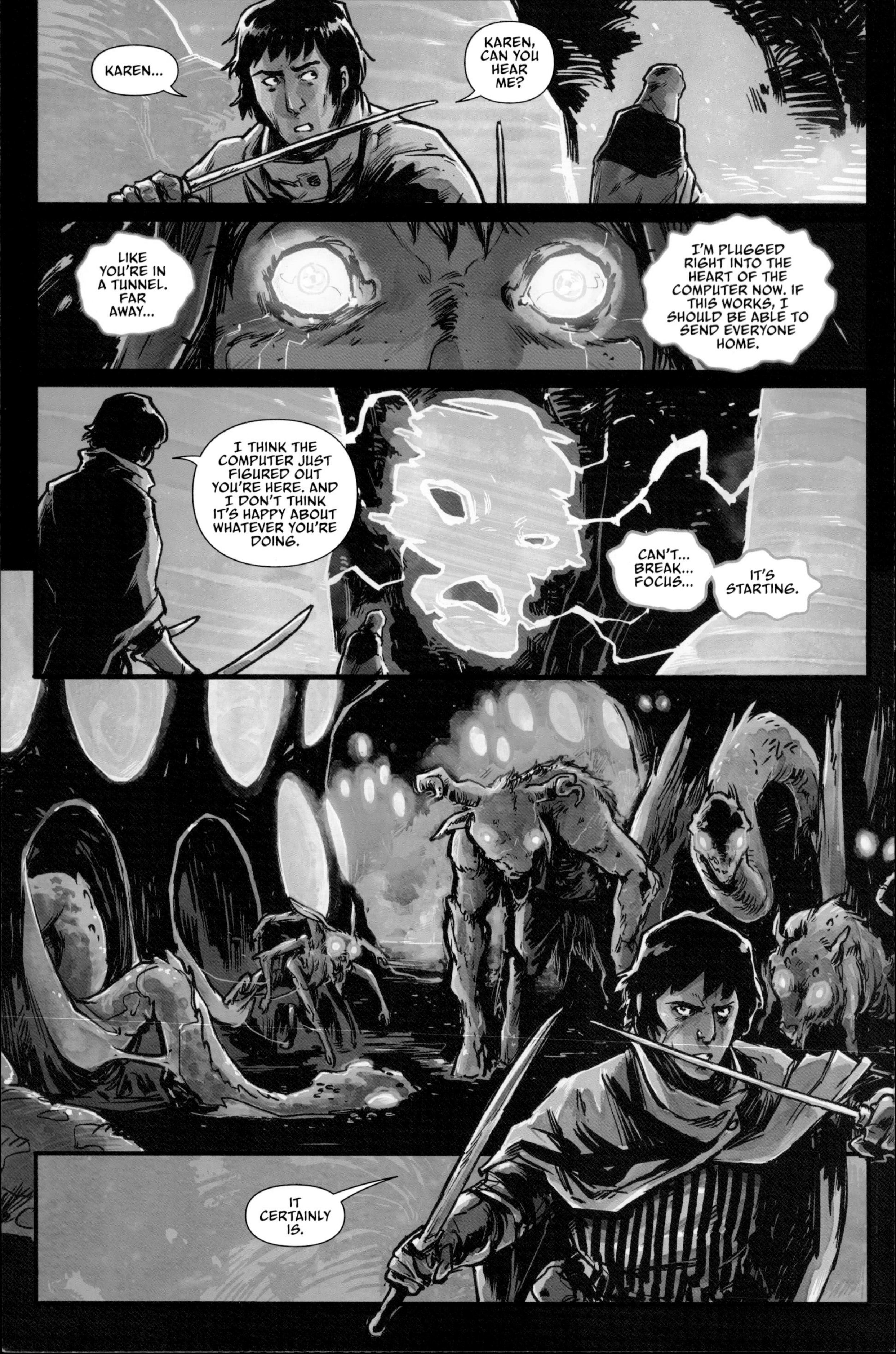
KAREN...
KAREN, CAN YOU HEAR ME?
LIKE YOU'RE IN A TUNNEL. FAR AWAY...
I'M PLUGGED RIGHT INTO THE HEART OF THE COMPUTER NOW. IF THIS WORKS, I SHOULD BE ABLE TO SEND EVERYONE HOME.
I THINK THE COMPUTER JUST FIGURED OUT YOU'RE HERE. AND I DON'T THINK IT'S HAPPY ABOUT WHATEVER YOU'RE DOING.
CAN'T... BREAK... FOCUS...
IT'S STARTING.
IT CERTAINLY IS.

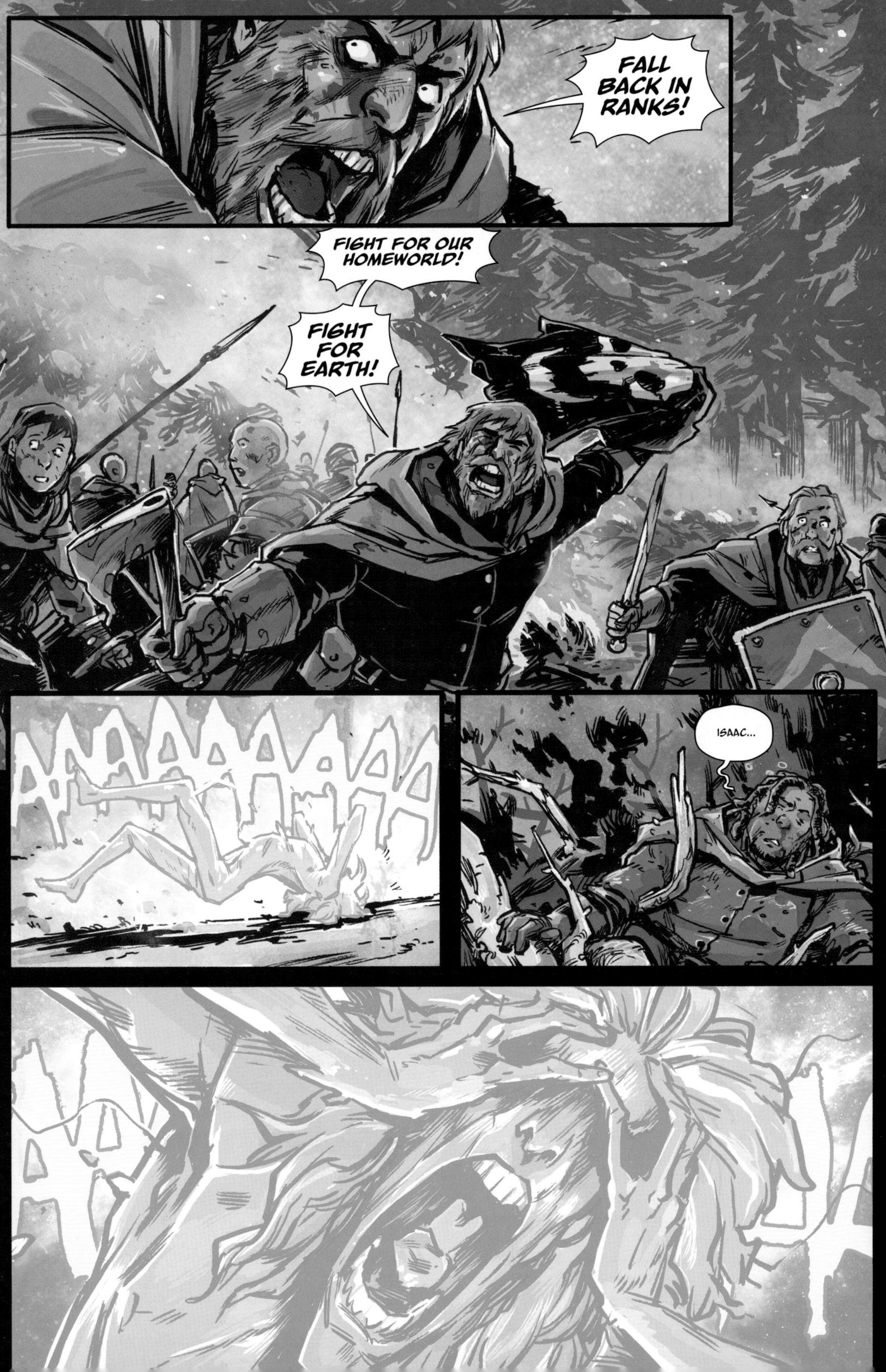
FALL BACK IN RANKS!
FIGHT FOR OUR HOMEWORLD!
FIGHT FOR EARTH!
ISAAC...

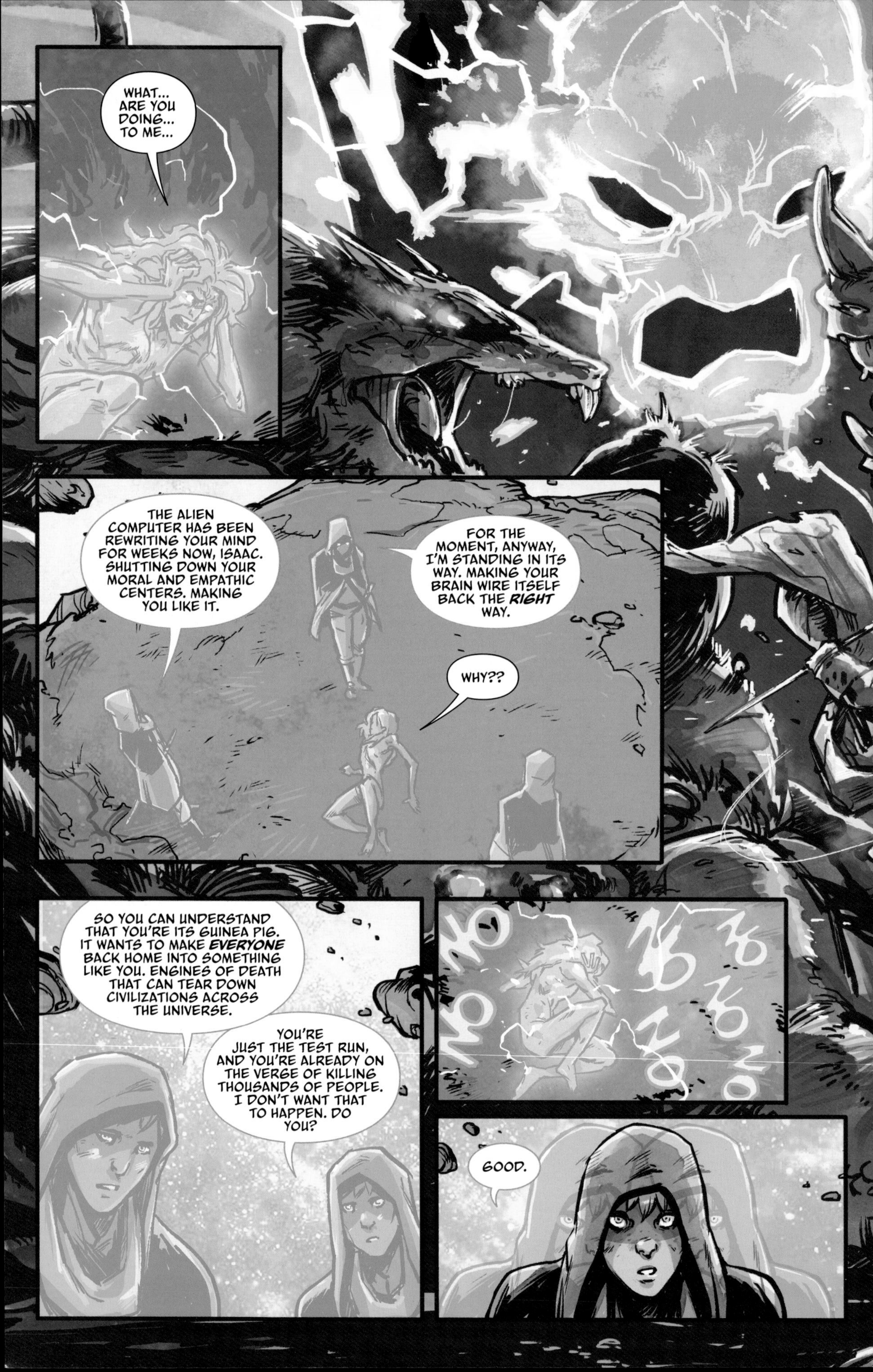
WHAT... ARE YOU DOING... TO ME...
THE ALIEN COMPUTER HAS BEEN REWRITING YOUR MIND FOR WEEKS NOW, ISAAC. SHUTTING DOWN YOUR MORAL AND EMPATHIC CENTERS. MAKING YOU LIKE IT.
FOR THE MOMENT, ANYWAY, I'M STANDING IN ITS WAY. MAKING YOUR BRAIN WIRE ITSELF BACK THE *RIGHT* WAY.
WHY??
SO YOU CAN UNDERSTAND THAT YOU'RE ITS GUINEA PIG. IT WANTS TO MAKE *EVERYONE* BACK HOME INTO SOMETHING LIKE YOU. ENGINES OF DEATH THAT CAN TEAR DOWN CIVILIZATIONS ACROSS THE UNIVERSE.
YOU'RE JUST THE TEST RUN, AND YOU'RE ALREADY ON THE VERGE OF KILLING THOUSANDS OF PEOPLE. I DON'T WANT THAT TO HAPPEN. DO YOU?
GOOD.

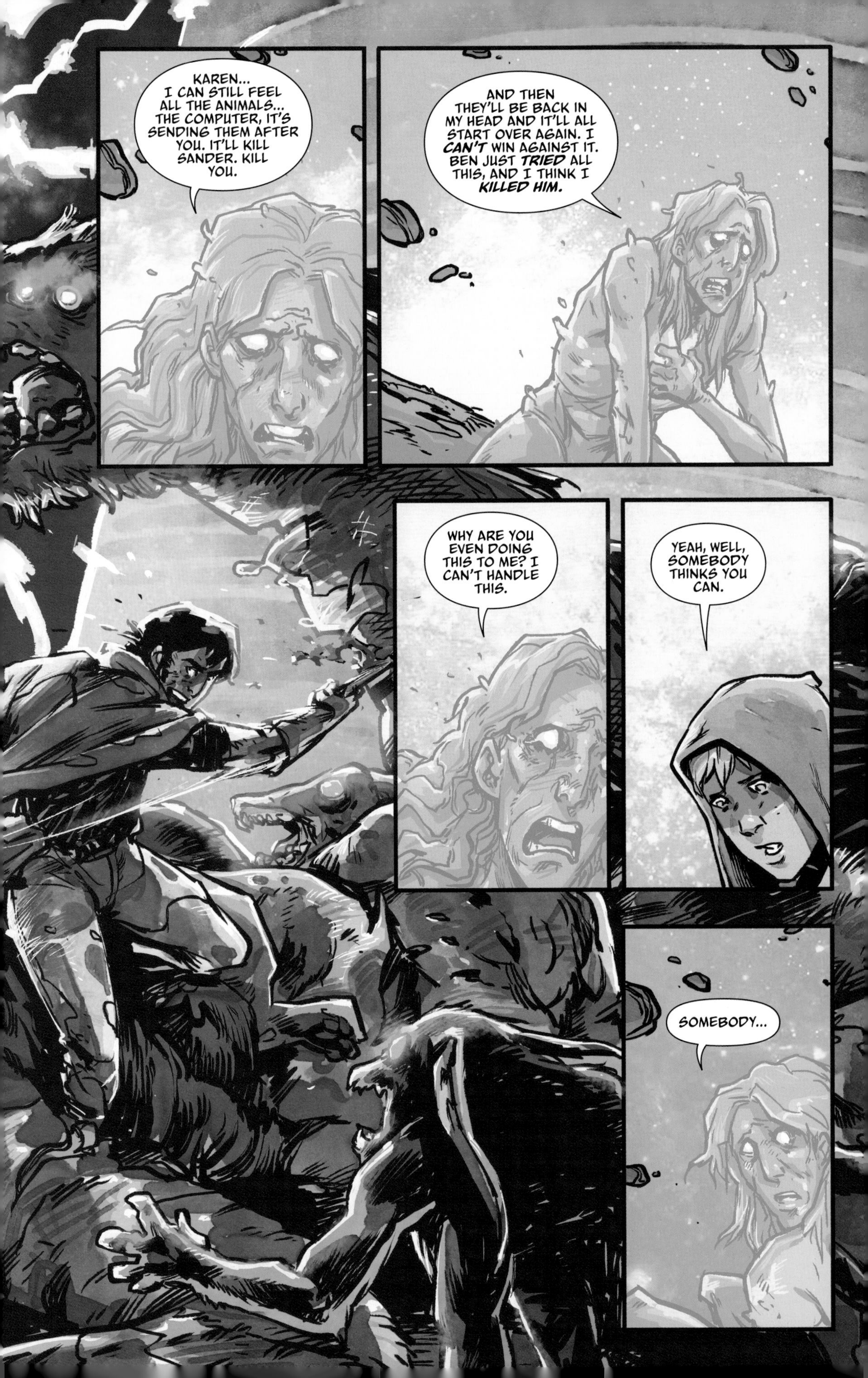
KAREN... I CAN STILL FEEL ALL THE ANIMALS... THE COMPUTER, IT'S SENDING THEM AFTER YOU. IT'LL KILL SANDER. KILL YOU.
AND THEN THEY'LL BE BACK IN MY HEAD AND IT'LL ALL START OVER AGAIN. I CAN'T WIN AGAINST IT. BEN JUST TRIED ALL THIS, AND I THINK I KILLED HIM.
WHY ARE YOU EVEN DOING THIS TO ME? I CAN'T HANDLE THIS.
YEAH, WELL, SOMEBODY THINKS YOU CAN.
SOMEBODY...

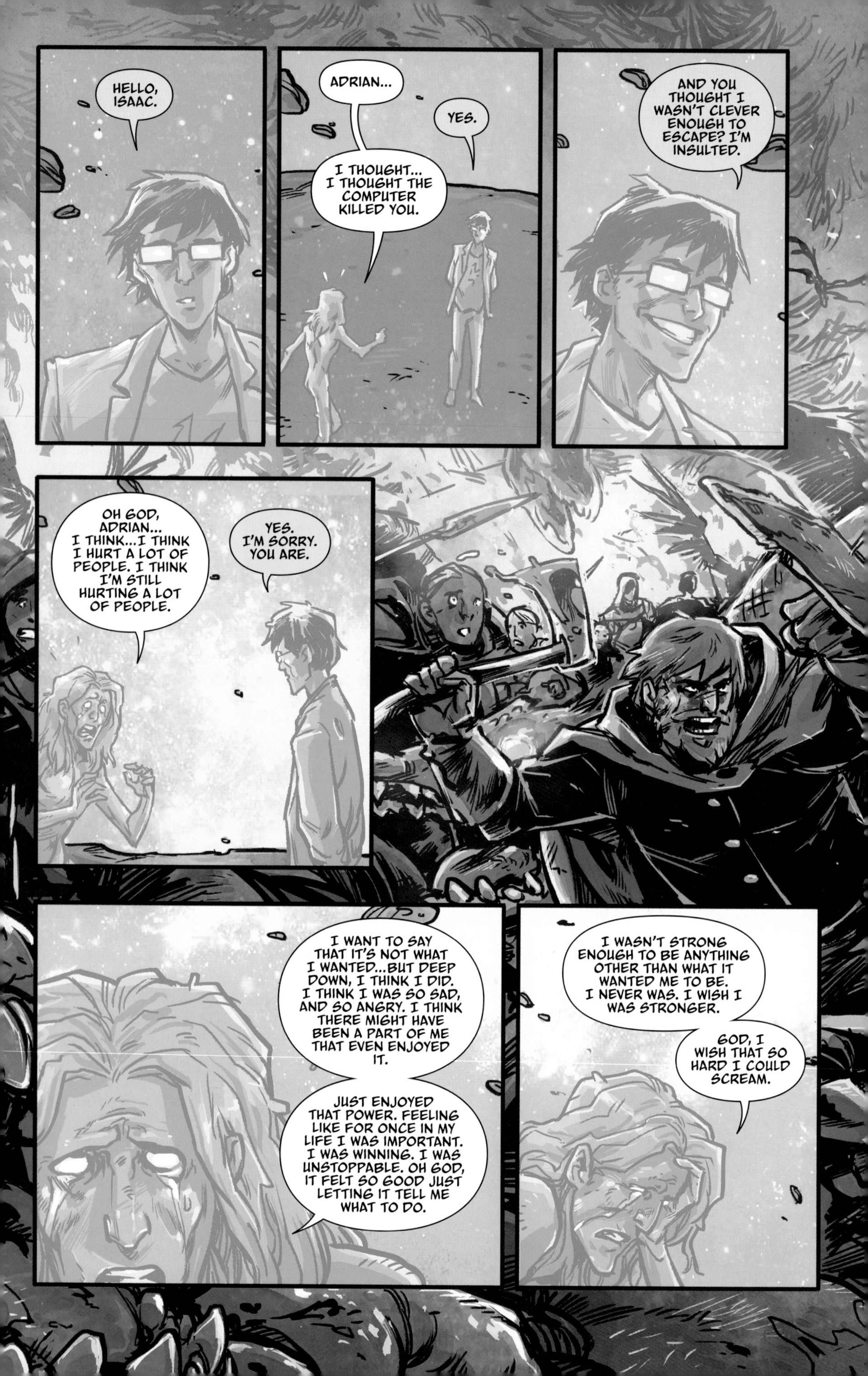
HELLO, ISAAC.
ADRIAN...
YES.
I THOUGHT... I THOUGHT THE COMPUTER KILLED YOU.
AND YOU THOUGHT I WASN'T CLEVER ENOUGH TO ESCAPE? I'M INSULTED.
OH GOD, ADRIAN... I THINK...I THINK I HURT A LOT OF PEOPLE. I THINK I'M STILL HURTING A LOT OF PEOPLE.
YES. I'M SORRY. YOU ARE.
I WANT TO SAY THAT IT'S NOT WHAT I WANTED...BUT DEEP DOWN, I THINK I DID. I THINK I WAS SO SAD, AND SO ANGRY. I THINK THERE MIGHT HAVE BEEN A PART OF ME THAT EVEN ENJOYED IT.
JUST ENJOYED THAT POWER. FEELING LIKE FOR ONCE IN MY LIFE I WAS IMPORTANT. I WAS WINNING. I WAS UNSTOPPABLE. OH GOD, IT FELT SO GOOD JUST LETTING IT TELL ME WHAT TO DO.
I WASN'T STRONG ENOUGH TO BE ANYTHING OTHER THAN WHAT IT WANTED ME TO BE. I NEVER WAS. I WISH I WAS STRONGER.
GOD, I WISH THAT SO HARD I COULD SCREAM.

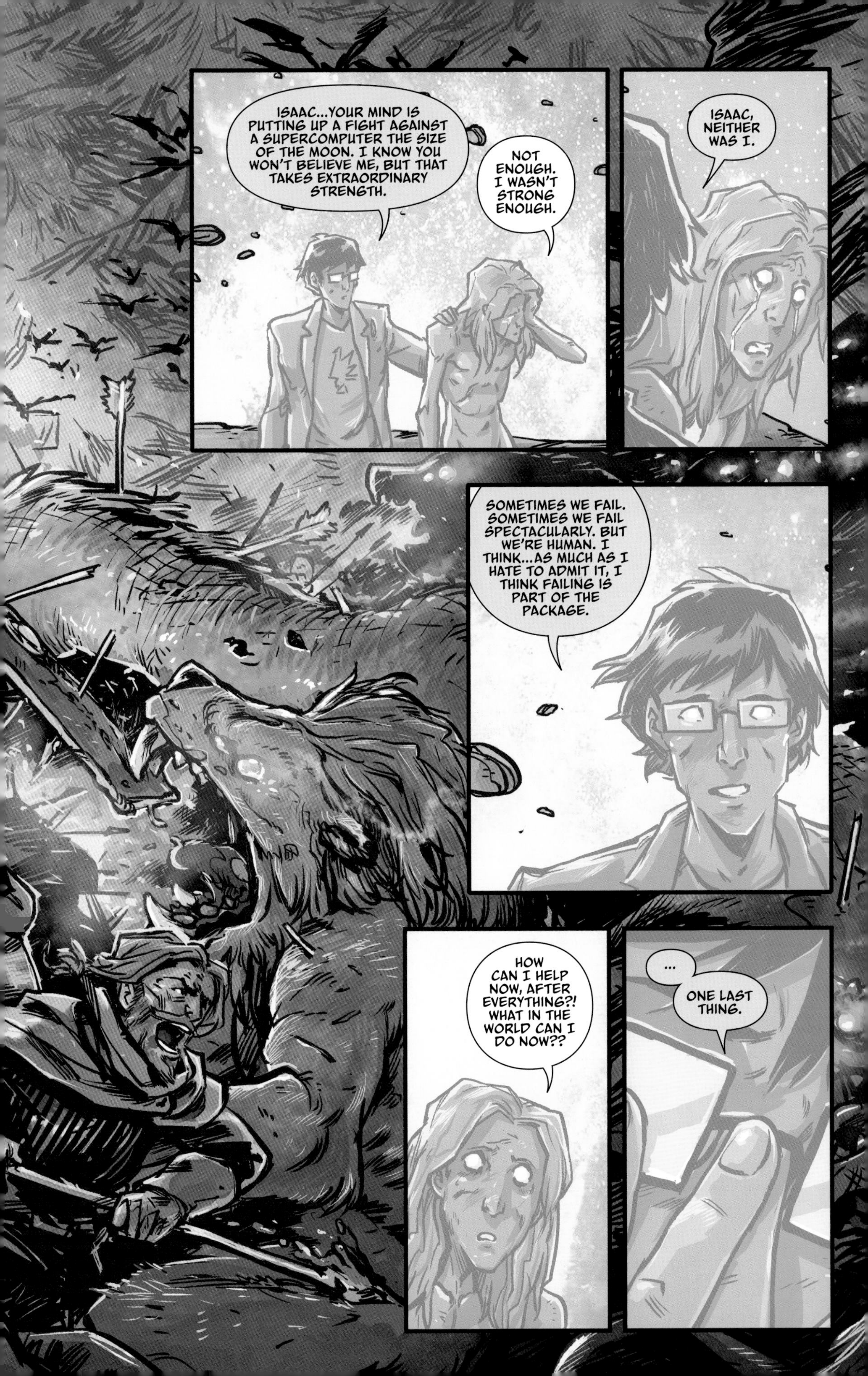
ISAAC...YOUR MIND IS PUTTING UP A FIGHT AGAINST A SUPERCOMPUTER THE SIZE OF THE MOON. I KNOW YOU WON'T BELIEVE ME, BUT THAT TAKES EXTRAORDINARY STRENGTH.
NOT ENOUGH. I WASN'T STRONG ENOUGH.
ISAAC, NEITHER WAS I.
SOMETIMES WE FAIL. SOMETIMES WE FAIL SPECTACULARLY. BUT WE'RE HUMAN. I THINK...AS MUCH AS I HATE TO ADMIT IT, I THINK FAILING IS PART OF THE PACKAGE.
HOW CAN I HELP NOW, AFTER EVERYTHING?! WHAT IN THE WORLD CAN I DO NOW??
...
ONE LAST THING.

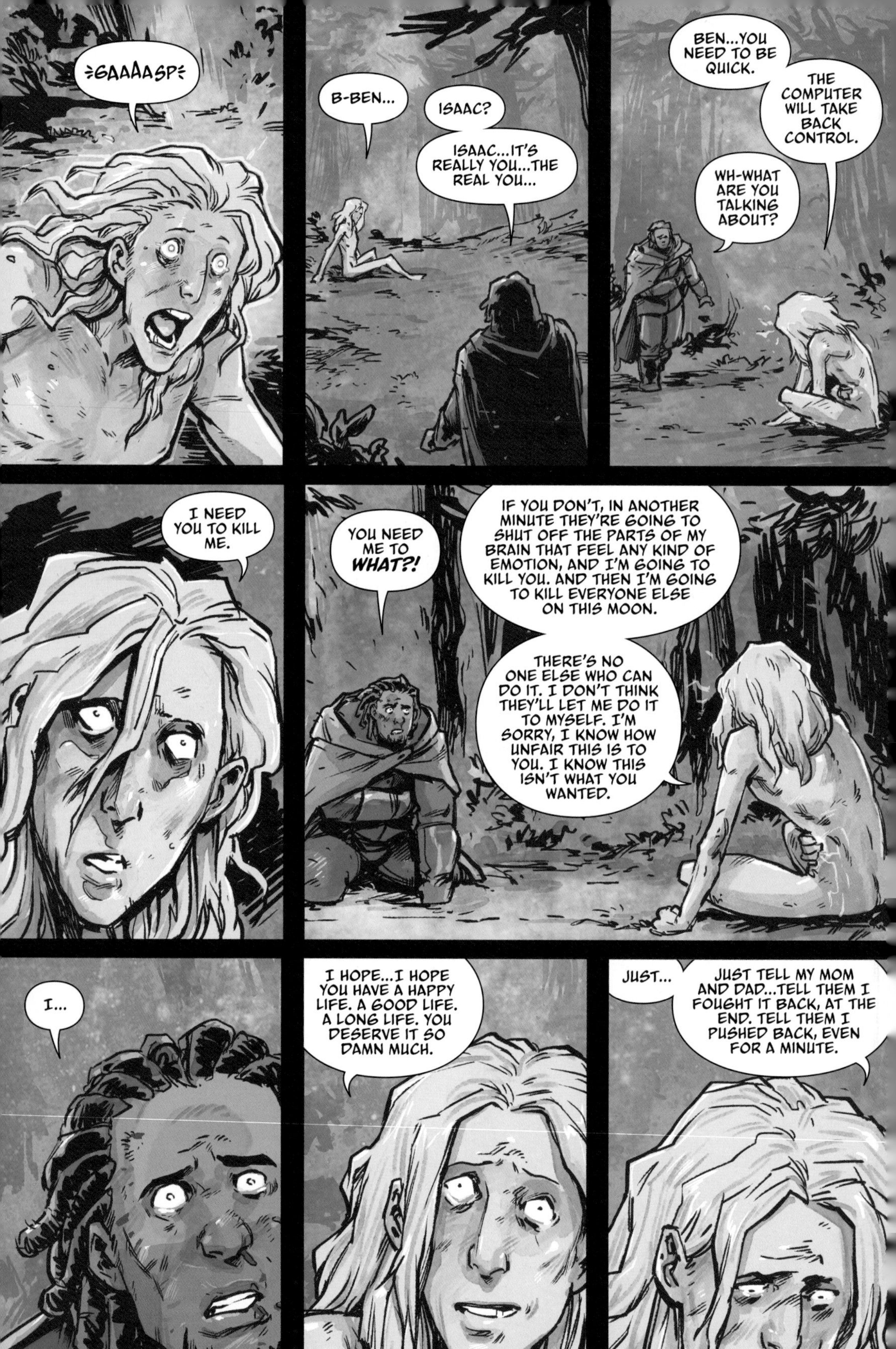

⁼GAAAASP⁼
B-BEN...
ISAAC?
ISAAC...IT'S REALLY YOU...THE REAL YOU...
BEN...YOU NEED TO BE QUICK.
THE COMPUTER WILL TAKE BACK CONTROL.
WH-WHAT ARE YOU TALKING ABOUT?
I NEED YOU TO KILL ME.
YOU NEED ME TO *WHAT?!*
IF YOU DON'T, IN ANOTHER MINUTE THEY'RE GOING TO SHUT OFF THE PARTS OF MY BRAIN THAT FEEL ANY KIND OF EMOTION, AND I'M GOING TO KILL YOU. AND THEN I'M GOING TO KILL EVERYONE ELSE ON THIS MOON.
THERE'S NO ONE ELSE WHO CAN DO IT. I DON'T THINK THEY'LL LET ME DO IT TO MYSELF. I'M SORRY, I KNOW HOW UNFAIR THIS IS TO YOU. I KNOW THIS ISN'T WHAT YOU WANTED.
I...
I HOPE...I HOPE YOU HAVE A HAPPY LIFE. A GOOD LIFE. A LONG LIFE. YOU DESERVE IT SO DAMN MUCH.
JUST...
JUST TELL MY MOM AND DAD...TELL THEM I FOUGHT IT BACK, AT THE END. TELL THEM I PUSHED BACK, EVEN FOR A MINUTE.

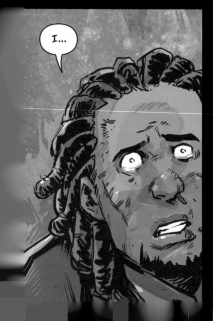

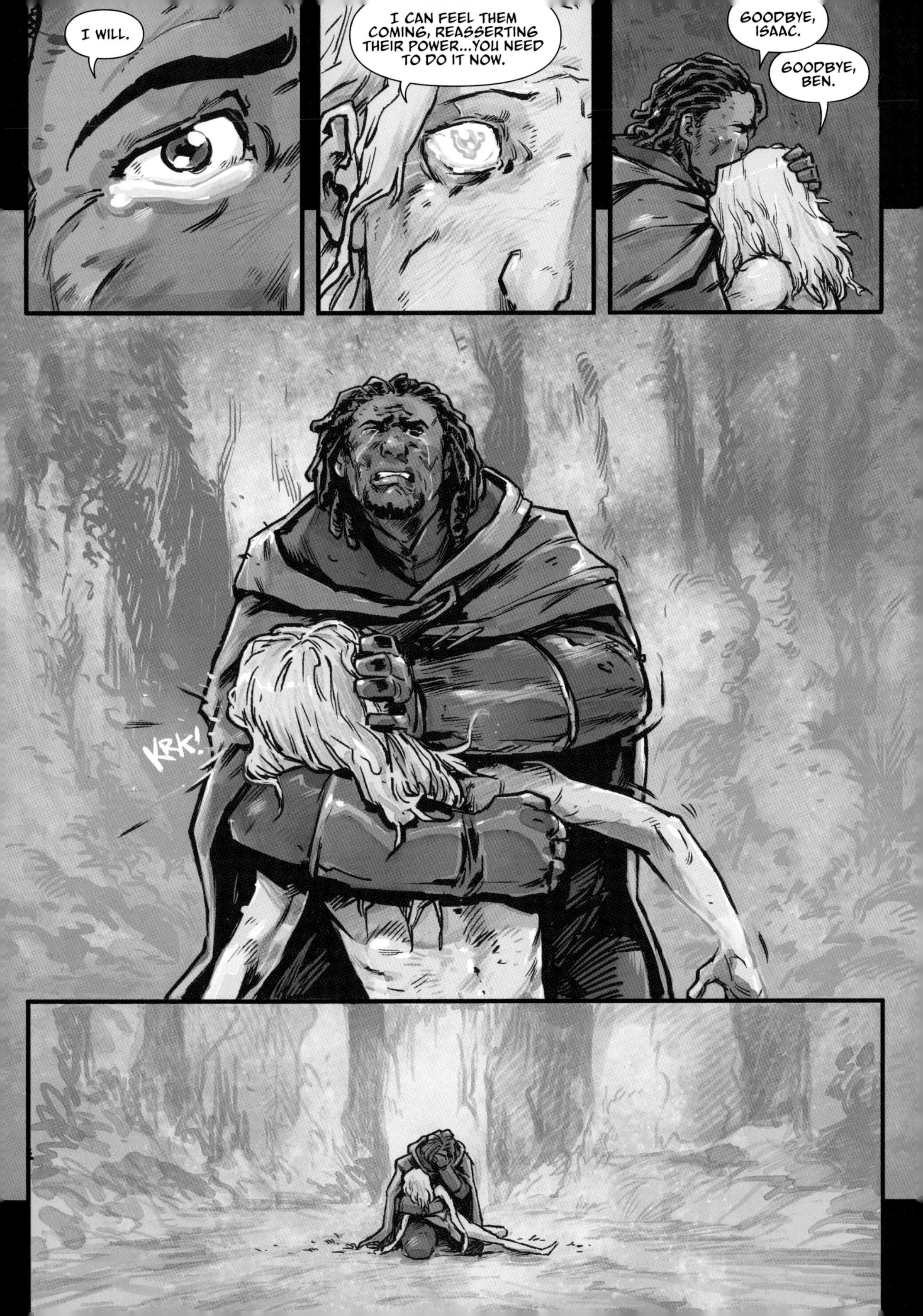
I WILL.
I CAN FEEL THEM COMING, REASSERTING THEIR POWER...YOU NEED TO DO IT NOW.
GOODBYE, ISAAC.
GOODBYE, BEN.
KRK!

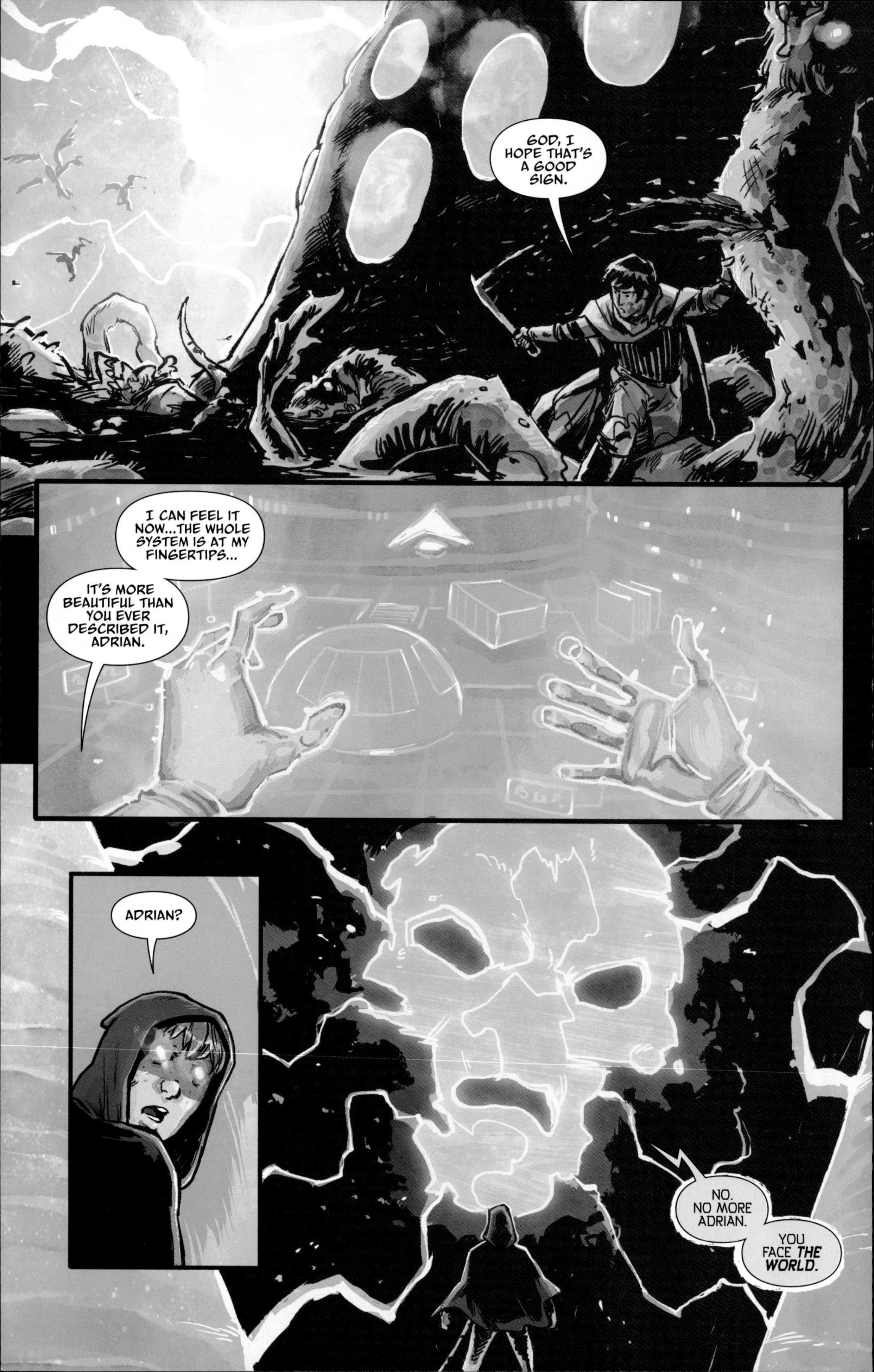
GOD, I HOPE THAT'S A GOOD SIGN.
I CAN FEEL IT NOW...THE WHOLE SYSTEM IS AT MY FINGERTIPS...
IT'S MORE BEAUTIFUL THAN YOU EVER DESCRIBED IT, ADRIAN.
ADRIAN?
NO. NO MORE ADRIAN.
YOU FACE THE WORLD.

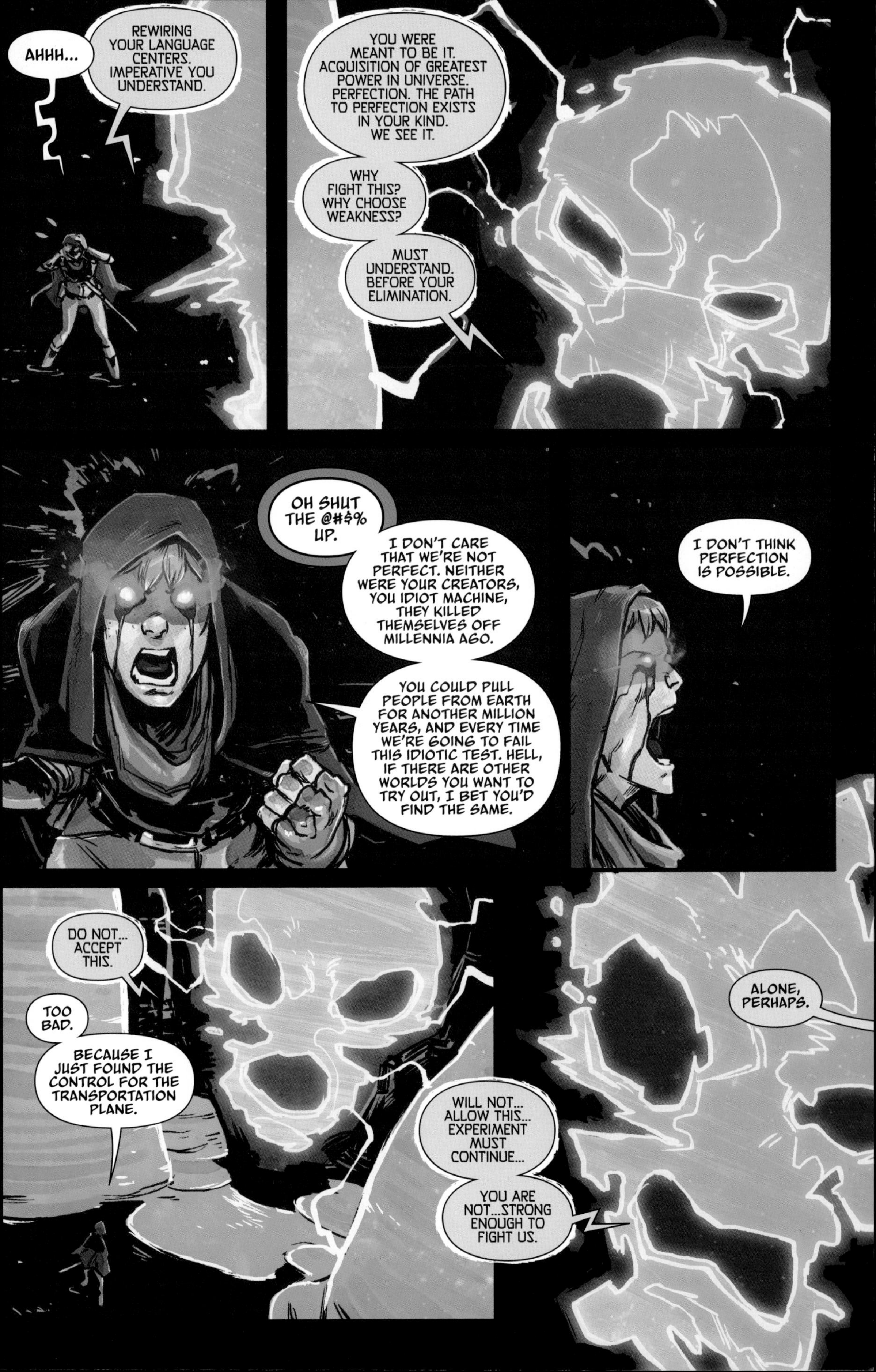
AHHH...
REWIRING YOUR LANGUAGE CENTERS. IMPERATIVE YOU UNDERSTAND.
YOU WERE MEANT TO BE IT. ACQUISITION OF GREATEST POWER IN UNIVERSE. PERFECTION. THE PATH TO PERFECTION EXISTS IN YOUR KIND. WE SEE IT.
WHY FIGHT THIS? WHY CHOOSE WEAKNESS?
MUST UNDERSTAND. BEFORE YOUR ELIMINATION.
OH SHUT THE @#$% UP.
I DON'T CARE THAT WE'RE NOT PERFECT. NEITHER WERE YOUR CREATORS, YOU IDIOT MACHINE, THEY KILLED THEMSELVES OFF MILLENNIA AGO.
YOU COULD PULL PEOPLE FROM EARTH FOR ANOTHER MILLION YEARS, AND EVERY TIME WE'RE GOING TO FAIL THIS IDIOTIC TEST. HELL, IF THERE ARE OTHER WORLDS YOU WANT TO TRY OUT, I BET YOU'D FIND THE SAME.
I DON'T THINK PERFECTION IS POSSIBLE.
DO NOT... ACCEPT THIS.
TOO BAD.
BECAUSE I JUST FOUND THE CONTROL FOR THE TRANSPORTATION PLANE.
WILL NOT... ALLOW THIS... EXPERIMENT MUST CONTINUE...
YOU ARE NOT...STRONG ENOUGH TO FIGHT US.
ALONE, PERHAPS.

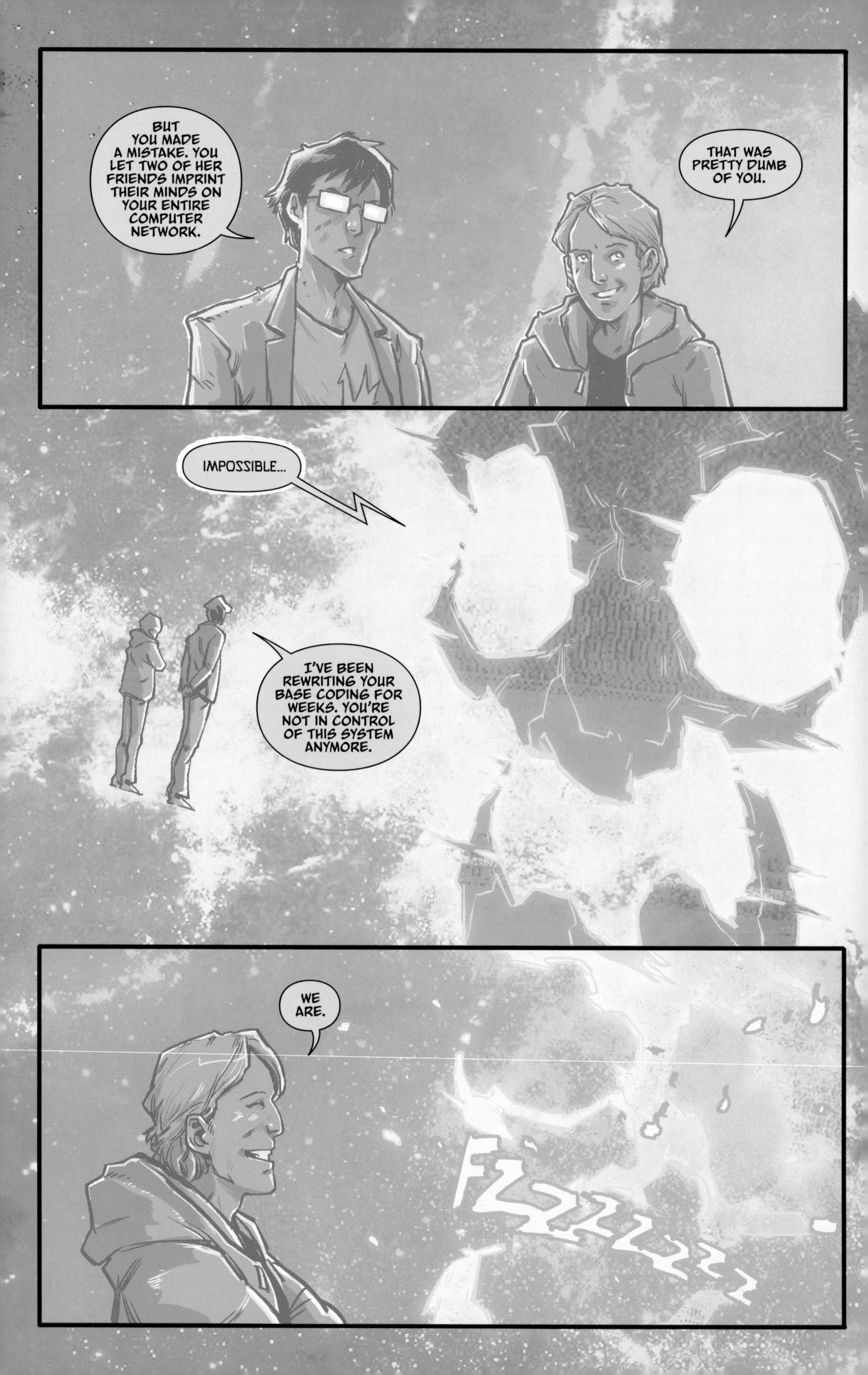
BUT YOU MADE A MISTAKE. YOU LET TWO OF HER FRIENDS IMPRINT THEIR MINDS ON YOUR ENTIRE COMPUTER NETWORK.
THAT WAS PRETTY DUMB OF YOU.
IMPOSSIBLE...
I'VE BEEN REWRITING YOUR BASE CODING FOR WEEKS. YOU'RE NOT IN CONTROL OF THIS SYSTEM ANYMORE.
WE ARE.
FZZZZZZZ

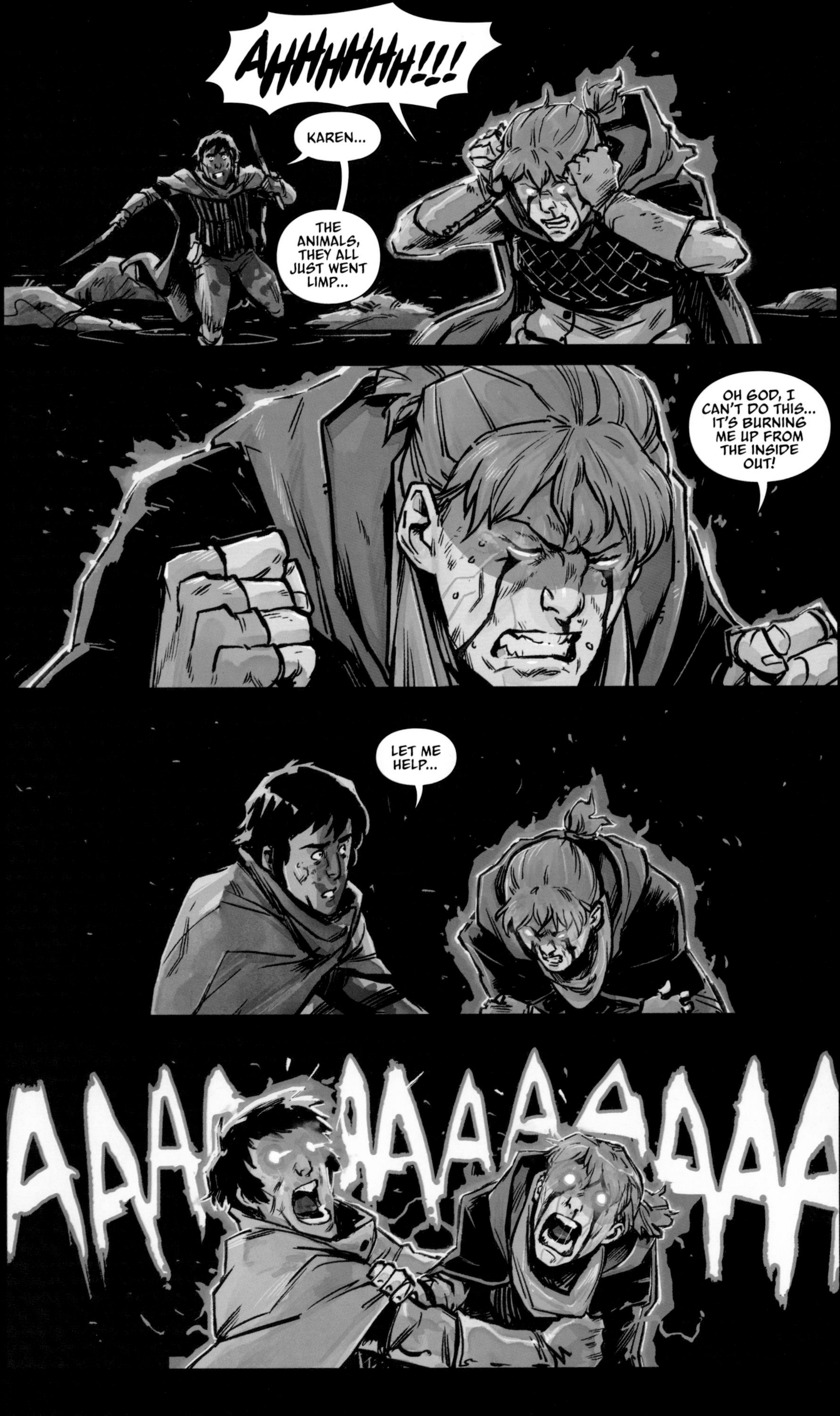
AHHHHHH!!!
KAREN...
THE ANIMALS, THEY ALL JUST WENT LIMP...
OH GOD, I CAN'T DO THIS... IT'S BURNING ME UP FROM THE INSIDE OUT!
LET ME HELP...
AAAAAAAAAAAA

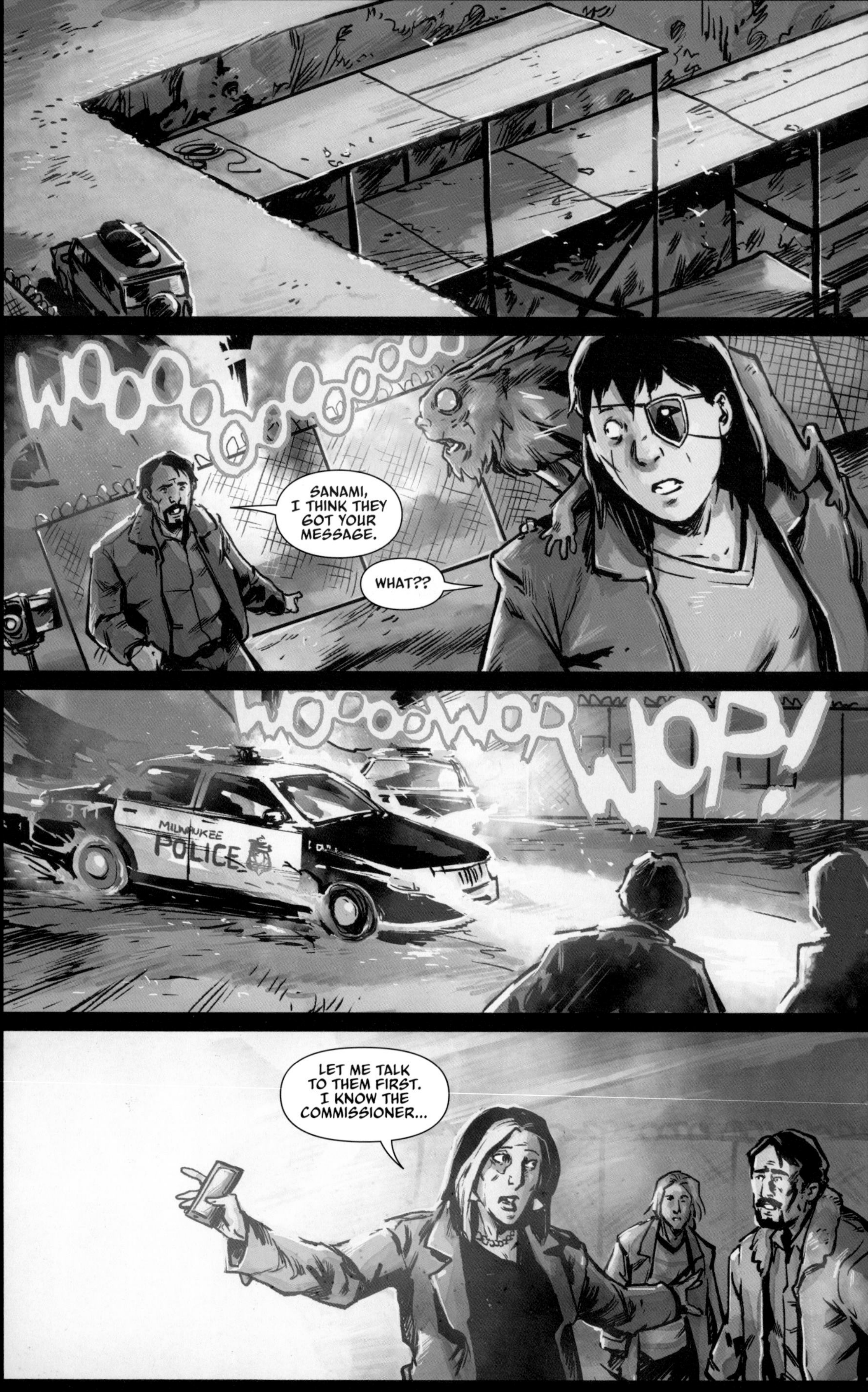
WOOOoOoOOOO
SANAMI, I THINK THEY GOT YOUR MESSAGE.
WHAT??
WOOoooWOP WOP!
MILWAUKEE
POLICE
LET ME TALK TO THEM FIRST. I KNOW THE COMMISSIONER...

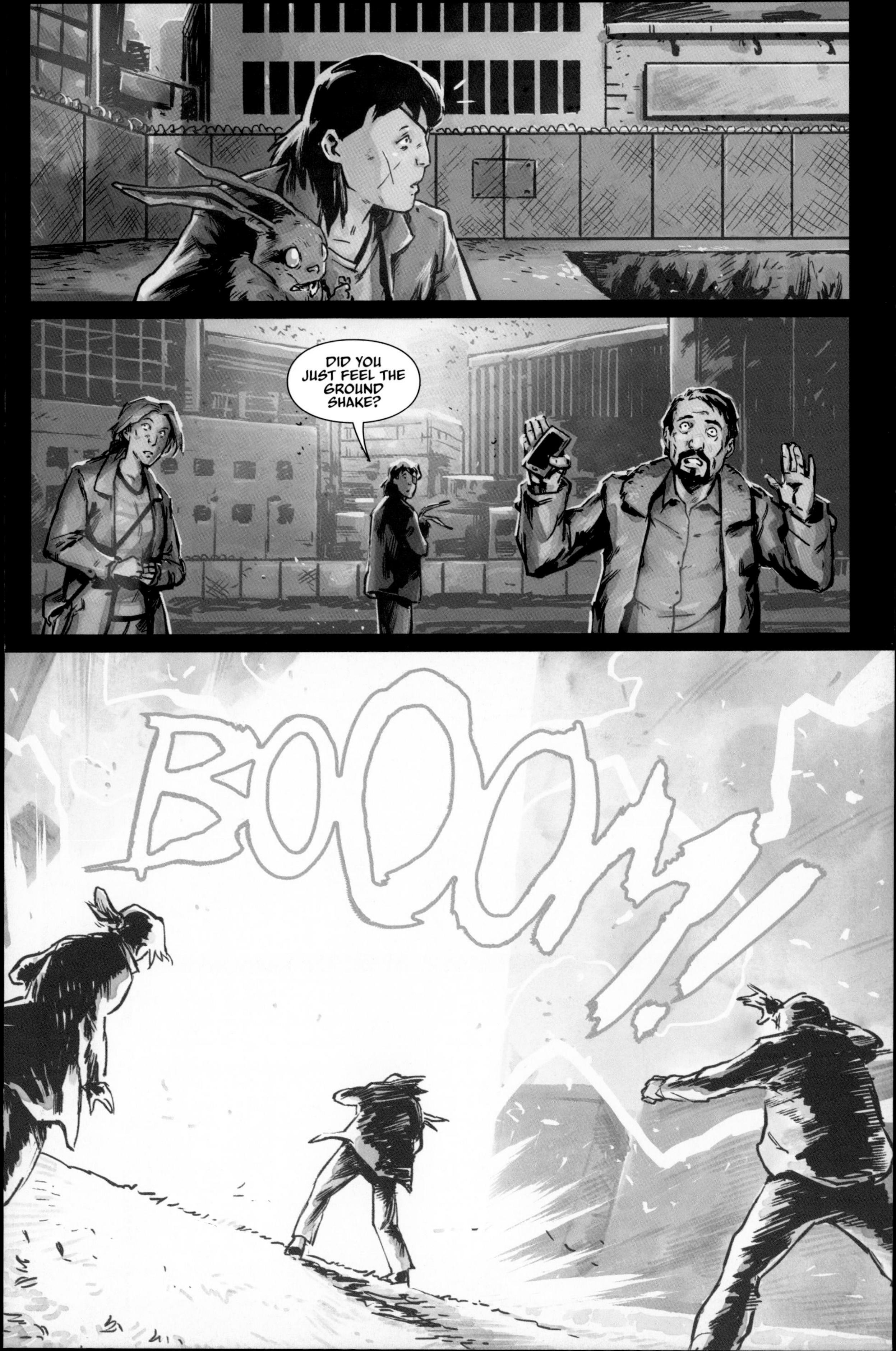
DID YOU JUST FEEL THE GROUND SHAKE?
BOOOM!!

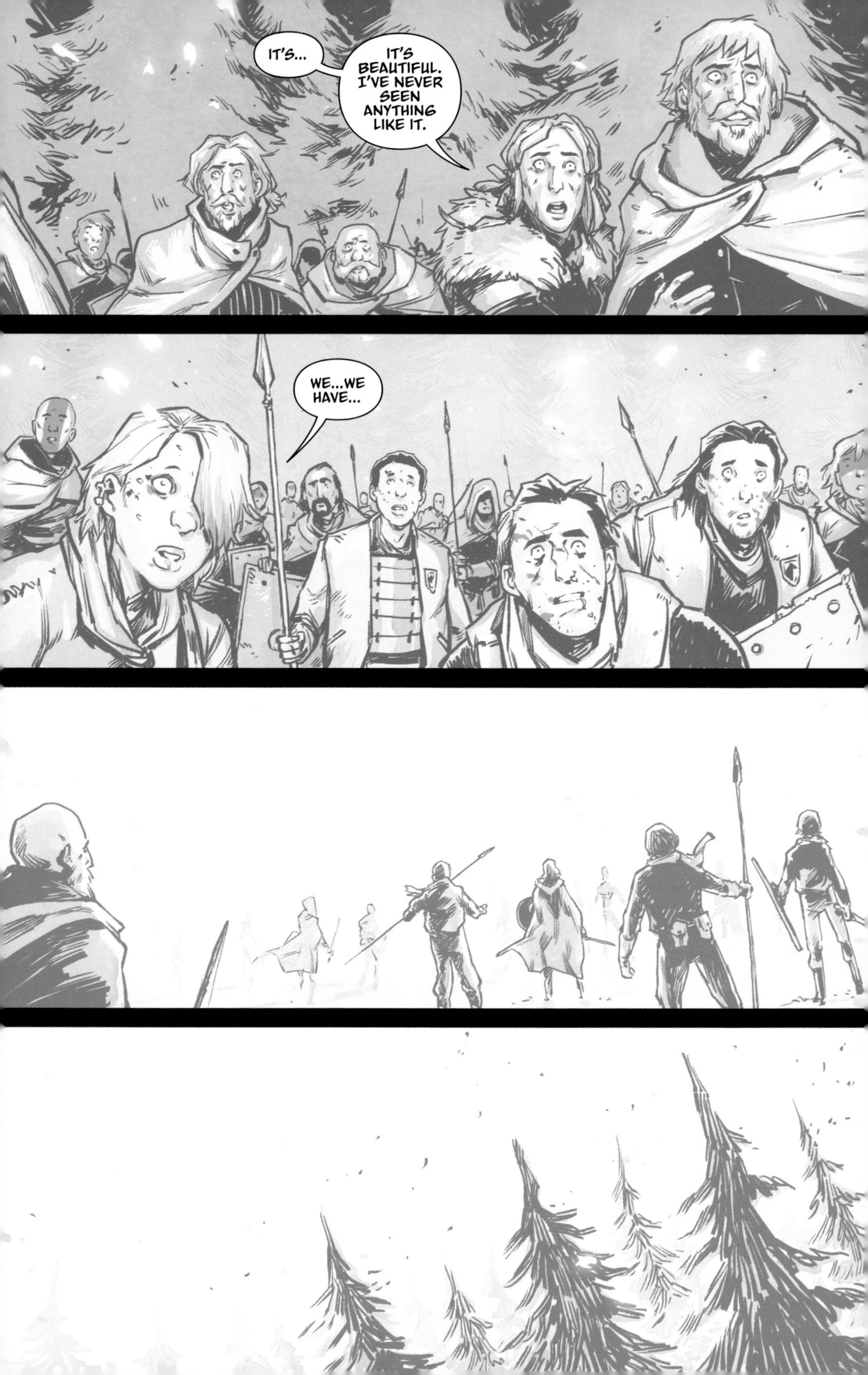
IT'S...
IT'S BEAUTIFUL. I'VE NEVER SEEN ANYTHING LIKE IT.
WE...WE HAVE...

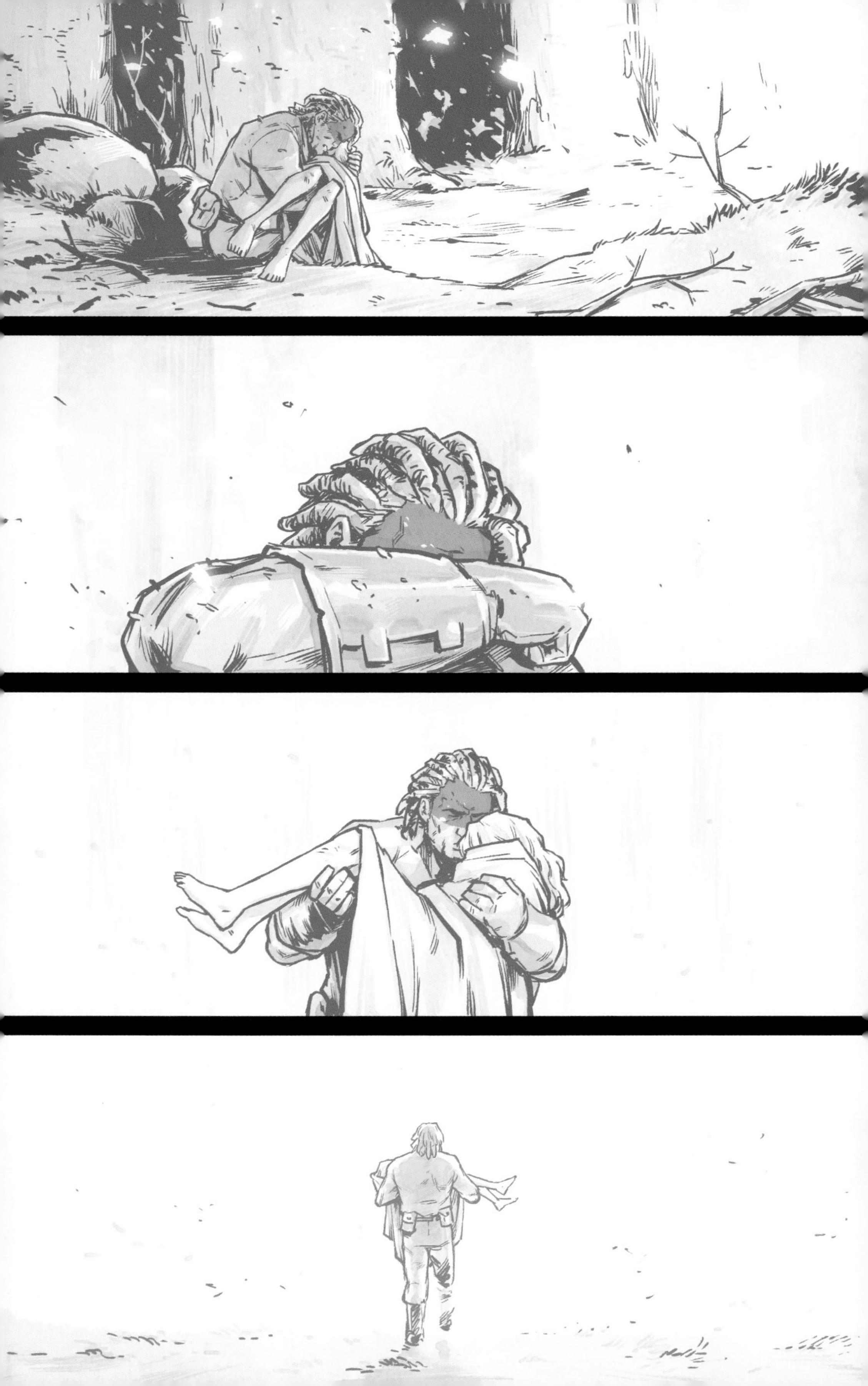

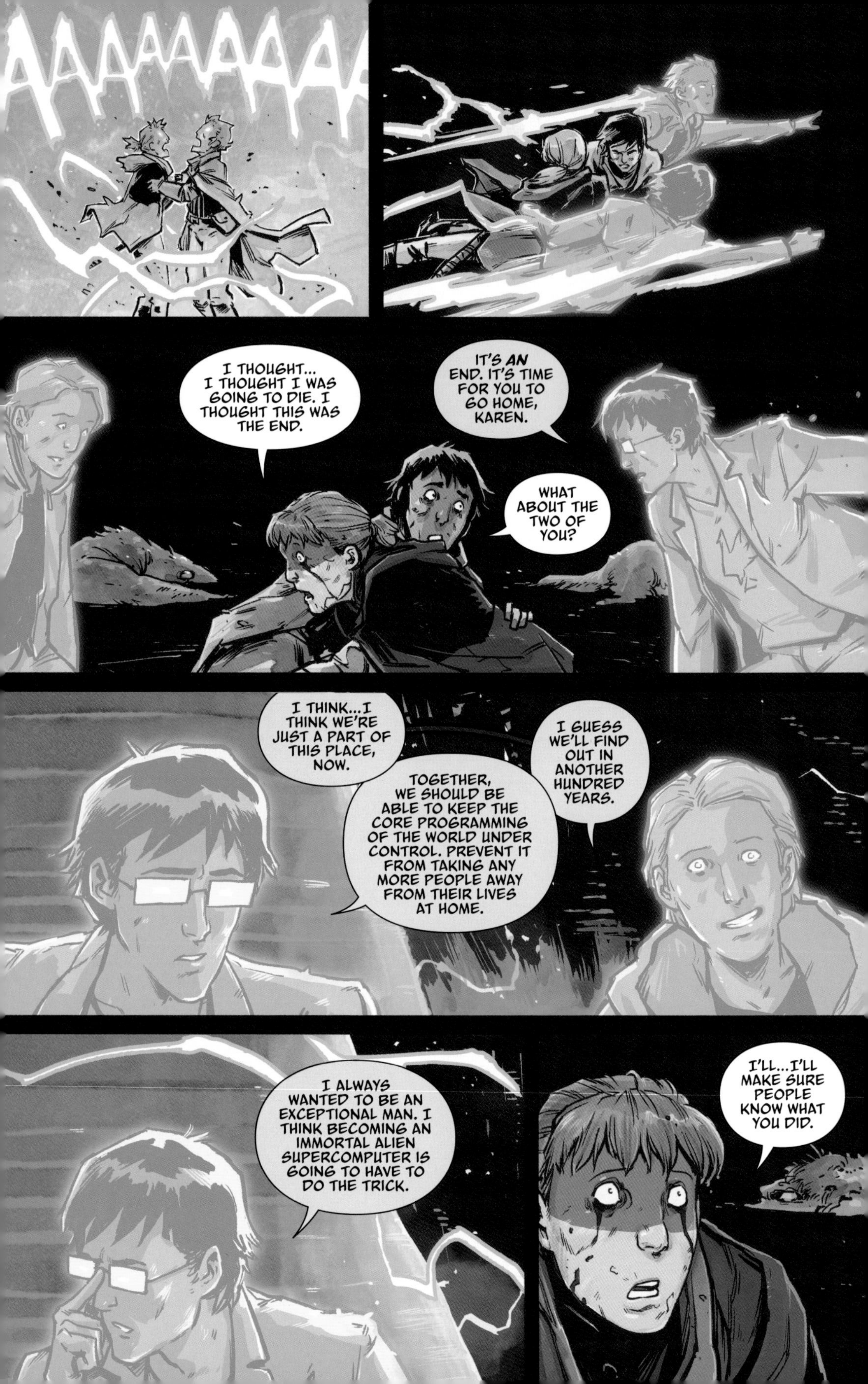
AAAAAAAAA
I THOUGHT... I THOUGHT I WAS GOING TO DIE. I THOUGHT THIS WAS THE END.
IT'S AN END. IT'S TIME FOR YOU TO GO HOME, KAREN.
WHAT ABOUT THE TWO OF YOU?
I THINK...I THINK WE'RE JUST A PART OF THIS PLACE, NOW.
TOGETHER, WE SHOULD BE ABLE TO KEEP THE CORE PROGRAMMING OF THE WORLD UNDER CONTROL. PREVENT IT FROM TAKING ANY MORE PEOPLE AWAY FROM THEIR LIVES AT HOME.
I GUESS WE'LL FIND OUT IN ANOTHER HUNDRED YEARS.
I ALWAYS WANTED TO BE AN EXCEPTIONAL MAN. I THINK BECOMING AN IMMORTAL ALIEN SUPERCOMPUTER IS GOING TO HAVE TO DO THE TRICK.
I'LL...I'LL MAKE SURE PEOPLE KNOW WHAT YOU DID.

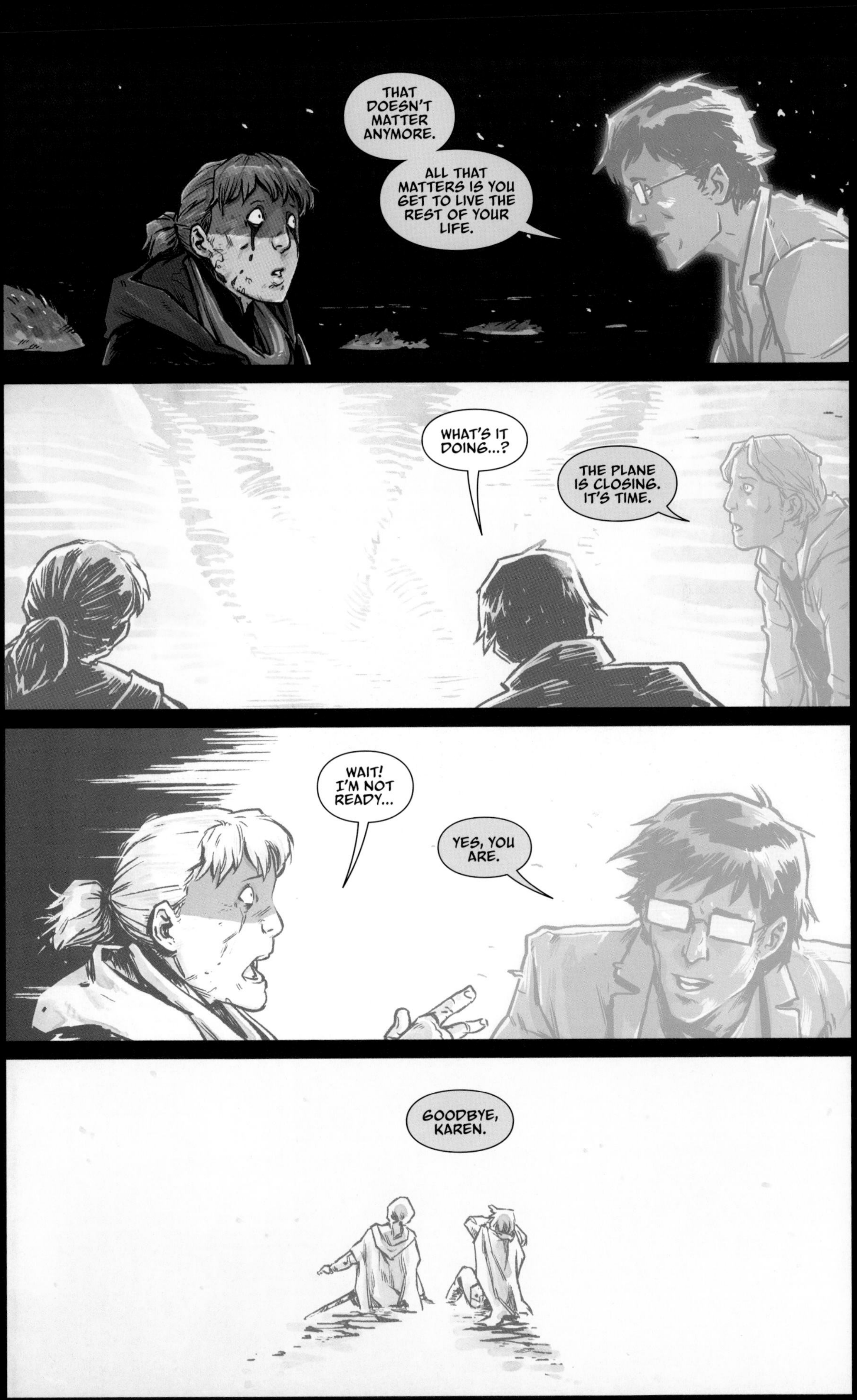
THAT DOESN'T MATTER ANYMORE.
ALL THAT MATTERS IS YOU GET TO LIVE THE REST OF YOUR LIFE.
WHAT'S IT DOING...?
THE PLANE IS CLOSING. IT'S TIME.
WAIT! I'M NOT READY...
YES, YOU ARE.
GOODBYE, KAREN.

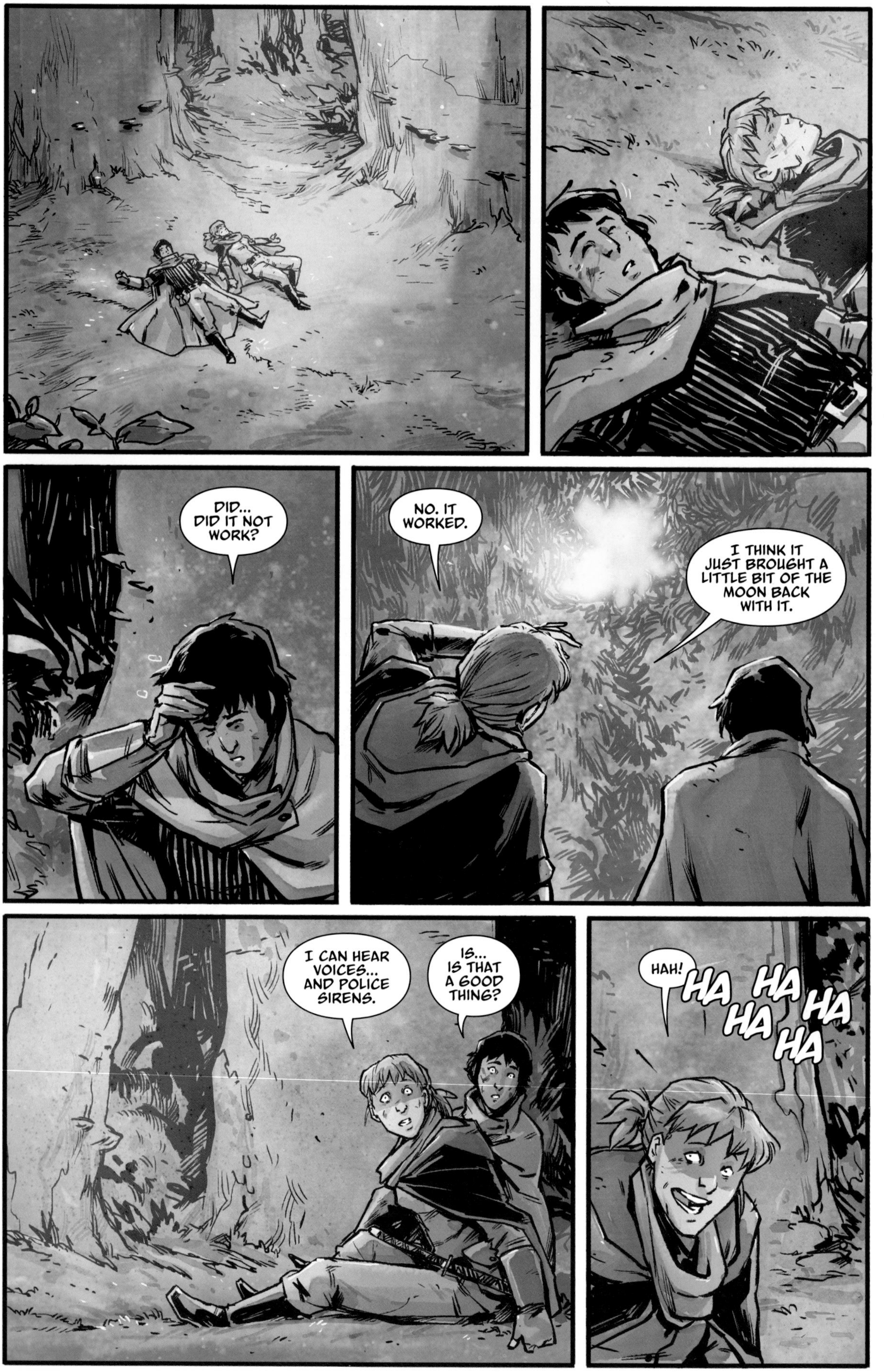
DID... DID IT NOT WORK?
NO. IT WORKED.
I THINK IT JUST BROUGHT A LITTLE BIT OF THE MOON BACK WITH IT.
I CAN HEAR VOICES... AND POLICE SIRENS.
IS... IS THAT A GOOD THING?
HAH!
HA HA HA HA HA

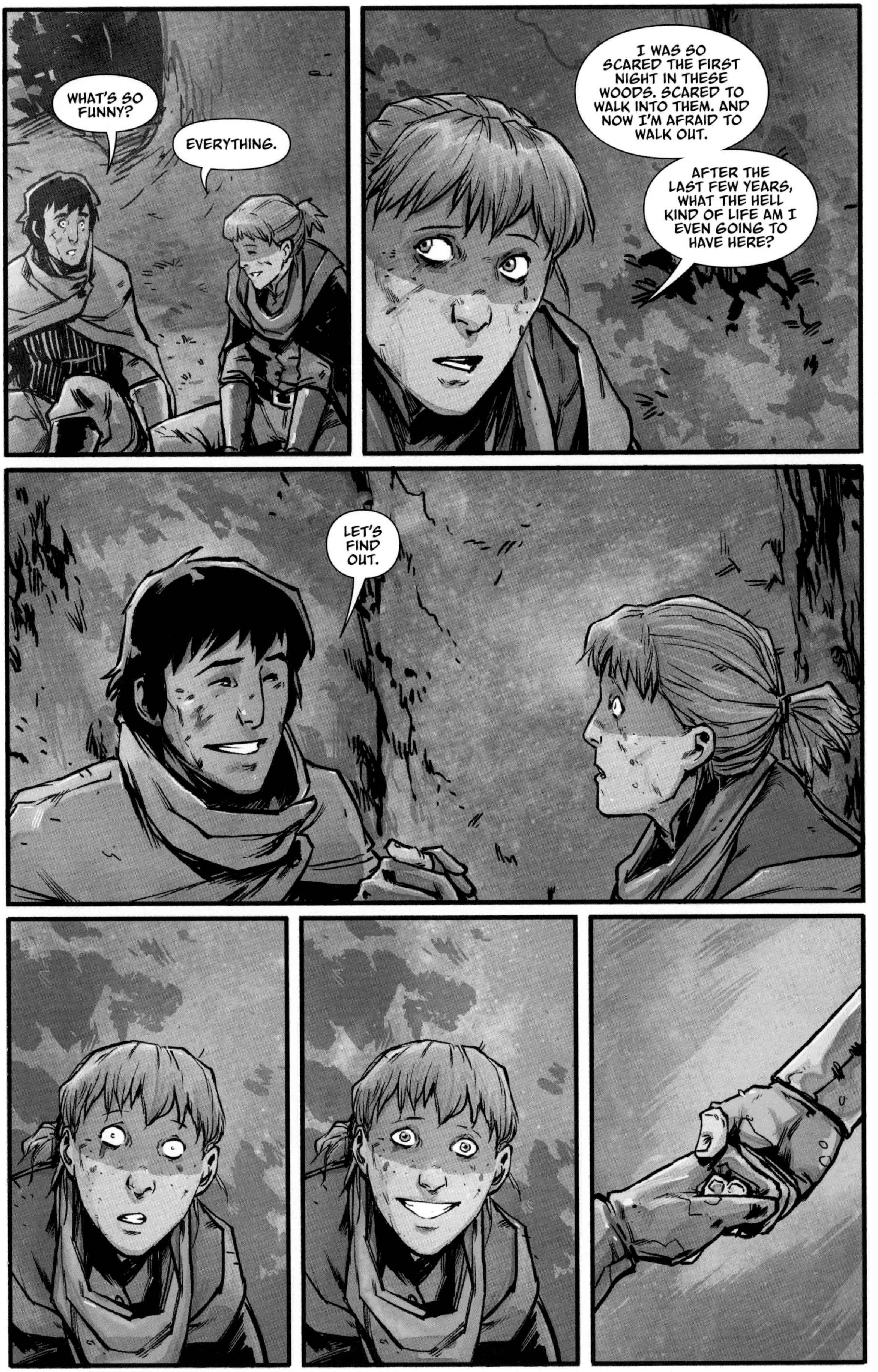
WHAT'S SO FUNNY?
EVERYTHING.
I WAS SO SCARED THE FIRST NIGHT IN THESE WOODS. SCARED TO WALK INTO THEM. AND NOW I'M AFRAID TO WALK OUT.
AFTER THE LAST FEW YEARS, WHAT THE HELL KIND OF LIFE AM I EVEN GOING TO HAVE HERE?
LET'S FIND OUT.

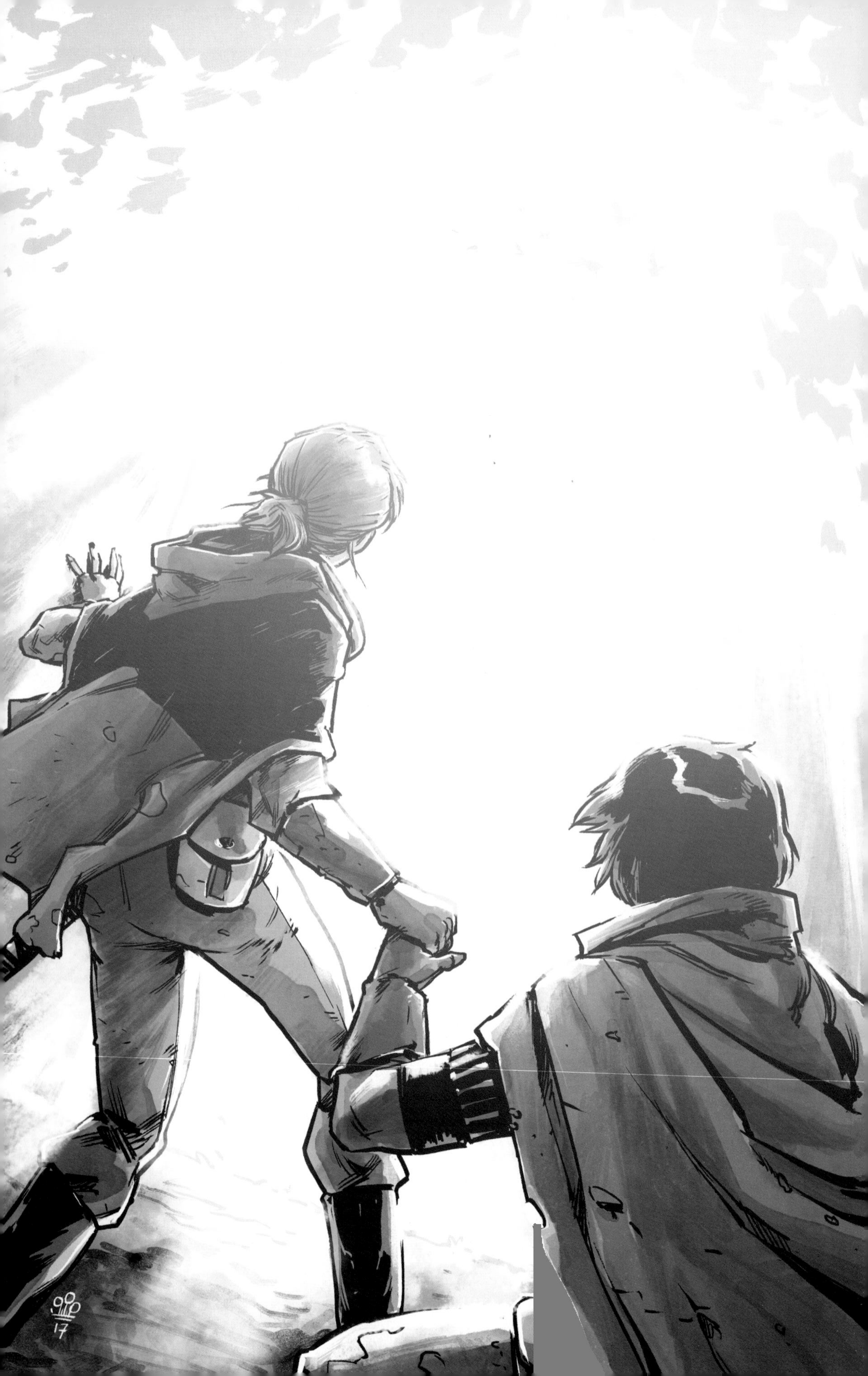

THE END.

COVER
GALLERY

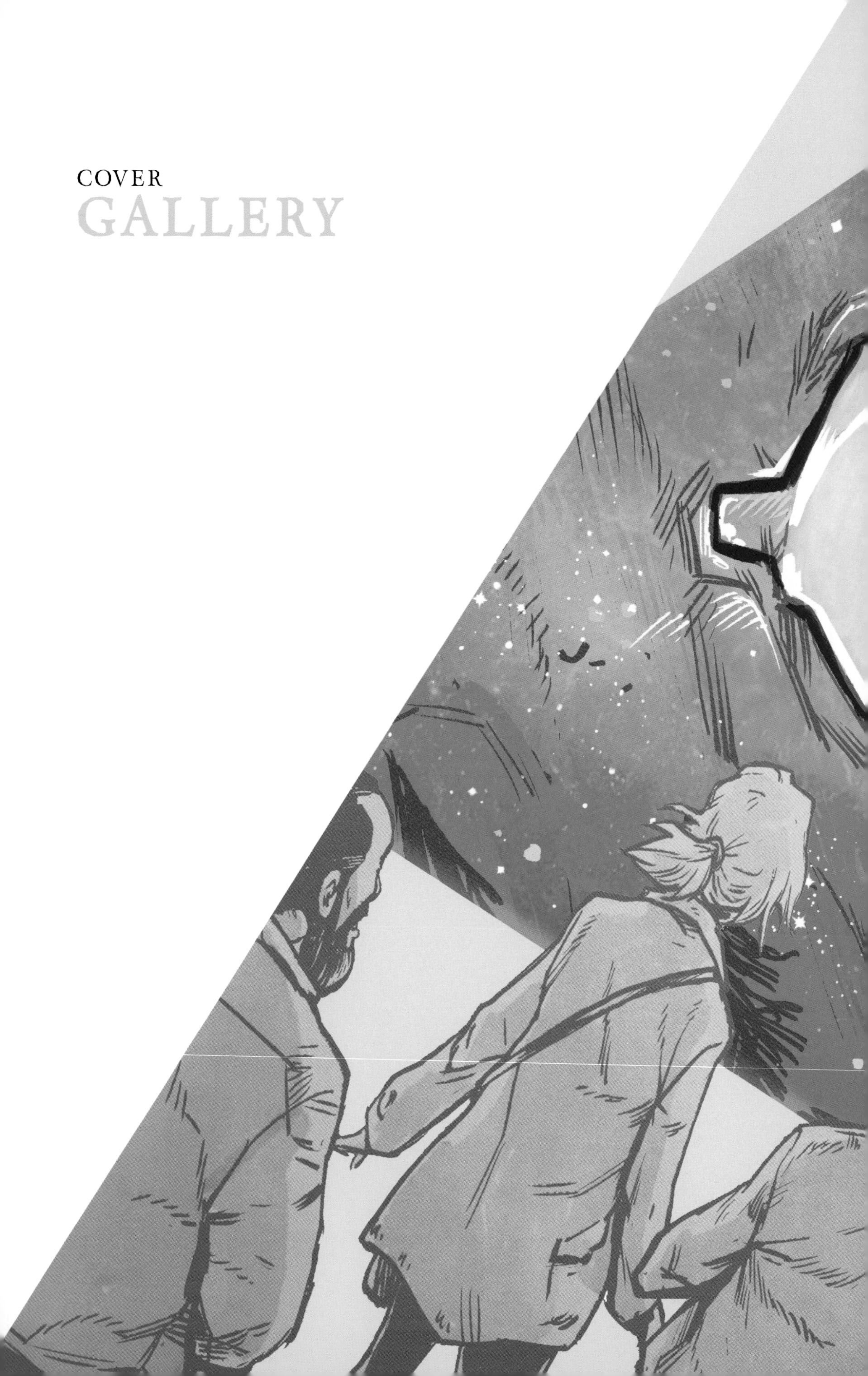

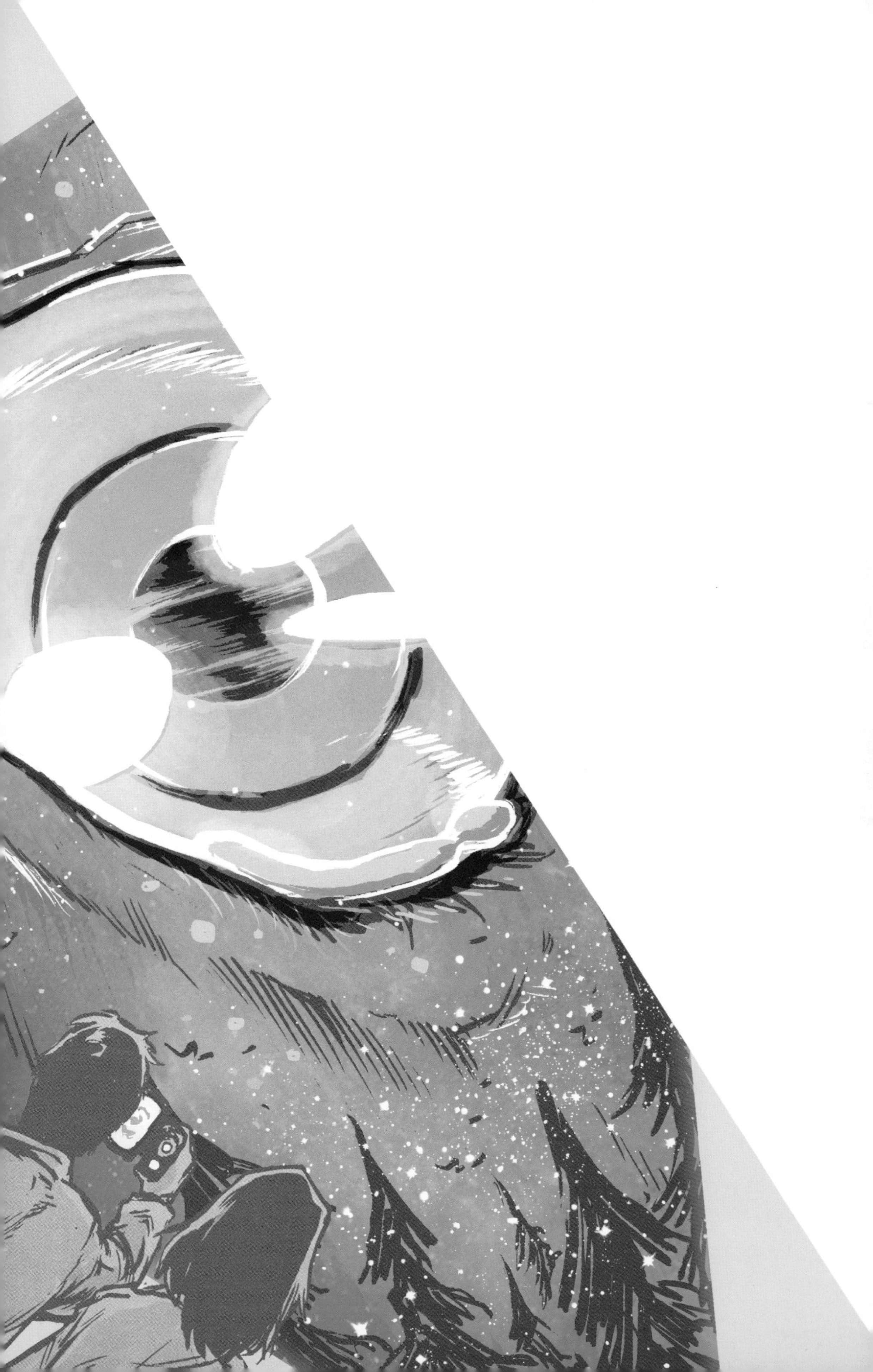

ISSUE THIRTY-THREE COVER **MICHAEL DIALYNAS**

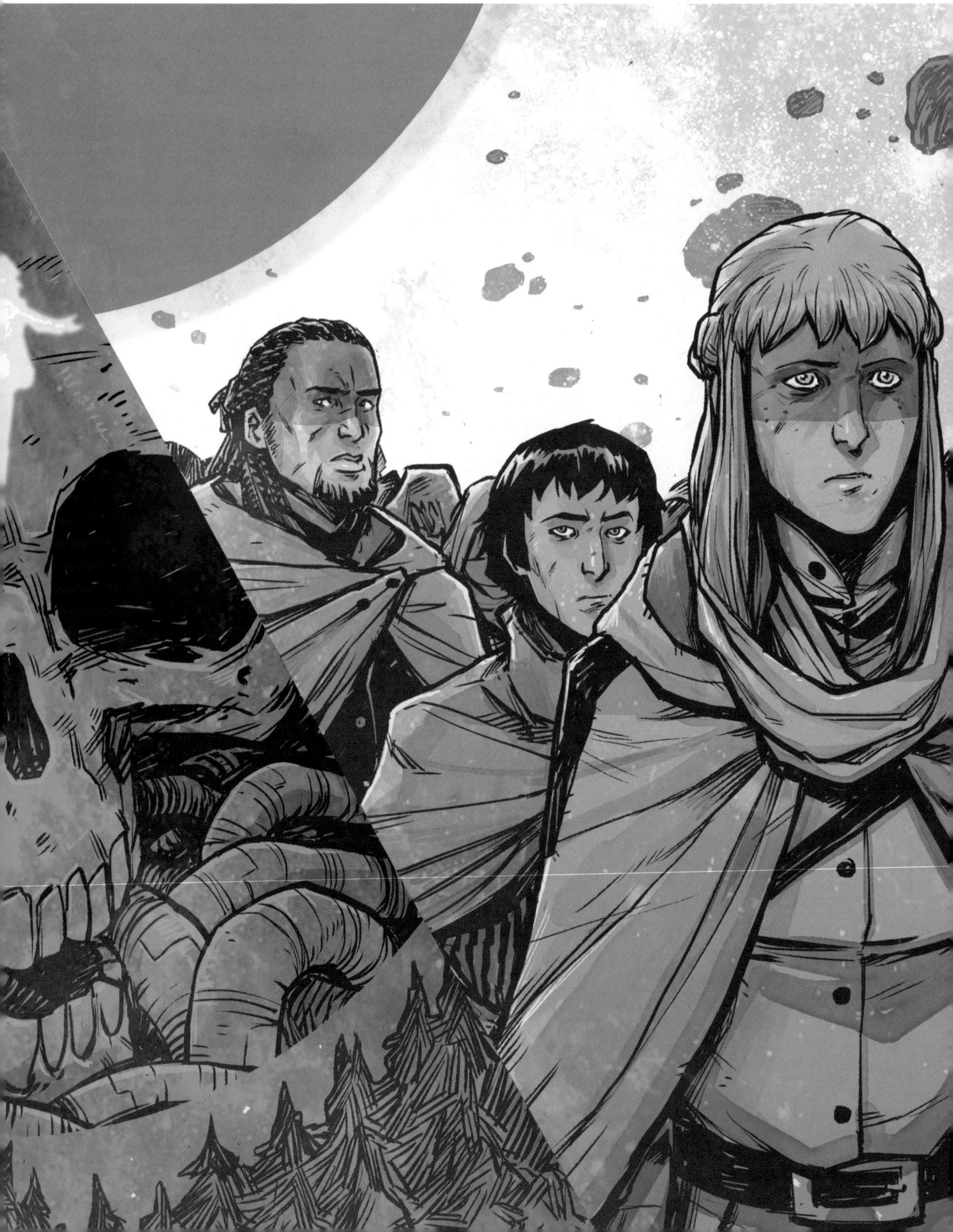

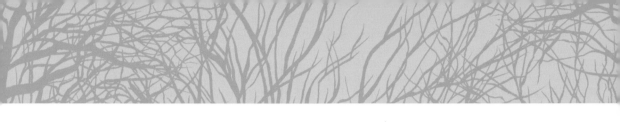

ISSUE THIRTY-FOUR COVER **MICHAEL DIALYNAS**

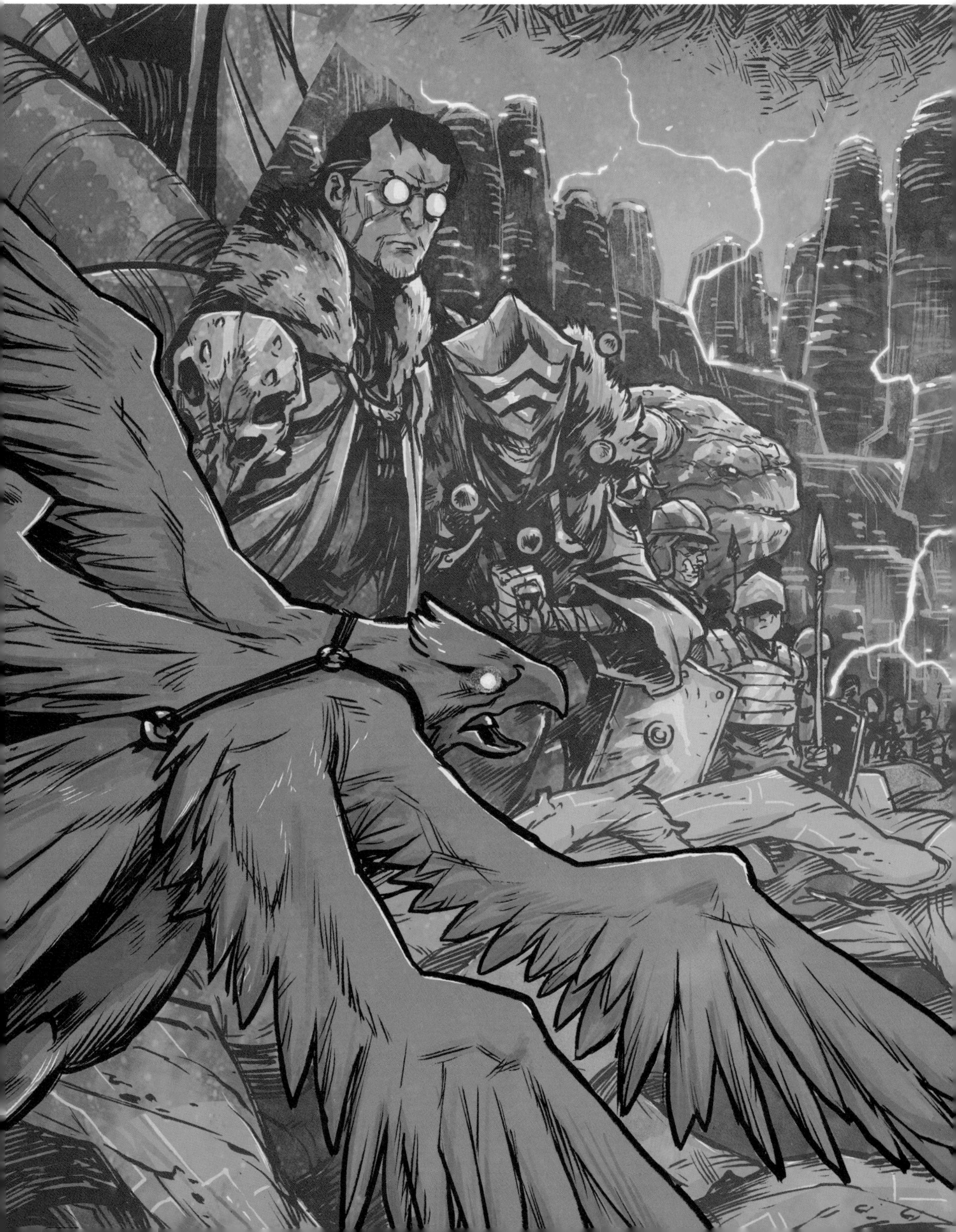

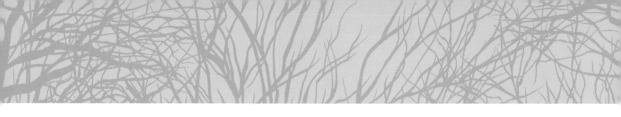

ISSUE THIRTY-FIVE COVER **MICHAEL DIALYNAS**

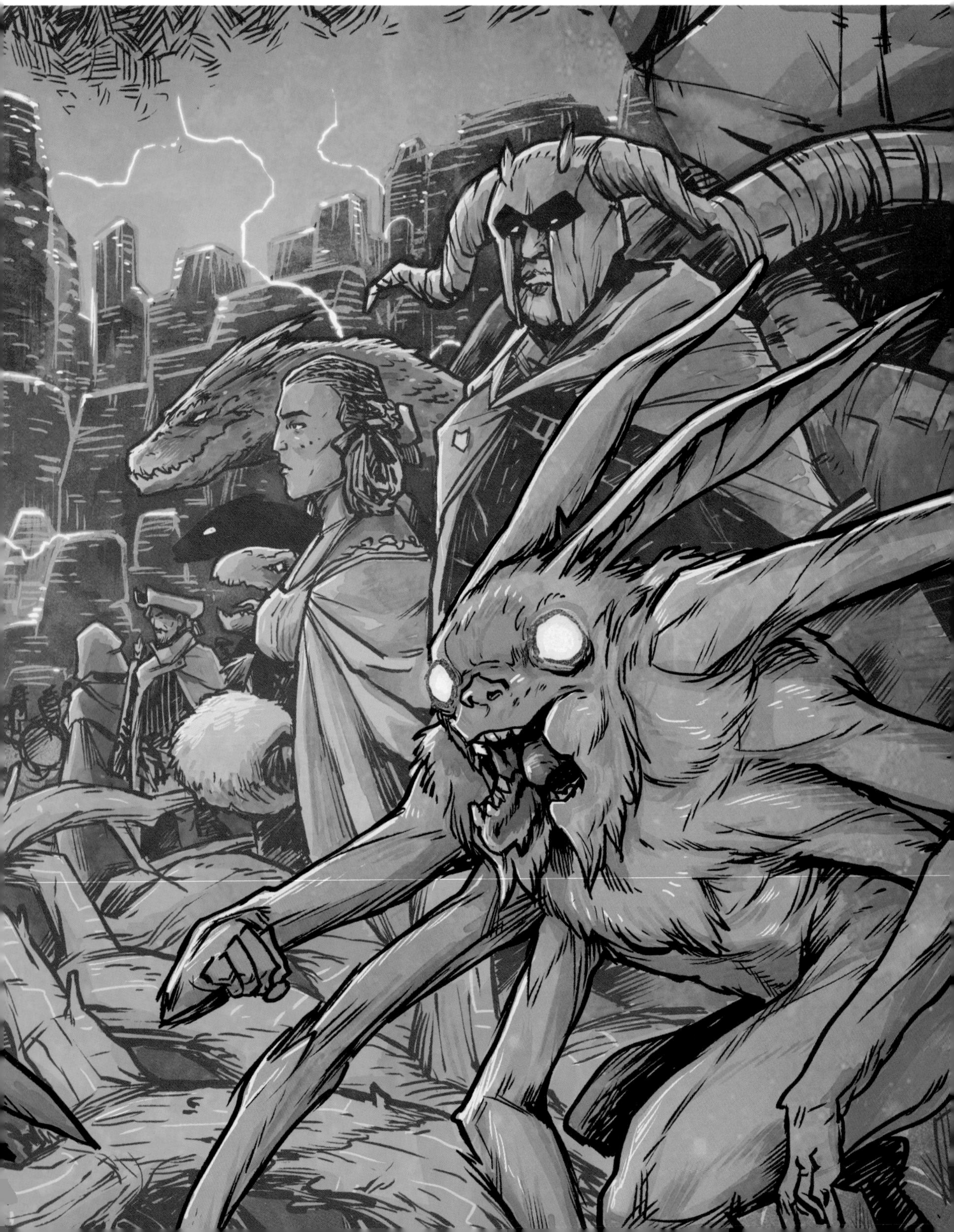

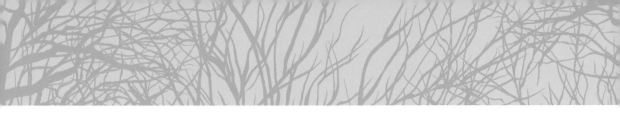

ISSUE THIRTY-SIX COVER **MICHAEL DIALYNAS**

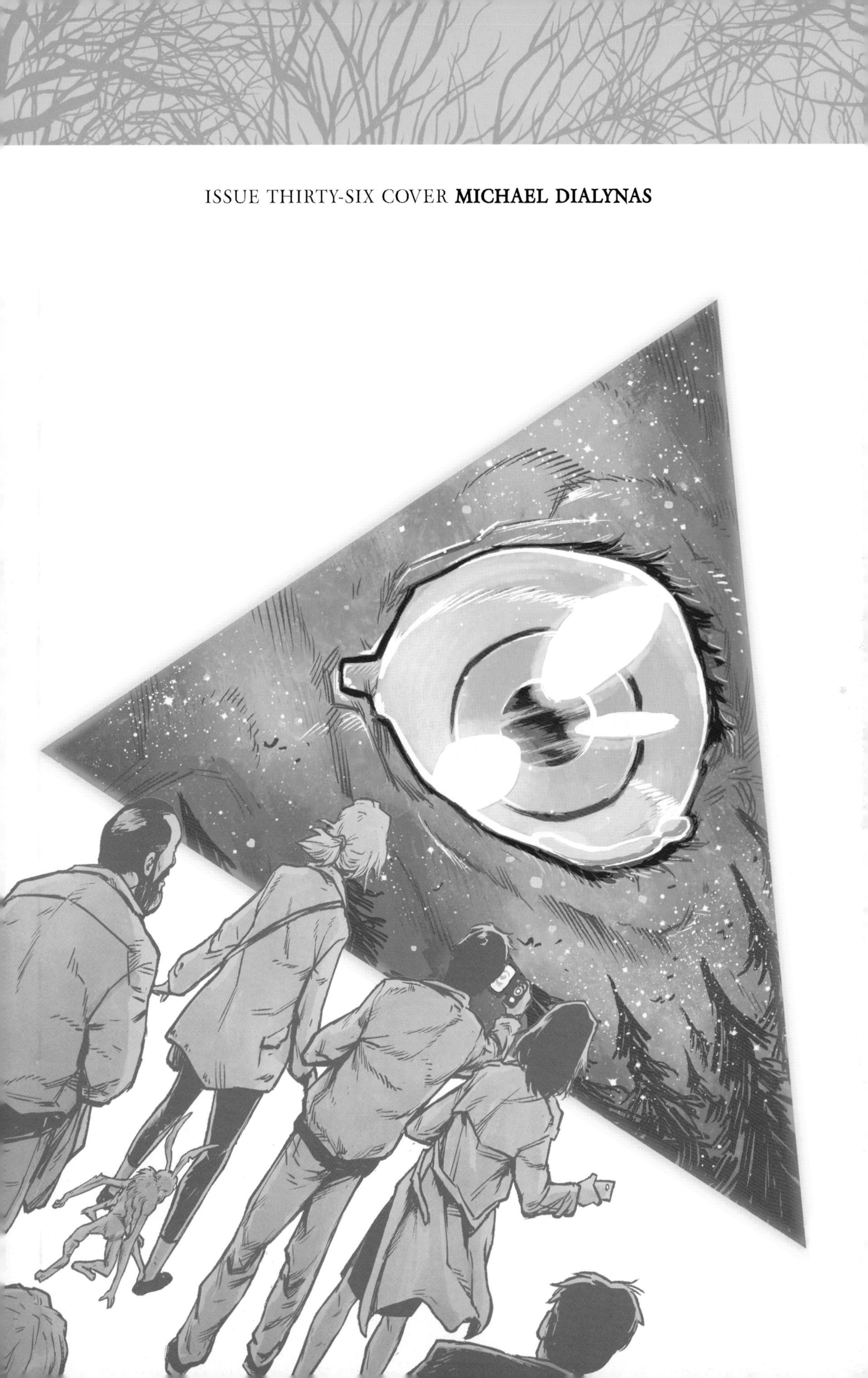

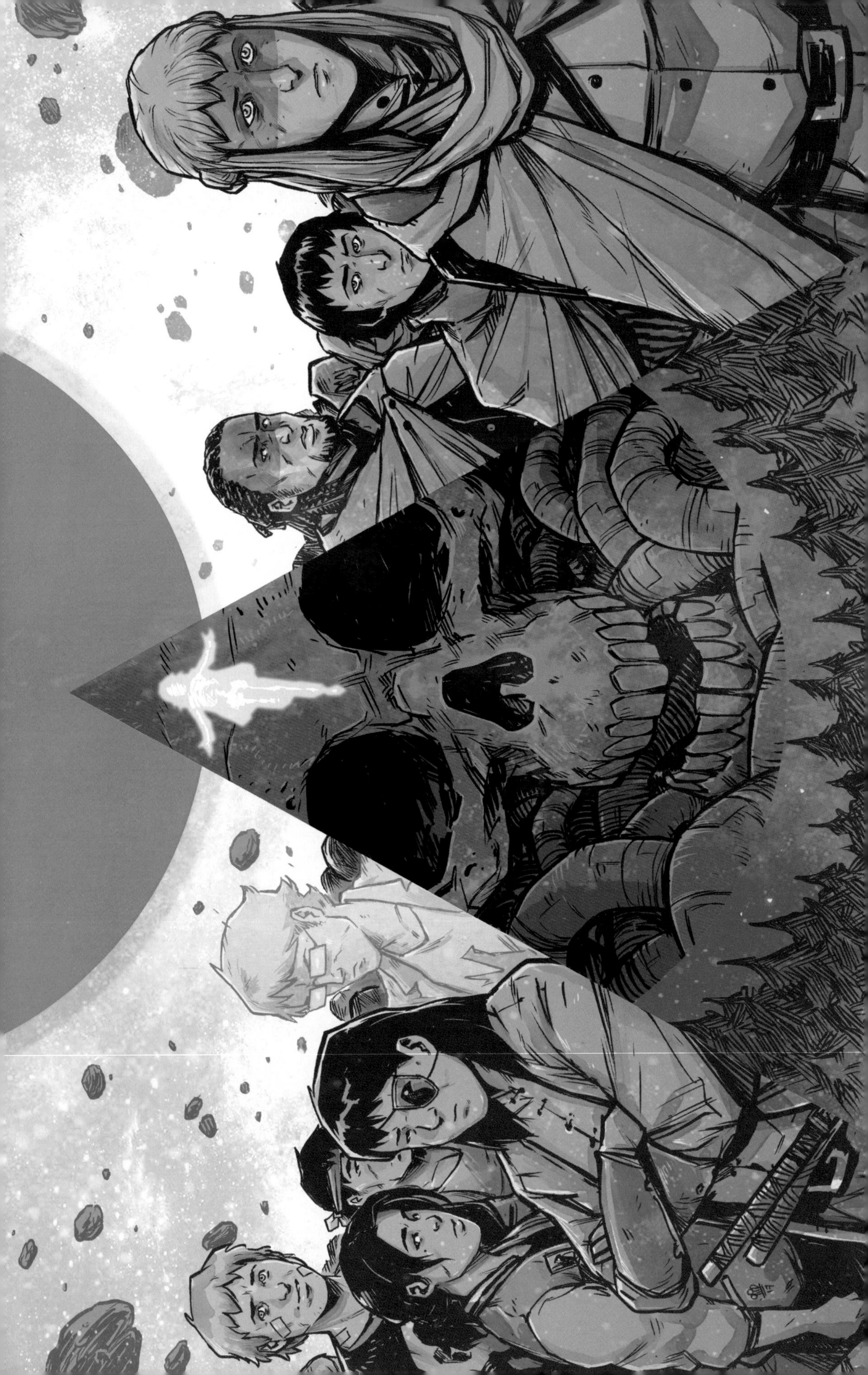

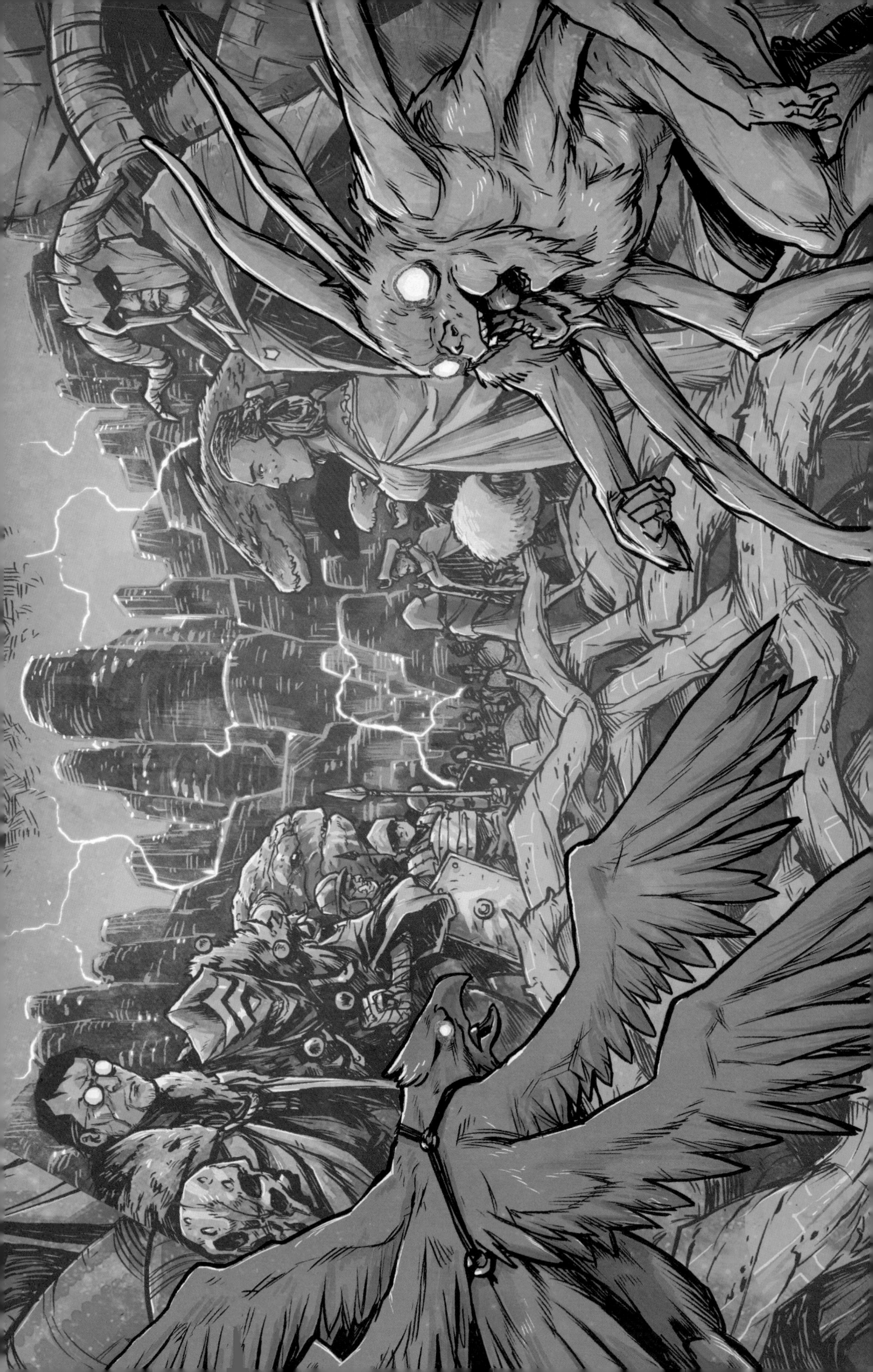

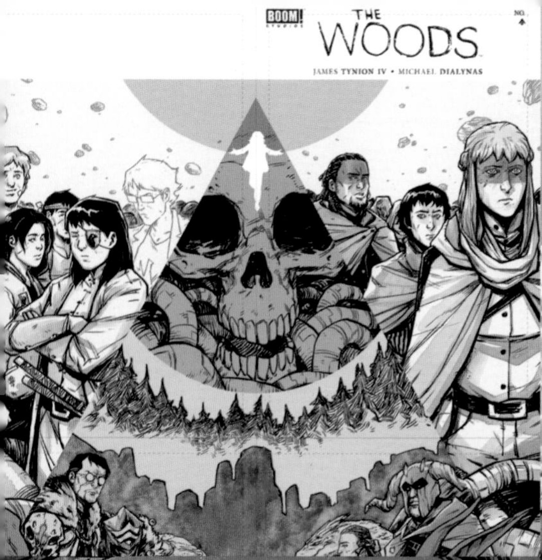
BOOM! STUDIOS
THE WOODS
JAMES TYNION IV • MICHAEL DIALYNAS

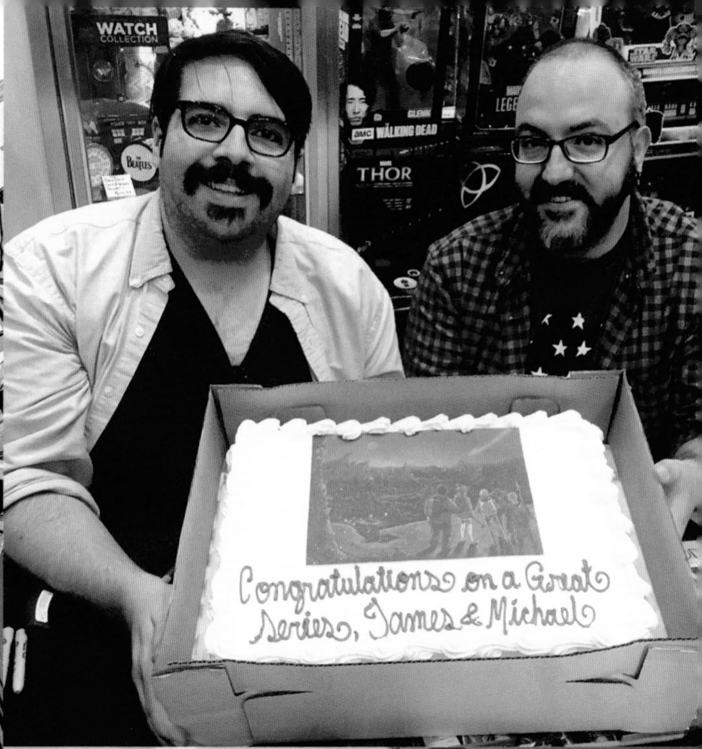
WATCH COLLECTION
WALKING DEAD
THOR
Congratulations on a Great Series, James & Michael

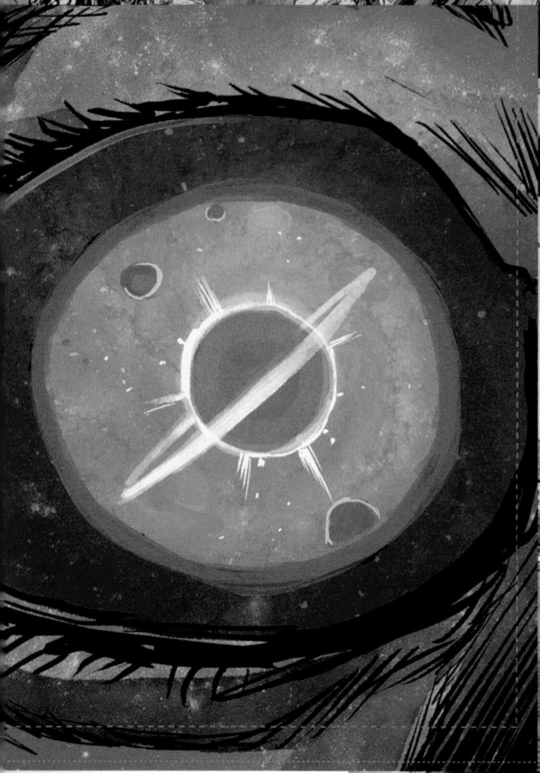

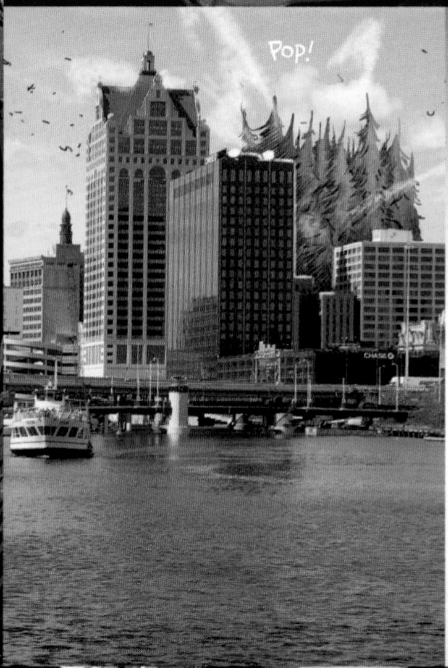
POP!

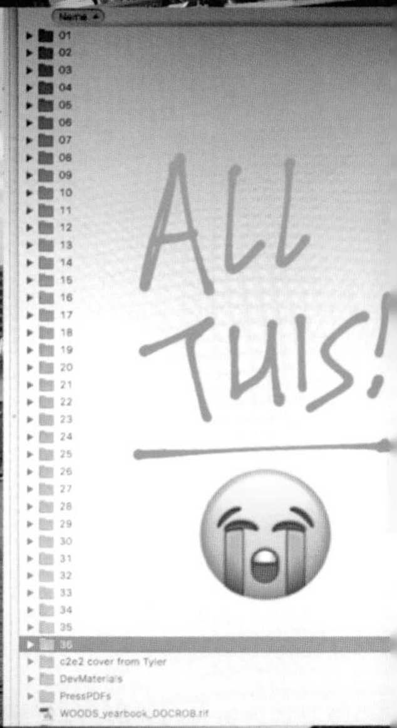
01
02
03
04
05
06
07
08
09
10
11
12
13
14
15
16
17
18
19
20
21
22
23
24
25
26
27
28
29
30
31
32
33
34
35
36
c2e2 cover from Tyler
DevMaterials
PressPDFs
WOODS_yearbook_DOCROB.tif
ALL THIS!

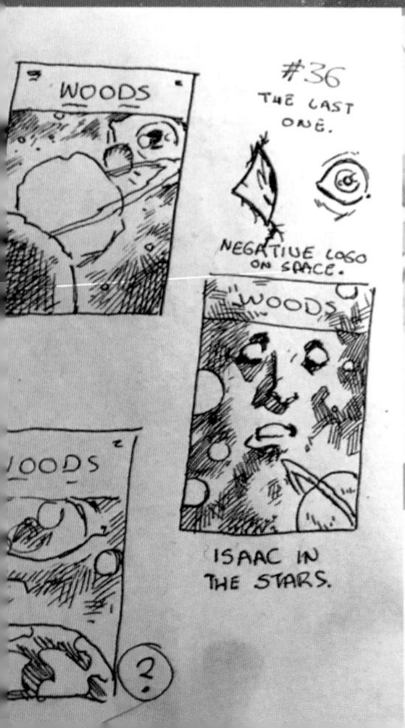
WOODS
#36
THE LAST ONE.
NEGATIVE LOGO ON SPACE.
WOODS
ISAAC IN THE STARS.
WOODS
?

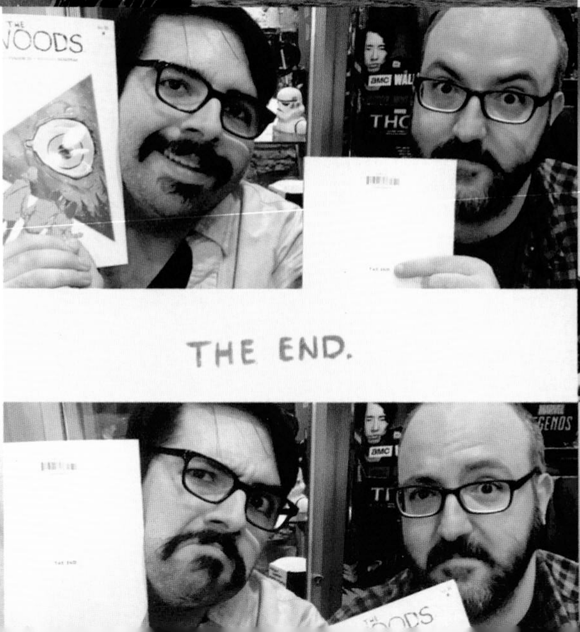
THE WOODS
THE END.

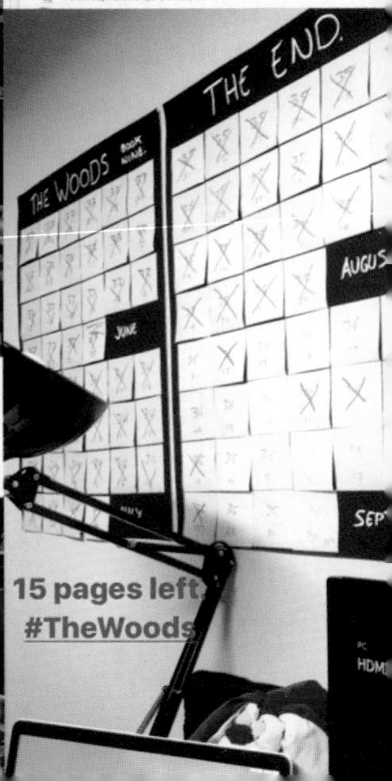
THE END.
THE WOODS BOOK NINE
JUNE
15 pages left
#TheWoods

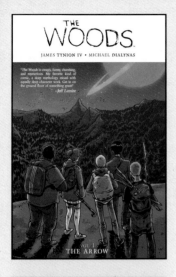

SERIES RETROSPECTIVE
OUT OF THE WOODS

On my hard drive, there's a file named *The Woods*, created on June 10, 2012. There are only a few lines of text in it, but this is how it starts. "Full midwestern high school is beamed to planet on the other end of the universe. Wooded planet. Lotsa problems and stuff." It's followed by a few brief, generic descriptors that would ultimately become the core cast of *The Woods*: Adrian, Karen, Isaac, Ben, Sanami, and Calder.

It would be another year and a half before my incredible partner Michael Dialynas would bring those characters to life in a few sketches that immediately captured the heart of the series. And a bit longer before the first issue hit the stands. Back then, I only had a few comic credits to my name. I was still working at a small advertising firm in New York City, moonlighting on a few small co-written projects for big publishers, unsure what my next steps would be. I still remember, late one night, pacing in my Manhattan apartment on the phone with my friend and mentor, Scott Snyder, when he asked me the most important question of my young career. "If you could only write one comic book for the rest of your life, what would that comic book be?" The answer wasn't meant to be my favorite superhero, but rather, what kind of series would encapsulate all my interests, all the core themes I wanted to play with, all the settings and genres I wanted to explore...

The question set my brain on fire. But a few months later, one afternoon, I opened a document and started to write a rough sentence about a high school transported into an alien forest, and the kids trying to figure out how to survive and how to get home. Ultimately, *The Woods* is a story about growing up (aren't all stories about teenagers?), but more specifically, it's the story of my life, the encapsulation of the first five years of my career, and all my interests and follies. It ends with an understanding that the process of growing up never really ends, it just changes.

By putting the last words of this series to the page earlier today, one part of my life is over. I'm out of the Woods. But that just means the next part of my life is ready to begin. And it means that it's time for me to ask myself the question all over again, and see what strange sentence might fall out and shape the next era of my life. Until then, my love goes to my co-creator, Michael, and my incredible editors, Eric Harburn and Jasmine Amiri. And to each and every one of you who came to the other end of the universe to see some "problems and stuff" unfold.

James Tynion IV
2017, NYC

After four whole years since being brought in on this book, I can honestly say that it sucks and feels weird to have finished drawing it.

I can look back and see myself evolve from Page 1 all they way to Page 794—*The Woods* is that series for me, the one where I grew up.

Since drawing the first pages in 2013, it became a huge part of my life—every month reading a new chapter from James, every day drawing a new scene, getting to create new weird creatures, seeing Doctor Robot interact with things in the background of pages, seeing the characters grow in real time, from high schoolers to young warriors desperately fighting for a chance to go home again.

And now that they are home, I feel that this chapter in my life has ended.

Just like for the kids of Bay Point, things are going to be different and better from here on, and I hope the next book I work on will capture me the way *The Woods* did.

Thank you James, Eric, Jasmine, Ed, the real Bay Point kids.

Michael Dialynas
2017, Athens